A Manager's Guide to Current Issues in Information Systems

Frédéric Adam
and Ciaran Murphy

BLACKHALL
Publishing

BLACKHALL PUBLISHING
26 Eustace Street
Dublin 2
Ireland

e-mail: blackhall@tinet.ie

ISBN: 1 901657 46 9

A catalogue record for this book is available
from the British Library.

Printed in Ireland by
Betaprint Ltd

A Manager's Guide to Current Issues in Information Systems

Contents

Section 1:
Information Systems for Managers

Section 2:
Managing IT

Section 3:
The Electronic Revolution of Business

Section 4:
Information Systems for More
Effective Organisations

About the Authors

Frédéric Adam is a college lecturer in the Department of Accounting, Finance and Information Systems at University College Cork in Ireland. He is also a senior researcher with the Executive Systems Research Centre (ESRC). His main research interests include the role and use of information in organisations and the study of the decision making processes of top managers. His research has been published in a number of journals including the *Journal of Strategic Information Systems, Decision Support Systems* and *Systèmes d'Information et Management*. He also regularly acts as a consultant in the areas of information systems implementation and information systems for top managers.

Patrick Bowe is a Research Associate of the Executive Systems Research Centre (ESRC). His research interests include data warehousing, workflow management systems and groupware. He has developed a prototype workflow management systems which has been successfully tested in a number of Irish organisations. He now works as an IT specialist in the banking industry.

Tom Butler is a telecommunications engineer with Telecom Éireann, Ireland's major telecommunications service provider. He has been a visiting lecturer at UCC since 1997. His research interests include information systems development, CASE, user participation, organisational change and the implications of IT for the emerging knowledge-based theory of the firm. His research has been published and presented at several international conferences and he has a number of forthcoming book and journal publications.

Cathal Casey is a college lecturer in the Department of Accounting, Finance and Information Systems at University College Cork (UCC). He is also a senior researcher with the Executive Systems Research Centre at UCC where he is actively involved in research and consultancy in many areas of MIS. His research interests include decision support systems, expert systems and the evaluation of investments in IT.

Valerie Coatnoan is a Research Associate of the Executive Systems Research Centre at University College Cork. Her research is focused on electronic commerce and the commercial potential of the internet.

Pat Finnegan is a lecturer in Management Information Systems at University College Cork and a senior researcher with the Executive Systems Research Centre. He holds a PhD from the University of Warwick (United Kingdom). His research interests include inter-organisational systems, electronic commerce and IS planning.

Brian Fitzgerald is senior researcher at the Executive Systems Research Centre (ESRC) at University College Cork and is currently an Associate Editor of *The Information Systems Journal*. He holds a PhD from the University of London and he is actively involved in applied research projects in the areas of systems development approaches, foundations of the IS field and executive information systems. His work has been published in various books and international journals, including *The Information Systems Journal*, *The Journal of Information Technology* and the *International Journal of Information Management*. He has presented his research at many international conferences and seminars. Having worked in industry prior to taking up an academic position, he has more than fifteen years experience in the IS field.

William Golden is a lecturer in the Department of Accountancy and Finance at University College Galway, Ireland. He holds a PhD from the University of Warwick (United Kingdom). His research interests include inter-organisational systems, electronic commerce and flexibility.

Joseph Haslam has lectured in University College Cork since he graduated in 1994 with a BComm, having majored jointly in Management Information Systems and Public Administration. He was awarded a MSc in July 1996. His research interests include disaster recovery planning, uses of multimedia and links between IS managers and IS researchers. Since 1997, he is working as a software developer in industry.

Margaret Healy is a college lecturer with the Department of Accounting, Finance and Information Systems, University College Cork, Ireland. Subsequent to obtaining her primary degree, she worked for a number of years with a major, international Irish food ingredients company. She is currently working on a doctoral thesis investigating capital investment systems in high-technology industries.

Clive Hotham is Professor of Information Management at City University Business School (UK). After six years as a Director of Finance and IT, he moved to the Business School in 1988. He carried out a major research project for the Institute of Directors, examining the IT needs of executives and he authored "Executive Information Systems and Decision Support Systems". His 1993 research study "Improving the Performance of Workgroups through IT " has become a bestseller and has been translated into French. He is the inventor of the BFS (business facilitation system) – an intensively computer supported environment for executive workgroups and has a large number of publications, lectures and broadcasts in the UK, the US and continental Europe. He is also an international adviser for the Executive Systems Research Centre (ESRC).

Colin McCormac is a lecturer in Management Information Systems in University College Cork, Ireland. His MSc and PhD were in the area of computational intelligence. His research interests currently include: neural networks, data mining, education information systems and intelligent tutoring. He has designed a number of Web-based education systems and developed software to operate them. He has published a text book in the area of Web-based education systems as well as a number of related papers.

Ciaran Murphy is Professor of Management Information Systems at University College Cork where he is the head of the Department of Accounting, Finance and Information Systems. He is also the Director of the Executive Systems Research Centre (ESRC) which he founded in 1990. He has many international publications and books and regularly presents his work in international conferences in the US, the UK and continental Europe. He also acts as a consultant on IT matters for large, Irish organisations and has advised the Irish government on educational matters in the area of IT.

John Murray is a Research Associate of the Executive Systems Research Centre (ERSC). After working with the Australian Defence Industries in Sydney, he is now back in Ireland where he works as a systems analyst. His research interests include internet technologies and software engineering.

Brian O'Flaherty is a College Lecturer in Information Systems in the Department of Accounting, Finance and Information Systems at University College Cork. In addition he works as a senior researcher with the Executive Systems Research Centre (ESRC). He has previously worked in the telecomm-unications industry as a software designer. His current research interests include computer-mediated communication, the internet and client/server technologies.

Jean-Charles Pomerol is a Professor of Computer Science in the Laboratoire d'Informatique of Université Pierre et Marie Curie in Paris, France. After a Doctoral Thesis in optimisation, he has spent the last twenty years researching decision support and knowledge-based systems. He has co-authored three books in these areas and has many publications in international journals such as the *European Journal of Operational Research* and the *International Journal on Human Computer Studies*. He is the editor of the *Journal of Decision Systems* and has participated in the development of numerous knowledge-based systems now in use in industry.

Arthur Stanley is a research associate of the Executive Systems Research Centre (ESRC). He now works in industry as a software developer. His research interests include client/server technologies, HTML and data warehousing.

Howard Williams is a Research Associate of the Executive Systems Research Centre (ESRC). He has over 30 years experience in the computer industry and has worked in Ireland, England, Germany and the US, for a number of computer manufacturers and automation systems suppliers. He has also lectured information systems in University College Cork for many years. His interests include programming languages and application development methodologies, and his main research focus is in soft computing and related business applications of neural networks.

Introduction

The Executive Systems Research Centre (ESRC) is one of the largest and most active research centres in Ireland in the area of information systems (IS). It was created in 1990 in the Department of Accounting, Finance and Information Systems at University College Cork in order to support the accumulation of IS expertise amongst a pool of leading-edge specialists there and to provide an organised framework for staff to carry out further research in IS. Since then, much useful research has been carried out, ranging from the most theorectical to the most applied and the expertise and experience accumulated have reached such a level that we decided to assemble it in the form of a book that can be distributed to a wide audience. This book presents the most applied and managerially oriented aspects of this research in a structured way and contains sixteen chapters, which are divided into the four sections listed below.

1. Information Systems for Managers.

2. Managing Information Technology (IT) Resources.

3. The Electronic Revolution of Business.

4. Information Systems for More Effective Organisations.

As no book can really attempt to be exhaustive in this volatile, fast-moving area, some IS topics, such as object-orientation or databases, are not specifically dealt with even though they are mentioned in some of the chapters. We feel it is more interesting to try to provide readers with a coherent and structured picture of what they should know about information technologies (IT) if they are to be able to understand and anticipate the contribution that information systems can make to the way they work.

And everyone must now seek to achieve this goal because, at this point in time, it is quite certain that the ability of the employees and managers of an organisation to understand and apply IT is essential for its success. There is abundant evidence of the impact of the effective use of IT as some companies apply new technologies with great success while others fail to achieve any benefits. It is our experience that the 'reactive approach' to IT, whereby managers wait and see what new developments are implemented by their competitors, no longer works. There is now too much novelty reaching each of us too quickly for such behaviour to be effective. As a result, managers must be more proactive in assessing what technology can do for them and experiment with new tools and techniques. This search for opportunities can no longer be left to IS professionals alone because the greatest opportunities for IT usage lie at the core of the different functional areas of organisations and only people who understand the specific needs of these areas can think creatively about new applications of IT. Thus, the role of business managers in introducing IT has become paramount.

But mangers will only be able to play such a leading role when they are sufficiently aware of the available technologies – not that they should become programmers, data communication specialists or database experts – but they should be capable of understanding the progress and evolution of IT, anticipate its potential contribution and shape its future applications in their organisation. Books, such as this one, are beneficial to individuals who feel that they are in a position where they must understand more about IT so that they can fully take part in the discussions about the contribution of IT to the future of their organisation.

We believe that this book will be particularly useful to any manager or employee of an organisation or administration who feels that they should understand more about information technologies or who, faced with new developments in their department or office have an urgent need for more information about a particular topic. The chapters in this book will provide such people with the fundamental facts about the application of IT and will also provide relevant examples of what happened in organisations where these applications were implemented. Some chapters also present recent surveys of what happens in commercial organisations which can be used by managers to 'benchmark' the way things are being done in their own organisation. Other chapters provide specific guidelines for implementing better information systems based on the first-hand experience acquired by members of the ESRC involved in consultantcy projects. Finally, most chapters suggest further reading that can be sought by readers who need to probe more deeply into the issues addressed.

If you think this is just another book about IT, think again – our future will involve more, rather than less, reliance on information technologies.

Frédéric Adam and Ciaran Murphy
March 1999

Section 1

Information Systems for Managers

This first section is made up of the four chapters listed below.

1   *Supporting Managerial Decision Making.*
2   *Business Application of Expert Systems.*
3   *Soft Computing for Soft Information Systems.*
4   *Executive Information Systems: Meeting Top Managers'*
     Information Needs.

The section deals with a number of concepts relevant to the development of information systems that support the work of managers and examines the kind of systems that have been used in organisations to support the decision making and the strategic planning activities of managers. It also addresses the difficult issue of how to design computers systems that are able to process the type of information that managers need most: the softer information.

In a number of instances, such information systems for top managers have proved crucial to the competitiveness of modern organisations because of the increased visibility and control that they give managers on the operations they must supervise. Thus, many top managers have dreamt about replicating the widely publicised decision support systems/ executive information systems (DSS/EIS) success stories.

However, the development of these systems has proved a real challenge because computers are very good at handling vast amounts of data, but very poor at replicating the way managers use and present information. Thus, much analysing and programming must be completed before any system can be developed and this makes information systems that attempt to tackle the information needs of executives, particularly risky investments, as described in this section.

1
Supporting Managerial Decision Making

Jean-Charles Pomerol and Frédéric Adam

INTRODUCTION

Decision Making

Decision making has long been regarded as one of the core activities of managers. It is also considered the most important one as the quality of managerial decision making (sometimes combined with a bit of luck) often determines the health of organisations. As a result, there has been a strong incentive for IS specialists to endeavour to develop computer systems that can support decision making activities. This movement started as early as the 1970s with systems that were reasonably crude in technical terms and has continued right through to the current time with varying degrees of success.

One of the great difficulties in developing systems that support managerial decision making, resides in the fact that many organisational decision processes are not of a continuous nature: i.e. at each instant, managers are not making a decision about every aspect of their organisation. The continuity assumption, which makes sense for someone driving a car or for controlling an industrial process, does not apply to a CEO making a decision to purchase new facilities. Decision systems are, unfortunately, much easier to develop when they deal with continuous decision situations.

More specifically, the difficulty arises because managers making decisions often do not receive feedback on their choices until months have past, i.e. after the environment (competition, market, etc.) has responded to the changes implemented. In addition, the decisions made can rarely be revised in the meantime because they involve investing in new assets that cannot be renegotiated or moved easily. For these reasons, understanding and modelling managerial decision making are inherently difficult activities and developing decision support systems is even more difficult.

Decision Support Machines

A decision machine is an automaton that applies a one to one correspondence between a diagnosed current state (the way things are at the certain point in time) and a particular action. The word 'decision' is, in this case, not totally accurate because the decision has already been made by the designer of the system when writing the program. However when managers are unaware of how the program operates, or when it is so sophisticated that it is impossible to look through its operations, these machines can be regarded as decision machines. Numerous such machines already exist in the context of almost continuous decision (control of industrial processes, underground or train driving, etc.).

However, programmed decision machines, which relate the current state to a specific action, do not reproduce all the complexity of human decision making. Such systems may have some undesirable effects so that managers may not wish, for various organisational reasons, to embody the entire decision process in a computer program. The first obstacle on the road to a 'decision machine' is that, in many concrete situations, the set of all the possible current states cannot be described fully. Thus, the human decision maker is always indispensable, working in an interactive mode with the machine, mainly because unexpected (not programmed) states might occur. Emergencies and accidents are often created by the bad recognition of the current state (wrong diagnosis). The designers of decision support systems are therefore confronted with the paradoxical problem of having to develop systems capable of helping people in situations that neither the user nor the program can foresee. This is a difficult challenge in the development of decision support systems.

Another fundamental reason, that of accountability, presents a significant hurdle for the concept of decision making machines. In all areas, experts are individuals whose knowledge puts them at the cutting edge of difficult decision situations. In such cases, it can be expected that some wrong decisions will be made and the expert is then the person responsible for the consequences. Legal and financial responsibility will always require that someone takes ownership of a decision made by a machine, a responsibility few people would take unless they were very confident about the accuracy of their machine's diagnosis.

Reducing Uncertainty with 'What-if' Analysis

Coping with uncertainty (i.e. dealing with situations where many parameters are not known, such as what customers want, or anticipating the future) is the key to good management. Although various attempts have been made to help managers cope with uncertainty, many decision makers are not satisfied with the proposed 'rationalist' methods because in real situations, events are either very interdependent and/or the probabilities they occur remain unknown (e.g. What is the probability that the price of oil will be higher in three months than today?).

In this perspective, managers must internally simulate potential actions and make a decision. This kind of prospective reasoning is called a 'what-if' analysis and has been regarded for a long time as the main function of decision support systems (DSS). This is the popular reasoning of the type: "If I do that, they will react like this and I will do this if the price increases." What is important in scenario reasoning is to be able to develop many scenarios and to assess, at least approximately, their probabilities. Thus, supporting people in decision making amounts mainly to helping them foresee the consequences of their potential actions.

In many case, a 'what-if' analysis (or more accurately a 'scenario reasoning') should produce two outputs:

(a)   all possible outcomes in a given time-frame;

(b)   the probability or plausibility of each outcome.

The decision maker reviews these potential outcomes, then makes a decision based on his preferences and triggers his actions in accordance with the chosen scenario. This will involve resolving trade-offs between the value of a given outcome and its risk. Unfortunately, for non-aided decision makers, scenario reasoning leads to an explosion of the number of alternatives to consider and the factors to take into account and it is almost impossible for a single individual to handle the long, precise and diverse scenarios involved. This is the very reason why support from machines is necessary.

WHAT IS A DSS?

There are many ways to describe DSS technically, but whatever way is selected, a number of difficulties must be addressed. The first difficulty is that DSSs are, more often than not, ad hoc systems designed for a particular purpose. This leads to definitions of DSSs, which state that DSSs are systems intended to support a decision maker or that enable a manager to solve problems, in their own personalised way.

Thus, decision support implies the use of computers to:

(a)   assist managers in their decision process for semi-structured tasks;

(b)   support, rather than replace, managerial judgement;

(c)   improve the effectiveness of decision making, rather than its efficiency.

The obvious drawback of such definitions is that, while they clearly describe what a DSS is meant to do, they are weak at describing how it should do it and do not provide any clear guidelines for DSS development or usage.

DSS has also been associated with artificial intelligence (AI). This novel vision of DSS amounts to viewing DSS applications as essentially problem solving applications. It is illustrated in Figure 1.1, which shows the typical structure of a DSS application.

Representation Levels in DSS

Another way to think about DSS is to consider the degree to which the problems tackled are clearly represented in managers' minds. These representation levels are characterised by a certain level of abstraction and a specific way of thinking. They can be compared from two points of view: the degree of abstraction of the problems tackled and the degree of formalisation of the problems.

Thus, the five representation levels can be illustrated with the following description of the problem handling process.

1.   At the top level, representations are mainly cultural and psychological; managers are more or less aware of what a problem involves, but its expression is mostly beyond lan-

Figure 1.1: Typical Architecture of a DSS

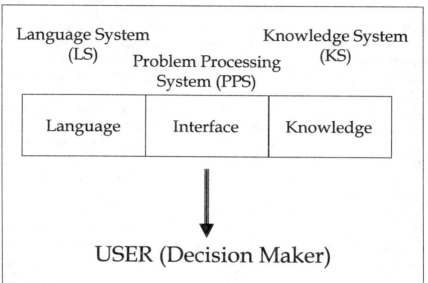

[Reproduced with permission from Editions Hermes, Paris]

guage. It is at this level that the problem is shaped.

2.   At this level, the representations become explicit and the problem can be broken down into a number of sub-problems, some of which can be formalised. The structure of the problems is still partial, rather than detailed, and managers will refer to 'the marketing function' or 'the marketing process' without being able to formalise processes in greater details.

3.   At this level, decision makers are able to define the structure of the problems they must solve. They are able to put forward models that can be used for the investigation of the alternatives they will pursue.

4.   At this level, the decision makers will perform sensitivity analyses with the models they have defined in the previous stage so as to determine which input values are the most suitable.

5.   Finally, at the lowest level, managers decide upon the most suitable values and the representation of the problem they must solve is stable and fully operational.

The process described here is a top-down process whereby the structure of the concepts investigated is refined from one level to the next until decisions can be made. Levels 1 and 2 are generally considered to be strategic levels of reflection, handled by top executives, whereas the other three levels correspond to more operational and tactical levels. It is worth noting that, at the top level, the decision maker has total freedom to decide on a direction to follow. This is obviously a very important stage of the decision making process as the only factors limiting the horizon of the decision maker are either psychological (unconscious) or cultural (e.g. his/her educational background). This stage is all the more important because it conditions the outcome of the decision making process. Avenues that are not envisaged at that stage are unlikely to be explored at a later stage. The manager's vision of the problem is then considerably refined at the second level to prepare for the formalisation of the third level were the manager enters the realm of "hard system thinking" where the representations and computational models must be fully stabilised. At the remaining levels, the manager will define the processing to be applied to the data and identify the most appropriate input values of the model.

ROLE OF MODELS IN DSS

Models constitute a very important component of DSS applications. The support the decision maker receives from the DSS being used comes mainly from the ability of the model to represent accurately and to simulate reality. Models are active in the search for solutions, a vision in sharp opposition with the idea that DSS merely follow the reasoning of the decision maker. The idea that reality can actually be modelled in a DSS raises a specific problem: if models get to such a level of sophistication, what role will the human operator play and will the DSS still need to be interactive? This underlines the limits of current knowledge in relation to models, which are, at best, incomplete, often simplistic and can only provide partial support to the decision maker. As such, they encompass the processing that can be applied to the data, a processing which reflects the knowledge of the developers of the system not the full reality of the environment of an organisation.

DSS applications will, typically, include a set of different models which are called in at the different stages of complex decision making processes or, alternatively, are used selectively depending upon the preferences of the decision makers. In this configuration, the DSS application will organise linking and passing parameters between the different models and provide an interface for the dialogues between the user and the DSS models. From the point of view of the user, the DSS is totally integrated in the sense that the user is faced with a single comprehensive, coherent tool aimed at supporting his or her decision making.

Models Most Frequently Used in DSS Applications

Many different kinds of tasks can be modelled or automated, hence the many different viewpoints adopted by developers of DSS applications. Mathematics alone offers a wide range of models ready to be applied, such as probabilistic models, statistical models, game theory, micro-economics models, etc. Operational research constitutes another abundant source of useful models in the context of an organisation, such as optimisation, economic order quantity, PERT, etc. Other domains can also provide interesting ideas for additional models: most notably, economics and accounting (see Chapter 16 of this book).

Looking at the range of tasks that existing DSSs have tackled, we can put forward a classification of the types of activities which often involve DSS applications. One of the most common tasks is that of analysing and statistically classifying series of events or figures. Many economical, or econometric, models enter that category, which also includes more qualitative kinds of analysis, such as competitor analysis and comparative strategy analysis based on games theory. More recent developments of DSS applications have even involved the area of negotiation and uncertainty analysis based on probabilistic and non-probabilistic decision trees.

Another common task involving DSS applications is forecasting, which can include various methods of projection of known, existing trends (econometrics models) and the prediction of customers' or competitors' behaviour using utility functions of the kind put forward by von Neumann-Morgenstern. These models are generally too normative to be really accurate, but their benefit is in enabling managers to 'predict' the reactions of a rational individual.

Other DSS applications are geared toward simulation, which is at the core of the activity of decision making (if everything was known about the future, the nature of decision making would be radically changed as little uncertainty would exist). Many econometric models and the Monte-Carlo methods are commonly used for these purposes. More recently, IS specialists have relied on expert systems to simulate the responses of the most complex systems, notably for the control of manufacturing processes (see Chapter 2 of this book).

Expert systems are also particularly strong in the area of evaluation or assessment especially when the data to be analysed is more qualitative than strictly quantitative. *Decidex* is an example of DSS which includes an expert system module for evaluating alternative scenarios. It enables managers to generate and select amongst a large number of possible actions and scenarios, the ones that have the most likely favourable outcome, based on possible outcomes and probabilities that might arise. Amongst these complex DSSs, which are aimed at supporting managers' choice, some systems may even be able to evaluate options in a multi-criteria environment, i.e. in a situation where a variety of somewhat contradictory criteria and conflicting goals must be pursued simultaneously. For example, *Multi-Decision* uses artificial intelligence to enable a manager to select interactively the most satisfactory actions within a set of scenarios and based on a large number of attributes.

Finally, DSS applications have been used very commonly in the area of optimisation, an area where most of the models of operational research provide the underlying theory for the search of optimal solutions under constraints. This remains one of the most traditional tasks of DSS applications, especially in cases where a credible, accurate mathematical algorithm can be applied and a quantitative solution exists.

In the 1980s, many DSSs included models of reasoning based on various degrees of artificial intelligence, for example in the form of an expert system module. Such systems are called intelligent DSSs. In spite of the early success of such concepts, the difficulties inherent in developing intelligent DSS (the huge costs associated with the large amount of knowledge required and, ultimately, their modest performances), have meant that these systems have gone out of fashion very quickly. Often, the task of reasoning is given back to the human decision maker, especially when there are additional problems, such as data entry (reading hand-written documents, etc.) or accountability. Users now seem to prefer more simple models based on large amounts of data.

In terms of simplicity, developers of DSS applications (especially end-users) have not neglected the fact that spreadsheets and simple, multi-dimensional modelling tools, such as *Lotus Improv*™ or *MS Excel*™ (database functions) are more than suitable for small DSS applications. They now represent the bulk of currently existing DSSs. Multi-dimensional spreadsheets use a simple data cube to generalise to n-dimensions the two-dimensional tables used by managers. Each cell in the model represents one item of data, such as monthly sales for a specific product on a specific market for a particular year. Users can then manipulate the data cube to display the information they want as a two or three-dimensional table depending upon the mode of representation available.

This method of manipulation of the data is particularly useful for organisations which deal with many products on many markets because it eases considerably the tasks of consolidation of accounting results and the forecasting/planning process. Individual markets and individual products can be monitored by managers without any additional burden for the operators who prepare the information displays.

Conception of DSS Models

In the early days of DSS modelling, systems were often geared towards the solution of one specific problem and were, therefore, based on a stable representation of this problem, i.e. a single model. These models, which were often very large, were solved according to a sequential series of specific steps.

1.　Initiation of session.

2.　Acquisition of the data.

3.　Execution of the model.

4.　Presentation of results.

This sequence is similar to that followed by many optimisation machines. This 'linear' conception of DSS was slowly discarded, however, based on more recent research that has put forward many novel methods for the resolution of problems.

Another source of evolution in the way DSS applications

operate came from user feedback. The old fashion attitude to DSS development, whereby analysts gathered information about the problem that must be solved and then retired to their offices to create the model and the interface of the system, is no longer acceptable. These practices resulted in many failures of DSS applications because users refused to use the systems that were developed for them or refused to follow the procedures specified by the developers. Problems would particularly arise in cases where models were developed without adequate attention being paid to current organisational practices and new procedures were too radically in conflict with theses practices. It follows that current practice must be used as a basis for the way the DSS will ultimately be used. This largely explains why expert systems modules, which give their users more flexibility in the choice of the methods followed, have rapidly become essential components of DSSs.

As a conclusion, the two main hurdles that DSS developers must overcome are:

(a) the creation of a non-linear method of solving problems;

(b) the resistance of system users to change the way they work.

These two obstacles can be addressed by establishing proper dialogue between the user and the system. The progressive, or evolutionary, development is another potential answer to the problems of user involvement and better prediction of the future uses of the system. The interactivity of the DSS will condition the degree of control the user has over the process of decision support and, ultimately, the degree of confidence the users have in the system.

An interactive session will typically be based on a number of stages.

1.   The user calls the decision support application.

2.   The data is acquired either from a database or from a series of answers provided by the user.

3.   The processing of the data begins.

In this last stage, the user retains control over the operation taking place. He can interrupt the process, go back, follow a different lead by altering input data or modifying the initial answers and can terminate the analysis at any stage he likes. Partial and final results can be stored and compared with the results of other simulations. Such an interactive model is obviously much richer than any linear model as described in the previous paragraphs; it is also much more in keeping with the way decision making takes place among managers.

Integration of Models in DSS

The models that are built into a DSS, exchange information with the database(s) to which the system is linked. In addition, models may also exchange data with other models within the system and several system architectures have been used to enable these exchanges. These architectures are studied in more detail in the next section, but some common principles of these architectures are presented below.

Models are stored in the DSS's model base, together with the programs applicable to the data processing required for these models. This model base also contains information about the input and output values of each model and the other variables which it uses for its calculations.

In simple DSS applications, relying on one single model, the only exchanges that take place are the exchanges of data between the database and the model. In multi-model DSSs, there is a need to integrate models in a coherent set, so that they are able to draw their information from the same data set (in order to avoid the duplication of data) and share their results. This creates a dilemma for DSS developers who are tempted to develop each model with its own data and its own conversations in isolation from the other models. While this is easier to implement, it may limit the usefulness of the DSS application considerably, because managers never think about one side of their knowledge in isolation from the rest of what they know. The DSS will not be efficient if much time is wasted transferring data from one model into another and updating input data and other shared variables. Therefore, the system must be able to switch from one model to another midway through processing data rather than run programs in isolation.

Another area of difficulty, in relation to the degree of integration of the different models within a DSS, involves the dialogue with the user. This is another area where the designer is faced with an alternative. The communication between the user and the system can be decentralised (so that each module or model has its own set of questions and answers) or they can be centralised (so that one specific module is handling all the communications between machine and user). Other DSSs have been developed with two separate levels of conversation:

(a)   general conversation;

(b)   model-specific conversation.

At the top level, the user may switch from one model to another or interrupt the execution of one model at a particular stage, whereas, at the other level, the user provides the input which is specific to the execution of the model currently being executed. This gives rise to a variety of different system architectures for DSSs. These architectures are presented in the next section.

ARCHITECTURES FOR DSS

The three fundamental components of DSS are:

(a)   the database;

(b)   the model base;

(c)   the interface/dialogue modules.

In practice, it may not always be so easy to distinguish between these components, but this basic architecture is nevertheless helpful in highlighting the basic issues in DSS design and, in particular, the requirements in terms of integration of the functions of DSSs. Based on the above, we can describe three main types of architectures commonly used for DSS as being:

(a)   the network of agents;

(b)   the centralised architecture;

(c)   the hierarchical architecture.

Networks of Agents

In a DSS of this kind, each model has its own database and its own integration and dialogue modules so that it represents a relatively independent agent, i.e. some kind of autonomous sub-DSS. The control of the network of agents is carried out by a special integration module (see Figure 1.2) which is not aware of the processing going on in the individual agents and merely

Figure 1.2: Network of Agents

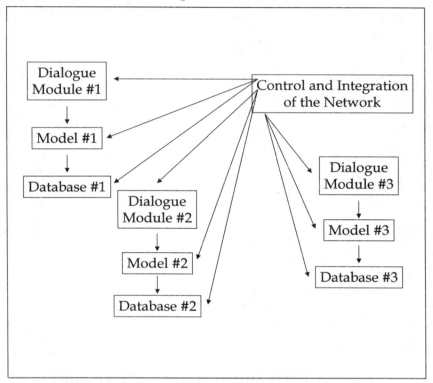

[Reproduced with permission from Editions Hermes, Paris]

manages the exchanges of data between the other components. The main advantage of this architecture resides in its great modularity, i.e. the ease with which additional modules can be built into the system. It remains that this ease of development is obtained at the expense of integration between the components, which is only minimum.

The network of agents is an open and adaptable architecture where modifications can be made within agents without affecting the other agents in the DSS.

Centralised Architecture

In this structure, all modules rely on a centralised dialogue module and a single database (see Figure 1.3).

The main advantage of such architecture resides in the excellent integration between the modules that it enables. The

Figure 1.3: Centralised DSS

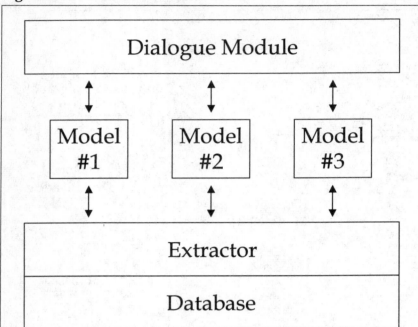

[Reproduced with permission from Editions Hermes, Paris]

unique dialogue module is a source of comfort for the user and the look and feel of the system is the same throughout. In addition, the unique database facilitates considerably the exchanges of data between modules. Control definitely resides with the user and is enforced by the dialogue module.

The main drawback of such architecture is its lack of flexibility. The design of the dialogue and control module can be very complex if it is to allow the same level of interaction between the user and the individual modules as, for example, a network of agents. This lack of flexibility becomes very obvious as the DSS evolves to accommodate additional models. The dialogue and control modules and the database must be fundamentally rewritten or redesigned to reflect these changes.

Hierarchical Architecture

In many ways, the hierarchical architecture is similar to the centralised architecture. The main differences are that the dialogue module is divided into specific sub-modules and that the database contains two layers with a view to facilitating the modification of the DSS.

The dialogue function of the DSS is divided into two layers. The top layer is the general dialogue module, which is concerned with the communication between the system and the user, and the communication between the modules. The second layer is composed of a series of model-specific dialogue modules, which serve as interface between each model and the rest of the application. The overall control of the DSS is taken care of by a supervisor module, which acts as an intermediary between the model-specific dialogue modules and the general dialogue module and co-ordinates the switches between modules. In this case, the models do not exchange any data or parameters among themselves and neither do their dedicated databases (see Figure 1.4). It is worth noting that, even though the supervisor's role seems to be comparable to that of the network controller in Figure 1.2, they differ quite fundamentally from each other. In order to perform its task, the supervisor must be aware of the nature of the data manipulated and the computations taking place within each of the models, a requirement that does not exist for a network controller.

Figure 1.4: Hierarchical DSS

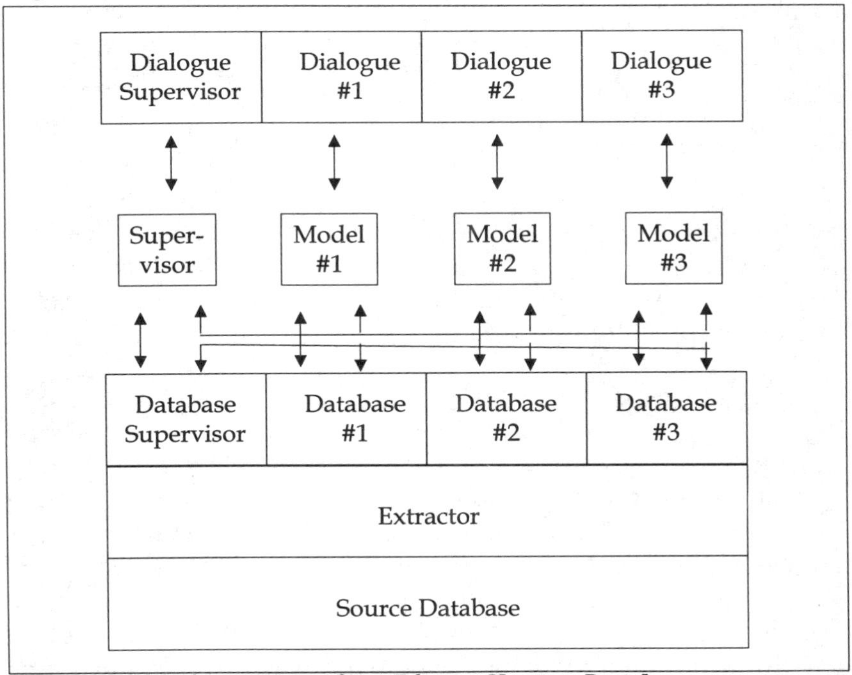

Hierarchical architectures have been used in many existing DSS applications, especially in cases where the different models in the systems are radically different in their structure and the way they operate. In such cases, it becomes interesting to separate the models and to give them access only to the data they can process.

In this kind of DSS, the user controls the application through the supervisor which has its own dialogue routines and enables the switch between models. The search for specific results (e.g. 'what if' analyses), by contrast, is done at the level of individual models. Some data exchanges among the different models can be organised using the supervisor which may copy the data from one model into its own dedicated database before passing them across to another process in another model.

This kind of architecture tends to cumulate the advantages of the networked and centralised architecture: unique dialogue modules giving a consistent interface and greater ease of use to the user, possibilities to exchange data and excellent integration on the one hand, and ease of adaptation and further development on the other. In the case where additional models must be added or removed, modifications must only be reflected in the supervisor and its two associated components (dialogue and dedicated database).

DSS DEVELOPMENT ENVIRONMENTS

Several options are available to developers of DSS applications who want to contribute to the decision making of their organisation. They will enable applications to be developed either by IT staff or directly by the managers/users.

Turn-key DSS

Turn-key DSSs are systems which include fully developed models and complete databases and can be used immediately by a decision maker. They are opposed to DSS generators which enable a user to develop a system to support a decision. DSS generators are dealt with in the next subsection.

In turn-key DSSs, the number of different models is often small, or even limited to one. The flexibility does not reside in the choice of many models, but in the ability to change a large number of parameters within these models, to run a wide range of simulations and to provide a wide variety of interpretations. The type of problems best handled by such DSSs will involve repetitive decisions with a specific approach to decision making, e.g. the selection of manuscripts by a publisher (around 100 different books accepted per year, a wide but known set of parameters and a formal presentation of each case). The value of such a system will reside in its ability to enable a subtle interpretation of the selection rules so that the decisions made are not stereotypical. This flexibility will be obtained by enabling the decision maker to include a wide range of parameters and variables in his or her analysis so that many different scenarios (i.e. paths to a decision) can be followed and the outcome of the evaluation is directly related to the specificity of each alternative considered.

At the end of the day, the flexibility of turn-key DSSs must rest with the decision maker. The quality of their intuition, the amount of knowledge they possess about the problem must be allowed to contribute to the decision making process, which requires that the DSS is open to new inputs and new parameters and that the interface between the user and the system must enable a high degree of interaction.

DSS Generators

DSS generators are systems that can be used to quickly develop a DSS of a certain kind or for a certain kind of task, e.g. the production of economic forecasts. These types of systems enable users to build a number of statistical or economical models based on existing templates and to adapt them to a specific decision situation.

In a generator, flexibility is a function of the number of templates of models available. The dialogue module must also be able to accommodate a great variety of types of interaction and handle many types of messages. Naturally, the flexibility of such systems also resides in the ability of the user to implement some variations in the inputs and variables used by the system. In other words, a DSS generator is a system that gives users the capability to modify the structure of models. As such, it is very close to expert systems generators.

At the same time, the development of DSS applications is not so straightforward that one DSS generator will offer solutions for all problems. A given generator will always be geared toward the support of a certain kind of decision situation and the models it proposes might not be very varied. In many cases, the models proposed will be similar and offer the user the capability to change the parameters used in certain type of model rather than radically change the structure of the model.

Tool Boxes

An alternative to turn-key DSS applications and DSS generators which brings more flexibility to their users, consists in providing them with a set of tools aimed at enabling them to develop their own DSS application from scratch. In some cases, this is achieved by providing a toolbox, made of building blocks more or less directly usable whereas, in other cases, it is achieved by providing a complete development environment not very different from the normal programming packages available under *Windows*™ (e.g. *Visual Basic*™). These development environments will include screen generators, code generators, libraries of codes and models and a database engine. Special programming languages must be created in order to enable users to code their models in the form of programs or routines. Such environments naturally require greater skills from the users, especially technical knowledge and programming skills, if users are to be able to develop complete DSSs from scratch. Otherwise, IS staff will be assigned the task of developing the DSS application based on ongoing dialogue with its would-be users.

CONCLUSION

The most significant weakness of DSSs, as regards executive use, remains in the lack of confidence of executives in the models used. The idea that decision makers need sophisticated models is probably wrong. Staff in charge of the preparation of decisions can probably use complex models, but high-level executives who most commonly make final decisions are too busy to train with and use difficult systems. On the contrary, they appear to prefer simple systems that they trust and understand and that display very timely 'punchy' information. More often, the data required to make the best decisions will already reside in some form or another in the database of the organisation and what is needed is a device to filter, display and to warn executives about important variances.

This resulted, throughout the 1980s, in a shift from DSS systems, including sophisticated prescriptive models, to simpler systems with attractive display and dialogue functions. A mere information filter seems more valued by executives than complex models and quick reaction to problems is more useful than sophisticated look-ahead; hence the increased popularity of the concepts of 'data warehousing' or 'data mining' both of which emphasise the ability of organisations to make the fullest use of the information they possess.

Nevertheless, many kinds of non-strategic but important problems must be tackled in organisations, many of them of a recurrent nature. In cases where the time available to deal with each case is limited, decision making must be delegated and DSSs become very useful. They can speed up the process and help managers enforce rigour and consistency in the decision making process.

2
Business Applications of Expert Systems

Cathal Casey

INTRODUCTION TO EXPERT SYSTEMS

Since the 1980s, expert systems (ES or knowledge-based systems) have represented one of the most exciting developments in information technology for the business community. The phenomenon of expert systems means that, for the first time, computers are being used to assist a person's thinking rather than merely processing data or providing information to think about. Expert systems provide users with the opportunity to be a little wiser, not just better informed. They carry computer support of decision makers a step further than any other type of information system. Specific definitions of expert systems are presented in Box 2.1.

Box 2.1: Defining Expert Systems

The British Computer Society's Group on expert systems proposed the following definition:

An expert system is regarded as the embodiment within a computer of a knowledge-based component, from an expert skill, in such a form that the system can offer intelligent advice about a processing function. A desirable additional characteristic, which many would consider fundamental, is the capability of the system, on demand, to justify its own line of reasoning in a manner directly intelligible to the enquirer. The style adopted to attain these characteristics is rule-based programming.

Other definitions include the following.

An expert system is a computer system which embodies human knowledge about some application area, stored in its knowledge

> *base in the form of* IF-THEN *rules, and is capable of making deci-sions or rendering advice which would normally require the at-tention of a human expert.*

An expert system is a computing system which embodies organ-ised knowledge concerning some specific area of human expertise sufficient to be able to fulfill its duty as a skilful and cost-effective consultant.

How do Expert Systems Work?

An expert system has four main components.

1.   A knowledge base, which contains the know-how or expertise.

2.   An inference engine, which carries out the reasoning, i.e. it determines the way in which the rules from the knowledge base should be applied.

3.   A database which is used by the inference engine as its 'notepad' or short-term memory.

4.   The user interface, which handles the conversation with the user.

In simple terms an expert system works by asking questions of the user and taking in responses as data. These are stored in the database. Then the inference engine applies the rules from the knowledge base to this data and thereby generates a conclusion. Figure 2.1 shows these components and how they interact. In addition to these basic components, most expert systems have the following additional components/features.

•   A developer's interface, which provides facilities for building and modifying the knowledge base.

•   An external interface, which allows for data to be passed to and from other programs and files.

•   Explanatory facilities.

•   The ability to reason with uncertain data.

Expert Systems: A Historical Perspective

The concept of ES has come about as a result of over 40 years of research in the field of artificial intelligence (AI), i.e. the scientific

Figure 2.1: Key Components of an Expert System

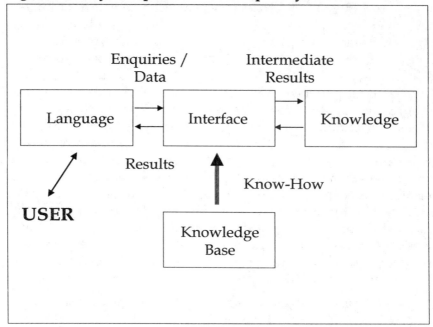

effort to build machines which, in some way, could be called intelligent. AI is the parent of ES: but the child has carved out a commercial presence far greater than the parent. Throughout its history the direction and emphasis of AI research has been changing, but the underlying goal has remained the same – to enable a computer to perform tasks which normally require human intelligence. Therefore, AI research has been concerned with many fields of investigation over the years: theorem proving, games, robotics, vision, natural language processing and expert or knowledge-based systems.

From these diverse fields of AI research, the area of expert systems has emerged as the one which is of most commercial or practical benefit. It was during the 1980s that interest in the business applications of expert systems soared. Even though much of the interest was media hype, genuine expert system professionals predicted the following.

Machines that lack knowledge seem doomed to perform intellectually trivial tasks, whereas those that embody knowledge and apply it skilfully seem capable of equalling or surpassing the best performance of human experts.

During the 1990s, this hype has died down somewhat. However, the opportunity to exploit expert system technology is now greater than ever before. This is partly due to technology advances (e.g. vast increases in the processing speed of PCs, *Windows*™ interfaces and increased connectivity of computers allowing seamless access to data from multiple sources), but it is mainly due to the ex-perience gained from expert system successes and failures over the last fifteen or so years. As with many fashionable areas of technology, the field of expert systems was initially hijacked by the media. This caused many companies to invest when the technology was not mature. There were many failures and some managers became disillusioned. As with all novel and fashionable concepts, the media raised public interest for a while and then quite suddenly dropped the idea for the next fad. But the history of any technology shows that people overestimate what it can do for them in its initial years, and underestimate what it can do in the longer run. At the start of the 1990s Edward Feigenbaum, one of the pioneers of expert systems, commented:

> *Much has been expected from expert systems and now, finally, we can say that much has also been delivered. Today expert systems assist human intellectual work over a wide range of tasks which are 'knowledge intensive' and 'information oriented'. Examples can be found in every area of corporate life from the office to the factory floor.*

Business Applications of Expert Systems

Expert systems applications often have a profound impact on the way that business is conducted, but they are systems that are only suitable for problems that are knowledge-intensive in nature. In fact the number of business problems which could be solved by using an expert system is likely to be quite small. However, when an expert system solution is suitable, the rewards are usually significant. This is particularly the case when the app-lication is of a strategic nature.

Consider for example the case of the Digital Equipment Corporation (DEC), where an expert system application allowed them to retain and improve their competitive edge in the mini-computer market. DEC's strategy of offering customised VAX mini-computers was under threat due to the difficulty associated with ensuring the correct configuration of the proposed computer system for each customer. It was a nightmare for human configurers to specify accurately the range of different options relating to things such as the number and type of terminals, plugs, channels, memory, hard disk configurations, peripheral options, interrupts, cabling and cabinet layouts. Human errors were common and the costs associated with correcting these errors after implementation was forcing DEC to move from their customised strategy to one of standardisation. However, in conjunction with Carnegie-Mellon University they developed an expert system for the task of configuration. The returns from such a system in monetary terms were, and still are, immeasurable. Not only did it multiply profits, it retained the productive distinctiveness of the business and as a result the goodwill and loyalty of its customers.

A typical application of expert systems is in the area of credit/loan approval. Such a system was developed by ITT Commercial Finance Corporation. The finance company estimate the returns from the system at several millions of dollars of savings in bad loan write-offs. American Express use a similar type of system called *Authoriser's Assistant* to approve or reject instantaneously requests for credit on their credit cards, which do not have credit limits. Their returns from the system are estimated to have been even greater than ITT's.

These areas of accounting/finance and taxation are ones where expert systems have made a significant impact. Typical of expert systems in these areas is a system called *Financial Advisor* which specialises in estate tax planning, ensuring that income and death taxes are minimised while providing related advice on investments and insurance cover.

These are just some expert system applications. Expert systems have been applied successfully to problems involving knowledge and human decision making skills in business areas, such as assembly, customer service, inspection, sales/marketing, personnel and production to name a few. Box 2.2 lists some further expert system applications.

Box 2.2: Some Applications of Expert Systems

- Auditing (accounting).

- Capital investment planning (finance).

- Career planning (management).

- Commercial loan application screening (finance and banking.
- Configuring computer systems (operations).
- Customer service representative training (marketing).
- Interpretation of new accounting standards (accounting).
- New venture decision making (marketing and management).
- Personal investment planning (finance).
- Product pricing (marketing).
- Sales management quota setting (marketing).
- Strategic planning (management and business policy).
- Tax planning (accounting and taxation).

Currently there are many business problems awaiting the application of an expert system. The problem is that the people dealing with them do not realise that an expert system might be a viable solution to their problems. It is this identification gap which the next section of this chapter addresses.

APPLYING EXPERT SYSTEMS TO SUITABLE PROBLEMS

It is important to raise awareness of the scope of expert system technology among business people in order to enable them to recognise the types of problems which could be solved using expert systems. For this purpose, this chapter harnesses the experience gained on existing expert system projects in order to answer questions about expert system application.

When should an Expert System Solution be Sought?

The most common reasons for developing an expert system are to:

- preserve knowledge that might be lost through the retirement, resignation or death of a company's acknowledged expert in any field;

- 'clone' an expert mechanically so that his/her knowledge could be disseminated;

- store information in an active form, a knowledge base, rather than a passive one, a textbook or manual;

- give novices an aid that would help them to think in the same way as more experienced professionals;

- create a mechanism that is not subject to human failing, such as fatigue, and can hold up in positions where information must flow constantly.

Maintenance of the expertise level within organisations is often a problem. Organisations are often adversely affected when experienced staff members leave or retire. Once knowledge is encapsulated in an expert system, it is a relatively permanent resource and can be used after the departure of valuable staff members. In addition, experts usually benefit from developing an expert system, because development enhances and clarifies their decision making processes.

What Role do Expert Systems Play in Decision Making?

There are numerous roles which expert systems can play. Firstly, an expert system can be used to replace a practising expert. Expert systems have been developed which equal, and often exceed, the performance of human experts. For example, NL Baroid, a company in the drilling services business, developed an expert system called *Mudman* to analyse mud samples. The system was successful because, in the drilling service business, consistency is an important determinant of successful decisions. In addition, decisions need to be made quickly in that domain.

Similarly, in the medical arena *Mycin* is an expert system which has proven itself capable of consistently making more accurate diagnoses than medical practitioners in the areas of bacteraemia and meningitis, two infectious diseases which can prove fatal. But *Mycin* is not in widespread use. This is due to a problem of accountability. In the case of *Mycin*, who would be responsible for the death of a patient which occurred as the result of a mistaken diagnosis from a machine? The issue of account-ability is likely to limit the use of expert systems in the role of re-placing experts.

In some circumstances an expert system may be able to serve as a *substitute* or *additional* expert, when human experts are scarce or unavailable. This would be most useful in remote locations or when junior staff have only limited call on an expert's time. In the latter case, the expert system could handle routine or commonly executed tasks which require expertise, freeing the expert to concentrate on more important tasks which require his unique abilities.

American Express *Authoriser's Assistant* is an example of an expert system deployed as an *assistant* expert in the area of credit authorisation. American Express credit cards have no set spending limit. This feature is ideal from a competitive perspective, but determining the credit level for each customer poses a stiff administrative challenge. Each time a customer makes a large purchase, the merchant phones American Express and an employee then has to make a quick judgement call. Authorisation requests outside the normal buying pattern require a search of their databases for more information. The expert system performs that search and makes recommendations to the person who makes the authorisation decision. The entire process takes only seconds; the merchant is still on the phone. With an expert system in an assistant role, the user is fully involved in the decision making process and takes final responsibility for the decision. The expert system assists the user in the decision making process by providing intelligent information on which to base the decision.

An expert system can serve in an *advisory* role. Here the expert system provides answers and suggestions, on which the user is expected to act. However, care is required in developing expert systems which provide users with advice, particularly if the task is a responsible one. Above average staff will tend to rebel if the expert system provides erroneous advice and below average staff will tend to deny their responsibilities, by projecting the blame for poor performance onto the system.

Expert systems can be used in a *learning* or *training* capacity, as a source of know-how. If an expert system contains a body of high quality knowledge, trainee users, in addition to having access to the systems suggestions and solutions, can learn about decision making by having access to the know-how which is applied by experts in their decision making. As a result, trainee users are better equipped to make skilful decisions, and may gradually become more expert themselves.

What Types of Problem Benefit from Expert System Solutions?

Expert systems have, in the past, been considered a panacea for all problems. This is due in no small measure to extravagant media hype. One expert system developer commented that certain media coverage of expert systems and artificial intelligence in general meant that the expectations of users and experts alike were totally outlandish. The main success factor for the effective delivery of an expert system is the selection of a suitable problem. Trying to make an expert system fit where it should not is an exercise doomed to failure. Expert system applications are used mostly to solve narrow problems which require the application of expert knowledge and reasoning. Researchers have devoted much attention to the task of identifying attributes which indicate suitable problems. The following is a synopsis of such problem attributes.

- Expert system problems should involve a relatively small volume of logically complex operations, and in such problem areas there should be a relatively universal pattern of logic. Problems should not be too general or complex. In addition, they should be reasonably self-contained. The task should have a well-bounded domain of application and not be inter-linking or overlapping too much with related problems.

- Although the problems should relate to narrow domains of knowledge, they should be non-trivial, high-value problems which are of importance to the functioning of the business.

- There should be at least one human expert who is acknowledged to perform the task well. The primary sources of the expert's abilities should be specialised knowledge, judgement and experience. The expert should be able and willing to articulate that knowledge and also to explain the methods used to apply it to a particular task. Problems where experts disagree about solution correctness should be ruled out.

- Assuming that it is technically feasible to develop an expert system solution for a problem does not automatically mean that the project should be undertaken: the project should be viable. There should be a return in terms of cost saving or revenue. The following are situations where expert system applications tend to be viable:

(a)   expertise is scarce or being lost;
(b)   knowledge is being applied inconsistently;
(c)   expertise is required in many locations;
(d)   there is an opportunity to sell expertise.

• It should not be possible to solve the task using conventional computing systems. It may seem that there is much similarity between conventional computing, whether used for data processing or decision support and expert systems. Both involve processing information on a computer. However, their uses are quite different. Conventional computing is concerned with handling data which might subsequently be used in a decision making process. Transaction processing systems take the first step by organising data and transforming it from one form to another. Decision support builds on this by allowing the manager to view data at a level which is convenient to him (e.g. as a summary, as a trend, or as a 'what-if' report), rather than at the basic level presented by data processing. However, the user still has to make a decision based on his own expertise, even though the data is presented in a much more useful form. Expert systems take the next step. They build on the results of data processing and decision support by assisting the user with the interpretation of data and forming a response. Rather than resulting in more data, an expert system generates suggestions for action. Therefore, expert systems provide a lever on the decision making process itself (see Figure 2.2). They represent a fundamental change from the way that computers are used in conventional systems (see Table 2.1 below for comparison with decision support systems).

Figure 2.2 The Role of Computer-based Information Systems in Decision Making

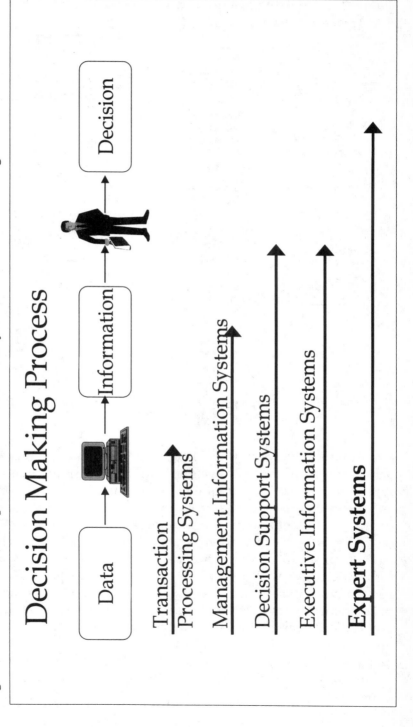

Table 2.1: Differences Between Expert Systems and Decision Support Systems

Attributes	DSS	ES
Objectives	Assist human decision maker	Replicate a human advisor
Who makes the recommendations	The human and/or the system	The system
Major orientation	Decision making	Transfer of expertise (human-machine-human) and rendering of advice
Query direction	Human queries the machine	Machine queries the human
Data manipulation method	Numerical	Symbolic
Characteristics of problem area	Complex, broad	Narrow domain
Content of Database	Factual knowledge	Procedural and factual knowledge
Reasoning capability	No	Yes, limited
Explanation capability	Limited	Yes

CONCLUSION

Expert systems are highly useful tools for business. They represent an advancement in the way computers support human decision making in that they incorporate human expertise, usually stored as 'if-then' rules, which they use to make decisions or offer intelligent advice about a specific type of problem.

The success of an expert system lies in its application to a suitable problem. In the past expert systems have been applied to problems for which they were not suitable, and there have been many application failures. Experience suggests that suitable problems are narrow ones where the solution depends on the application of specialised knowledge (or expertise) and that they are problems which are important to the functioning of the business. Finally, the entire project should be financially viable, i.e. the expert system should make, or save, money for the company.

3
Soft Computing for Soft Information Systems

Howard Williams

SOFT COMPUTING FOR SOFT INFORMATION

The growth of information technology (IT) feeds on an insatiable demand for information. The quality, accuracy and availability of information stored in myriad databases and transmitted via local and wide area nets provides a wealth of data that can be exploited by managers and professionals to inform their decision making. In the future, a higher proportion of information will be digital as newspapers, books, news services and mail are provided on electronic media.

As consumers of information, however, we very soon find that too much information overwhelms. When our focus of attention changes and the relevance of familiar information sources declines, we need to search new sources and trawling for data can be both time-consuming and tedious. It is more rewarding to talk to an expert, with at least the prospect of getting a few pointers in the right direction.

IT is identified with the measured, accurate data sets of rational scientific models – in fact, hard data. To a large extent, IT promotes hard data so well that soft data has not been a priority. Whilst hard data is useful, it is apparent that in the area of executive decision making, many executives base their actions on soft information. The success of executive information systems (EIS) in particular is critically dependent on providing information that satisfies a manager's perceived needs. For this kind of system, soft information is a priority. So let us first explore the distinction between hard and soft information.

Hard/Soft Information

Executives spend considerable time collecting soft information through a network of people inside and outside their organisation. As Henry Mintzberg says:

A great deal of the manager's inputs are soft and speculative –
impressions and feelings about other people, hearsay, gossip and
so on. Furthermore, the very analytic inputs – reports, documents,
and hard data in general – seem to be of relatively little importance.[1]

This soft information is used to identify problems and opportunities, develop agendas and build and refine mental models.
There is clearly no accepted definition of soft information; soft
information is simply contrasted with hard information as is
shown in Table 3.1. This table is characteristic of tables found in
the introductory chapter of MIS textbooks. Often this table is
related to three levels of management: operational, tactical, and
strategic, so that the operational manager is working with hard
data sourced from within his/her immediate environment and
concerned with production control, whereas the strategic manager is more concerned with external data, from personal
contacts or industry analysts related to long-term planning.
Generally, this table is used to emphasise that IT provides hard
data for structured problems and the role of IT in providing soft
data for unstructured problems is problematical.

Table 3.1: Hard/Soft Data Information Characteristics

Characteristic	Hard	Soft
Source	Machine resident often internal	Human, often external
Accuracy	High	Questionable
Degree of certainty	High	Low
Interpretation	Generally agreed	Subjective
Richness	Low	High
Ownership	Generally known	Often tightly held
Lifetime	Long	Short

1. Mintzberg, *The Nature of Managerial Work* (1973).

A better perspective of soft information may be gained by viewing information across a spectrum from hard to soft as shown in Table 3.2. Looking at these sources of information, we can indicate the ways in which such sources are used and may be supported in IT.

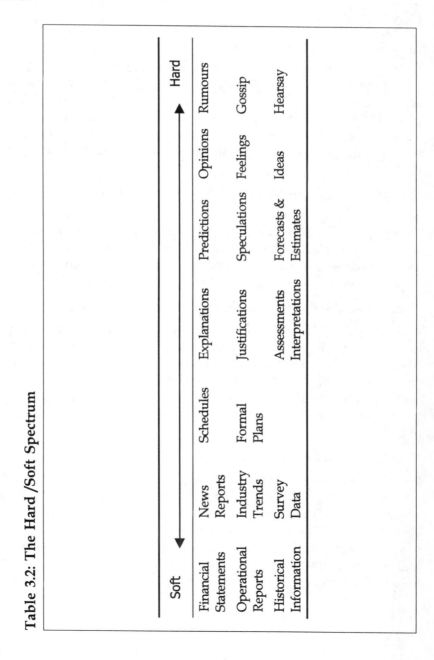

Table 3.2: The Hard /Soft Spectrum

Soft					Hard
Financial Statements	News Reports	Schedules	Explanations	Predictions	Opinions	Rumours
Operational Reports	Industry Trends	Formal Plans	Justifications	Speculations	Feelings	Gossip
Historical Information	Survey Data		Assessments Interpretations	Forecasts & Estimates	Ideas	Hearsay

News Reports, Industry Trends and External Survey Data

The majority of EIS systems should provide this kind of information in a readily accessible format. The individual user may either direct his/her search on-line or the system may maintain a profile of interests for each user and advise him of relevant stories as they are received.

Schedules and Formal Plans

Scheduling and planning activities are initially tentative and exploratory, so a small number of iterations under a review process are needed to achieve the best results. Once a schedule or plan is given legitimacy, via a formal sign-off, it drives the enterprise in a chosen direction. It establishes concrete goals and objectives and it will be used for highlighting achievements as well as deviations.

Explanations, Justifications, Assessments and Interpretations

This information helps to make sense of detailed hard data. This category of information provides a context and describes the processes responsible for hard data. It allows learning and development of expertise. The thrust of quality assurance and process improvement programs is to get this material documented.

Predictions, Speculations, Forecasts and Estimates

This category of information often provides the objectives and goals for tactical scheduling and planning. The sources of such data should be attributed so that users can refer to the original providers of this information to clarify their ideas and assumptions. It fosters a shared perception within the organisation and so supports the development of consensus concerning goals and objectives.

Opinions, Feelings and Ideas

E-mail and bulletin boards are the main vehicles for exchanging opinions, along with text annotation and voice commentary to screens. An advantage claimed for computer supported co-operative Work (CSCW), or groupware, systems, is that this level of soft information is encouraged in an anonymous environment. Peer pressure and power politics are reduced and consensus is easier to achieve.

Rumours, Gossip and Hearsay

In EIS systems, there should be provision for e-mail and bulletin boards and the question to ask is whether there are limits to the distribution of this material or limits to who enters the information. Some people may be hesitant about committing such soft information to writing and others will worry about whether this information is attributed to an author or is circulated anonymously.

The point which is emphasised by this presentation of a hard/soft information spectrum is that the level of abstraction or generalisation increases from left to right in Table 3.2 and likewise the degree of accuracy decreases. With an understanding of the distinction between hard and soft information, it is possible to think about the ways in which formal information is converted to soft information. We are all working in a real world where real facts and real processes interact in a maelstrom of complexity to generate streams of hard data. We absorb the facts, which are currently the focus of our attention, and which we can most easily interpret, against the models by which we understand reality and we try to find interpretations of facts that are novel or surprising. When it comes to reporting, we cannot deliver the accuracy or the detail of the original data, and we use our internal models to describe and explain cause and effect. At the boundaries of our areas of competence we are unreliable unless we adapt, improve and learn.

Now let us move from a human-oriented model of soft information generation to formal models that could be implemented in IT. In a soft communication channel, software agents receive, interpret and memorise a message in the context of simplified models: the message is not stored *verbatim*, as in a store and forward network node, but is stored in an abstracted form, later it is regenerated and transmitted forward. Hard information becomes vague, subjective – soft. The degree of communications success reflects the quality of the rules, or the training that the agents have received, and the accuracy and resilience of the models they use. Such a communication channel has software agents that are capable of some reasoning, abstraction, learning and memory. Agents filter the stream of hard input data to abstract relevant information. To implement such software agents we need to identify appropriate technologies in machine intelligence.

SOFT COMPUTING

The following quotation sets the context for soft computing.

It is believed that the most important factor that underlies the marked increase in machine intelligence nowadays is the use of soft computing to mimic the ability of the human mind to effectively employ modes of reasoning that are approximate rather than exact. Unlike traditional hard computing, whose prime desiderata are precision, certainty and rigor, soft computing is tolerant of imprecision, uncertainty and partial truth.

Soft computing has been coined as an umbrella term for a group of emergent technologies which relate to artificial intelligence. Under this umbrella term are grouped primarily:

- fuzzy systems;

- neural nets;

- genetic algorithms.

Although fuzzy systems have been on the research agenda since 1965, neural nets since 1943 (with a strong resurgence of interest since 1985), and genetic algorithms since 1975, there is growing evidence of convergence and textbooks are available treating the three technologies in an integrated fashion. What is behind each of these technologies, and how do they address the development of intelligent agents?

Fuzzy Systems

Traditional logic, taught since the times of Aristotle, is two valued (0 and 1 or true and false). An object or entity is either member of a set or it is not. Sets have hard boundaries. Using set theory, we can develop unions and conjunctions of sets which lead to Boolean Algebra and we can define axioms, propositions and predicates, which lead to formal theorem proving and formal descriptions. These are the foundations of hard IT.

One development of logic is probability theory, in which variables take on a value in the range 0 to 1, and the value is seen as a ratio of the number of times an event or outcome is recorded over a series of experiments. Probability theory aggregates results over many trials so that the probability of tossing an even dice is 0.5 and, if we have prior information that the dice is loaded, we can recalculate the probability. However, the outcome of any trial is not a probability. If we are tossing a dice, the outcome is definitely 1, 2, 3, 4, 5 or 6 and definitely not one of the remaining numbers. Each trial is measured in the context of a fixed number of outcomes, each with a hard boundary, so probability lies in the domain of hard systems.

The central idea behind fuzzy systems is to model uncertainty in set membership. Rather than postulating a black and white model of systems where everything can be tidily categorised by the set or sets of which it is a member, systems are seen to exhibit such variety that set boundaries are vague, subject to interpretation and coarsely defined. There is an uncertainty whether an object is member of a set or not and the uncertainty is measured by a fuzzy membership value in the range 0 to 1. By accepting that sets have fuzzy boundaries, models built on hard mathematics can be simplified, and may still perform realistically at reduced accuracy. So the goal of fuzzy systems is to model complex systems with some uncertainty, greater simplicity and improved resilience.

Fuzzy systems include one concept which lends itself to practical applications. This concept is the linguistic variable. The idea is that a variable such as *speed* is described by adjectives (and qualifiers as necessary) that have significance in certain speed ranges. The boundaries between each speed range are not precisely defined and may be approximated by the trapezoids shown in Figure 3.1. So each speed range is a fuzzy variable. Each range is associated with an adjective, so 20 to 50 mph is 'slow'. A specific speed, say 40 mph, may then be variously described as 'slow' or 'moderate'. This speed has a fuzzy membership value of 0.3 in the set 'slow' and at the same time a fuzzy membership value of 0.7 in the set 'moderate'. The value of the linguistic variable *speed* is characterised by a limited number of membership values in overlapping fuzzy sets. The effect is that a description of a speed as a vector of fuzzy membership values represents the vague, imprecise, subjective description of speed we often get in natural language. Linguistic variables provide the link between fuzzy systems and their users and designers. We will explore the use of linguistic variables in fuzzy controllers.

A fuzzy controller is shown in the block diagram of Figure 3.2. Sensors measure the state of the system under control. Each sensor signal corresponds to a linguistic variable, so each measured value is converted to a vector of fuzzy membership values. Taking a simple system with two linguistic variables, say

Figure 3.1: Linguistic Variable

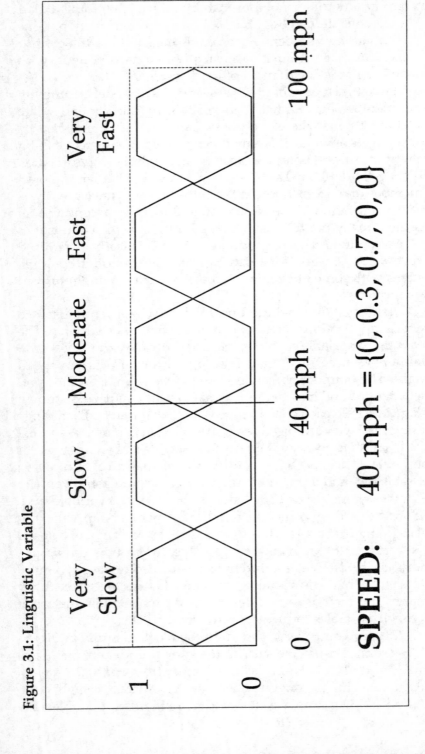

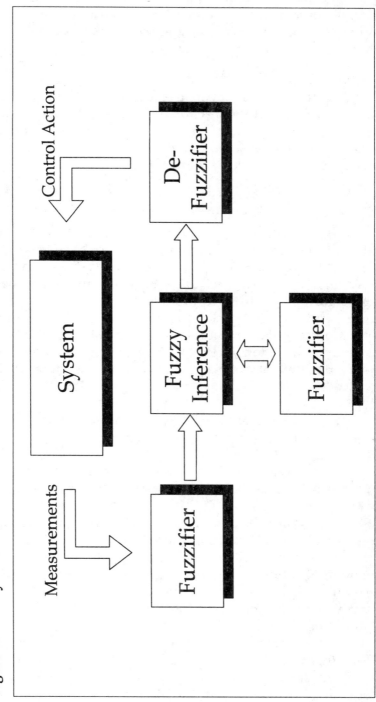

Figure 3.2: Fuzzy Controller

speed and *acceleration*, the state of the system is identified by an element of a two dimensional fuzzy matrix. If the state of the system is "speed is very slow and acceleration is moderate", this state is represented by the matrix element:

(speed = VS) AND (accel = M).

The elements of the fuzzy matrix are filled with the appropriate fuzzy controller output or action. These fuzzy entries are supplied by an expert or craftsman operator or on the basis of an intuitive understanding of system behaviour. The controller actions may also be expressed as rules of the type:

IF (speed = VS) AND (accel = M)   THEN (control = FP)

where (control = FP) may mean, say "set control fully positive".

One rule is written for each element of the matrix, so that the table or rules represent the built-in expert knowledge used to control the system. In operation, at time t, the measured variables *speed* and *acceleration* are fuzzified. Each rule which becomes true contributes a fuzzy component to the control signal. The composite fuzzy control signal is converted to a hard output value by a process of de-fuzzification. The controller repeats the cycle of control calculations, at times t+1, t+2, etc., so that any deviation between the actual and the desired state of the system is balanced by a control output, which brings the system back to the desired state.

An advantage of fuzzy controllers is that they require little formal or hard understanding of system dynamics as is the case for conventional controllers. Conventional control theory is based on mathematical dynamic models of a system which are generally linearised to obtain analytic solutions and, therefore, tend to work poorly in non-linear applications. The fuzzy controller on the other hand can be programmed to deal with non-linearity in a more intuitive and resilient fashion.

Fuzzy controllers are the largest sector of the market for fuzzy applications. The most significant investment in fuzzy systems is taking place in Japan, with America and Europe playing a catch-up role and, as Table 3.3 shows, the growth in applications in this decade has been accelerating. A survey in an IS journal in March 1994 identified three landmark fuzzy systems. The first dates from the early 1980s, when the Blue Circle Cement Company identified that the operation of their kilns was critically dependent on the skill and expertise of a limited number of operators and they were concerned that this pool of expertise could not be expanded to cope with a growing number of new kilns. Conventional control of kilns, in which lime is clinkered and the clinkered mass is then ground to form cement powder, was abandoned due to the lack of an adequate mathematical model. Instead, a fuzzy expert system called *Linkman* was used and the experience of skilled operators was captured in fuzzy rules. The first kiln to be controlled by a fuzzy system came on-line in 1982 and was then extended to all kilns operated by the company. This early application proved the feasibility of fuzzy systems.

Table 3.3: Commercial and Industrial Fuzzy Systems

Year	Number of Systems Implemented
1986	8
1987	15
1988	50
1989	100
1990	150
1991	300
1992	800
1993	1,500
1994	2,500
1995	large numbers

The second landmark application is the Sendai subway system in Japan. This system is an *Automatic Train Operations Controller* which provides speed control of trains between stations. The speed profile of the train consists of phases of acceleration, coasting and braking and the control needs to take into account such factors as the comfort and safety of passengers. Since 1986, the system has reduced the stop-gap distance between trains by 2.5 times, doubled the passenger comfort index and reduced power consumption by 10 per cent. As a result of the experience gained on such early systems, Japan is rapidly exploiting fuzzy technology both in control and in consumer products.

The third application is in a completely different area. The

Yamaichi Fuzzy Fund Manager is a financial application in trading systems. It handles 65 industries and a majority of the stocks on the Nikkei (the Japanese stock market) and it makes buy/sell decisions on stocks. It consists of about 800 rules which are reviewed monthly by a group of experts and maintained by senior business analysts. The system was tested for two years and in terms of the return and growth, its performance exceeded the Nikkei average by over 20 per cent. It has been used in commercial operation since 1988. Such fuzzy expert systems are another major market area for fuzzy systems.

The application of fuzzy theory requires a significant re-orientation of our thinking about set membership and operations on sets. A glance at textbooks on fuzzy logic will convince you that this reorientation will be tough. Some see fuzzy logic to be a paradigm shift as significant as Newtonian mechanics. Others are more pragmatic and can identify that fuzzy systems simplify process models so that they become more resilient, but less accurate. Remember the adage:

"Models should be as simple as possible, but not simpler."

Neural Nets

Whereas fuzzy systems are motivated by the imprecise boundaries around the meaning of words, neural nets are based on our understanding that brains store information in a distributed fashion across a network of brain cells called neurons. The activity of neurons is thought to be responsible for the emergent features of control, stasis, memory, self-consciousness and intelligence in animals. However, neural nets are a pale reflection of their neuron cousins. A model for a neural net node is shown in Figure 3.3.

The neural node, which is analogous to a real neuron, calculates a weighted sum of inputs. The weighted sum is 'squashed' to constrain it to the range 0 to 1 and this is the output value of the node. Many neural nodes are interconnected to form a net as suggested in Figure 3.4.

Figure 3.3: Neural Node

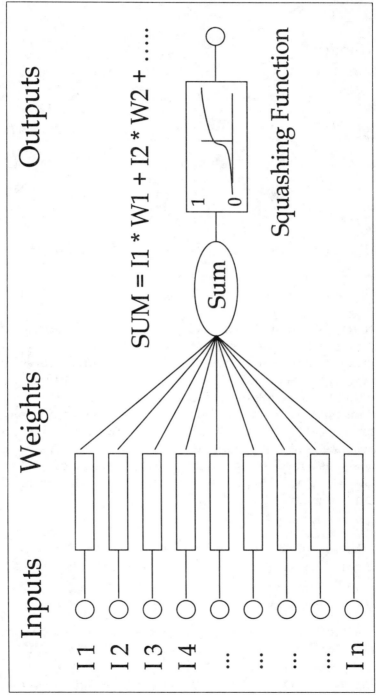

Figure 3.4: Neural Nets

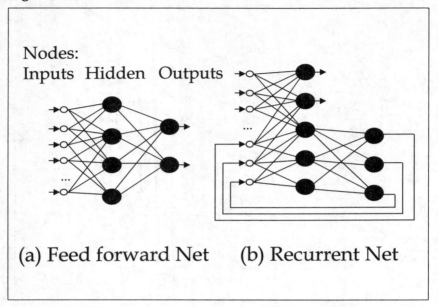

Nodes:
Inputs Hidden Outputs

(a) Feed forward Net   (b) Recurrent Net

Such nets consist of an input layer which distributes input values to one or more hidden layers and through to a final layer of output nodes. The essential feature of neural nets is that the weights can be modified, progressively through a training regime, so that the net provides a desired output response for given sample inputs. The reinvention of the back-propagation algorithm for weight training was the major stimulus for recent, reawakened enthusiasm for neural net technology. A net is characterised as a feed-forward net if nodes at each layer are connected only to the next layer. In a feed-forward net, the output (O1) is a non-linear function of the input values (Ii):

$$O1 = f (I1, I2, I3, ...In)$$

If there is feedback, the net is characterised as recurrent and the output (O1) is a more complex function of inputs (Ii) and outputs (Oi):

$$O1 = f (I1, I2, I3, ...In, O1, O2, ...Om)$$

The fact that nets are trained to respond correctly does not mean that neural nets learn. As yet, neural nets do not exhibit the reflexivity or self-awareness that is necessary for self-adaptation of weights; it is more appropriate to say that a net is conditioned to react to a stimulus and generate a desired response.

The distributed representation of knowledge and the ability to retrieve a conditioned response lead to features of neural nets that are extremely interesting to system designers. These are:

(a) tacit knowledge;

(b) associative memory.

Tacit knowledge is 'given wisdom' or experience. Tacit knowledge is knowledge for which we have no formal model against which we can validate or explain behaviour. Tacit knowledge is accumulated before understanding. When we use neural nets in systems, they are trained by the designer to appear intelligent because they have absorbed the designer's explicit or formal knowledge. Tacit knowledge is relevant to such system activities as function approximation and table-lookup. A function, or a table, expresses a formal relationship between input and output variables. If we can condition a neural net to provide the same output as predicted by the function, the net tacitly knows the function and behaves accordingly. Tacit knowledge is generally imposed on feed-forward neural nets and in the majority of applications, the training is performed by the back-propagation algorithm.

Associative memory is the ability to retrieve complete information from a partial representation. In general, recurrent nets are used for associative memory. In auto-associative nets, samples of complete information are imposed on the first layer of nodes and the net is trained to regenerate this complete information at the output nodes. After training, a partial input vector is imposed on the net inputs, the net is allowed to run until the outputs are stable, at which time the output is a correct representation of the complete information on which the net was trained.

The years 1980-1990 have been called the 'Neural Decade', being the period in which so many neural applications emerged. A survey in *IEEE Expert* for August 1996 looks in detail at four applications that perhaps exemplify the thrust of current neural products. The first is a neural integrated circuit (IC) that sells for about $5 and is designed for speech processing in toys and consumer electronics. The IC handles speech synthesis and speech recognition and is aimed at such applications as children's learning aids and speaker verification for car security systems. This device will currently recognise about a dozen words for speaker independent voice recognition and up to 30 words for speaker dependent voice recognition. Such a device can very easily be seen to provide another mode of communication between an executive and his computer and an alternative to the keyboard, mouse and screen display.

The second application is from IBM, which has developed a neural net that detects computer viruses on the boot sector of a floppy or hard disk. This is distributed with OS/2 and must run on minimal machines with little memory, so there is a premium on the efficiency of neural computation. The network was trained on about 200 known viruses and has caught about 75 per cent of new boot sector viruses that have come out since the product was launched. This is an intelligent utility which encapsulates as much tacit knowledge as was available at the time of its introduction, and behaves reasonably well against new threats.

The third application is face-recognition which humans are superbly adapted to perform but is one task that still defies formal explanation. In February 1995, the first pilot installation of a face recognition system for commercial use, took place in a bank's computer centre. The neural system compares a video camera image of a person's face against information supplied simultaneously by a security card and addresses the specific verification task: "Is the person in question identical to the cardholder." The system is right 99.5 per cent of the time. This application presents one approach to a tough pattern recognition problem and also potentially overcomes the disenchantment that infrequent users have with passwords.

The fourth application is in steel making, which is an industry with high peak demands for electricity in such plants as arc furnaces in which scrap iron is melted to produce high-grade steel. By combining conventional process models and neural nets, the power demands of the arc furnace can be optimised. At one site, the steel maker has cut US$1 million per year from his energy costs. Such optimisation applications in process control can save huge amounts of money and the soft computing approach is shown to out-perform conventional process models.

Neural nets have a simple computational overhead so they are easy to implement in hardware or software and their performance can be tuned or trained to provide the appropriate level of functional complexity.

Genetic Algorithms

Again, a biological analogy has been commandeered to describe a learning mechanism based on Darwinian evolution. Genetic algorithms stem from the need to solve complex optimisation or combinatorial search problems. The analogy suggests that a population of genes is propagated from one generation to the next in such a manner that following generations are fitter in the evolutionary niche in which they operate.

Each gene is seen as a possible solution. Between generations, new genes are created by crossover, mutation and similar genetic operations. The fitness of each gene in a new generation is evaluated against a performance measure for the problem at hand. The best genes are saved and poorly performing genes are eliminated. After perhaps many generations of adaptation, a successful gene represents a good, if not optimum, solution to the problem we are trying to solve.

Genetic algorithms can be seen to provide a directed search of a solution space with randomisation of intermediate solutions to avoid getting trapped in false minima. Genetic algorithms are based on a model which has wide significance for living systems and they do not depend on detailed hard or formal understanding of the optimisation problems they address. They characterise the type of technology that we would like to use to train soft systems. In current practice, back-propagation is by far the most popular method for training neural nets.

A comparison of these three technologies is attempted in Table 3.4. Together, these technologies score 'good' for each of the characteristics listed on the left. The table also includes an assessment of classical control theory and symbolic artificial intelligence. The table suggests that the three complementary soft technologies may out-perform classical control theory and symbolic artificial intelligence.

Separately, fuzzy systems and neural nets have been used to create intelligent systems. Both can be used for function approximation and function estimation, both are developed from a description of the required input/output relationship. They differ primarily in their knowledge representation. Neural nets have a distributed knowledge representation expressed by the weights between nodes. Tacit knowledge implies no formal structure and the internal operations of a neural net are essentially black-box. On the other hand, fuzzy systems represent

Table 3.4: Comparison of Technologies

	Fuzzy Systems	Neural Networks	Genetic Algorithms	Control Theory	Symbolic AI
Mathematical Model	SG	B	B	G	SB
Learning Ability	B	G	SG	B	B
Knowledge Representation	G	B	SB	SB	G
Expert Knowledge	G	B	B	SB	G
Non-linearity	G	G	G	SB	B
Optimisation Ability	B	SG	G	SB	B
Fault Tolerance	G	G	G	B	B
Uncertainty Tolerance	G	G	G	B	B
Real-time Operation	G	SG	SB	G	B

The fuzzy terms used for grading are good (G), Slightly good (SG), slightly bad (SB) and bad (B).

knowledge in a structured, rule-oriented fashion. Direct encoding of 'if-then' rules is a visible evidence of the knowledge representation. When developing a new system, we can decide which parts are suitable for fuzzy and which for neural implementation. The range and variety of application architectures obtained by using both techniques together is being exploited to improve current applications, like controllers, and to create new applications.

The combination of fuzzy systems, neural nets and genetic algorithms in a discipline called soft computing, can perhaps be seen as a trilogy of complementary techniques that have been brought together to develop intelligent agents. Fuzzy systems provide a theoretical framework for designing complex systems with uncertainty, neural nets provide memory and tacit knowledge and genetic algorithms are used to train such systems. Fuzzy sets and cellular computation allow for real simplification of complex systems. Providing the training data encompasses sufficient cases, the embedded, tacit or rule-based knowledge can demonstrate more resilience, and more 'intelligent' behaviour than hard systems. Particularly, at the interface between hard systems and human users, the use of linguistic variables and tacit knowledge can provide better cognitive match between the user and the machine.

Application of Soft Computing to Soft Information

We had suggested earlier that more and more hard data will be made available, and a function of soft computing is to filter the stream of hard data to make it more relevant or more easily assimilated by an executive. Two applications of fuzzy systems taken from the MIS domain, and treated in current textbooks, provide support for the argument that soft computing addresses the issue of soft data. These are:

(a) fuzzy information retrieval;

(b) fuzzy SQL.

Fuzzy Information Retrieval

This application applies to the interrogation of libraries of information containing complete documents – book, report or paper. When new material is catalogued, it is given an access code and is classified by subject. The classification is generally in terms of a list of keywords that are found in the title or the summary of the document. The classification is the basis for queries on the information system. A query is formulated in terms of keywords relevant to the user and those documents that best match the query are listed in response.

Retrieval of matching documents is a three step process. In the first step, a fuzzy thesaurus is constructed. All the keywords which classify documents are listed on the two dimensions of a square fuzzy matrix. Each element of the matrix is a fuzzy correspondence between the input keyword and the output keyword. Each element ranges between 0, if the keywords are clearly independent, and 1, if they are synonyms. The elements of the fuzzy thesaurus map the degree to which two keywords relate to the same concept. The thesaurus can be updated when new documents are entered into the system.

The second step is to match the keywords in the user query against all the keywords in the thesaurus. By composing the user keywords against this thesaurus, we get a set of user keywords and synonyms appropriate to the user query. The third step takes the expanded user query and composes it against the classification of each document in the library. The output of this fuzzy composition is a fuzzy correspondence between the user request and each document. Documents with a high correspondence are listed for retrieval.

Fuzzy information retrieval is a simple application of fuzzy sets. Both the thesaurus data and the classification data for documents are approximate, inexact, vague and subjective. But the theory provides an operation for set composition and this is used twice to provide a level of performance which is intuitively reasonable. Looking back at Table 3.2, this application might be expected to address the first breakpoint along the hard/soft spectrum. Hard data is filtered against a user query or a user profile maintained by the system. In practice, fuzzy information retrieval is the technology behind internet browsers which interface directly between the user and information sources on the net. It is questionable whether such browsers could be described as intelligent; any intelligence probably resides in the original choice of keywords for source documents and perhaps, significantly, in the creation of the fuzzy thesaurus. Which begs the question of what is machine intelligence anyway? I take the view that machine intelligence is a property of models that a designer has formalised as programs. Behind more complex intelligence there lie more complex explicit, rather than tacit, models.

Fuzzy SQL

In a distributed computing environment, a user has his own computer or workstation connected, via a network, to servers. The database server, in particular, may service databases which are local or remote. To provide an efficient utilisation of the network, and to download specific information to the user, the user creates a query asking for a subset of data in the database. The query language is generally the de facto standard 'Structured Query Language' SQL which permits statements of the form:

SELECT name, address, city

FROM customer

WHERE city = CORK

which, presumably, returns a list of customers in Cork. SQL provides hard data in return for hard, specific queries.

Fuzzy SQL provides an interface between a user and an SQL server which attempts to match the user needs expressed in softer more conversational terms. Often, a user trying to retrieve information will be in a learning mode, probing the environment, attempting to size a problem and building a mental model. In these circumstances, the user may not be able to formulate crisp SQL queries and it is the function of an intelligent agent to assist in this task.

Relational databases are based on a beautifully structured mathematical theory of relations and relational algebra, which includes operators such as project, union, join, etc., that are defined for hard sets. A fuzzy SQL begins by introducing modifications to the formal relational model. The first modification is to fuzzify elements of a relational table. Thus, in the relation *markets*, the elements *size* and *potential* are fuzzified.

Markets

Area	Size	Potential
east	large	good
west	(large, medium)	moderate
mid-west	small	(good, excellent)

Queries on this table can now refer to *size*> medium. Each column of a relational table may be fuzzified which really implies that the column identifier is treated as a linguistic variable.

The second modification is to fuzzify the join operation on relations. In SQL, constraints such as:

WHERE area1.potential = area2.potential

are crisp equivalencies. If potential is a linguistic variable, then potentials can be compared fuzzily. Two potentials are equivalent if they exceed a threshold fuzzy compatibility relation. With this modification, constraints can be expressed:

WHERE   area1.potential   =   area2.potential   WITH THRESH>0.80.

Fuzzification of the rich relational model can lead to dialects of SQL, which are less precise but more consonant with natural language. The relational model provides a highly consistent and formal approach to data storage and retrieval, so fuzzification leads us to products which lie higher up the intelligence scale. In terms of the hard/soft spectrum again, fuzzy SQL may be expected to help extract predictions, forecasts and estimates from hard data. I would like to draw the inference that the intelligence of soft agents is a function of the underlying formal models and fuzzification provides the abstraction of details to a level that is appropriate and attractive to an intelligent user.

Fuzzy information retrieval and fuzzy SQL are the workhorses of more complex soft MIS systems. Recently a fuzzy spreadsheet was announced with applications directed at scheduling, planning and decision making. The suggestion is that data for a spreadsheet model is retrieved from the environment using a combination of information retrieval and SQL.

CONCLUSION

Soft computing offers more than fuzzy systems and neural nets. Yet, the potential for soft applications resides in the imagination and creativity of their designers. Applications will result from critical awareness and expertise in a particular domain and a feeling for the needs of non-expert users of that domain knowledge. Soft computing provides an approach that builds on simplified models and tacit or rule-based knowledge to describe complex systems. If intelligence is equated with progressively more complex formal models, development of intelligent agents cannot be simple. It has been estimated that the development of one rule in an expert system costs about US$1,000 so even a simple system with twenty rules may prove expensive to build, unless supported by an analysis of the likely market potential. But the market will create more fuzzy products and we need some appreciation of the technology to be able to assess the claims made for these new products.

FURTHER READING

For further reading, I would recommend the paperback by Bart Kosko, *Fuzzy Thinking: The New Science of Fuzzy Logic*. The books on fuzzy systems are predominantly written from a science/ engineering perspective and directed to controller applications. All of the texts, and particularly those which cover both fuzzy and neural systems, can only be described as heavy. The impression I want to convey is that these technologies are being taken seriously in the science/engineering domain and that there is clear evidence that they are being exploited for new MIS products.

I have tried to establish the relevance of soft computing to soft data. In the context of the quotation from Clive Holtham:

The next generation will not just restructure existing hard data...
It will also attack the whole issue of soft data.

If this challenge is to be met, we are going to hear more about soft computing in the future. To summarise, the ideas contained in this chapter could be expressed as a warning to managers:

Beware, the future is fuzzy!

SOURCES

H Mintzberg, *The Nature of Managerial Work* (Englewoods Cliff: Prentice Hall) 1973.

B Kosko, *Fuzzy Thinking: The New Science of Fuzzy Logic* (UK: Flamingo) 1994.

4
Executive Information Systems - Meeting Top Managers' Information Needs?

Frédéric Adam and Ciaran Murphy

INTRODUCTION

In comparison to other sectors of activity, the universe of top managers has not been changed radically by the new technologies that have been developed in the last 30 years. This can be explained by one important factor: unlike many other users of technology, managers frequently have a choice over their dependence and use of new tools. Computers are a good example of this: if systems do not provide them with timely, accurate and relevant information, then managers will use alternative sources – or even make decisions without detailed information. This constitutes the primary characteristic differentiating executives from other users and explains why their relationship with technology is, in general, not straightforward. Thus, the history of data processing is replete with instances where researchers and vendors have claimed to have discovered *the* technology that will solve the informational problems of executives, only to fail to address the important issues in a manner that, at last, can convince manager-users that this is the right technology for them. At the same time, it is quite certain that the information needs of executives raise very real problems, evident in the abundance of reports that managers are "overloaded with data" yet "hopelessly uninformed". Recently, the internet phenomenon gave rise to similar mixed reactions as is explained in Section 3 of this book. Arguably, communication technologies, such as e-mail and mobile phones, have had instantaneous successes, but they also have failed to solve most of the problems they raise in terms of information and connectivity overload.

In this chapter, the now mature concept of executive information systems (EIS) is examined in terms of its potential in solving at least some of the problems raised by information systems for executives.

What are Executive Information Systems and Why are they Different?

Executive information systems, self-evidently, are systems aimed at addressing the specific information needs of top executives. In this, they have been compared to other types of systems previously developed, such as management information systems (MIS from the 1960s) and decision support systems (DSS from the 1970s), which have already been dealt with in Chapter 1. The founders of the EIS movement have insisted that the concept they put forward is radically different from anything that was attempted before from both a technical and marketing point of view, vendors and researchers have claimed that the new EIS approach brings radically novel solutions to the problems of executives. This may not be the case, as is shown below.

According to the proponents of EIS, the false assumptions inherent in the developments of the 'MIS era' (i.e. the 1960s and 1970s) included the belief that managers know their informational needs and that the linkage between better information and better decision making is evident. But, executives' jobs are characterised by an abundance of data that exceeds by far their processing capacity (approximately 40 hours of unsolicited readings and the same amount of solicited readings every week as described by one recent survey). Information systems for executives should, therefore, seek to isolate and present the relevant information in executives' diet instead of trying to complete it with more information. Also, there are no limits to executives' thirst for information (because they always need and want more), which means that development of information systems for them must be fundamentally different from the development of other types of systems.

However, an early definition of management information systems (MIS) dating from 1970 described it in the following terms.

A management information system is an organised method of providing past, present and projection information relating to internal and external intelligence. It supports the planning, control and operational functions of an organisation by furnishing uniform information in the proper time-frame to assist the decision making process.

From this stems the central problem with the concept of EIS. All the elements that the 'inventors' of EIS claimed to have been the first to introduce in the executive systems arena are already included in this 1970 proposition, as the comparison with a definition from the EIS era (dating from 1990) shows:

In essence, executive information systems are computer-based information delivery and communications systems for senior executives. They may bring the latest operating information, or the Wall Street results or external news stories or mail, to the desks of senior executives.

The vocabulary has evolved a little, especially in the domain of communications, but the fundamental project is exactly the same. It is also interesting to note that the system most cited by the proponents of EIS as an example of a successful EIS, (that of Ben Heinemann, the CEO of Northwest Industries), was discarded when its unique user retired in 1986. Thus, the revolution that was to occur based on EIS did not happen and it is now clear that computers will never be the sole source of information for executives regardless of the quality of the technology involved.

Problems that have occurred with EIS in industry include, in particular, the following.

* EIS cannot accommodate the working styles of all executives.

* EIS cannot easily provide the type of information executives need most: the soft information (see Chapter 3 of this book).

* Every technology has potential negative effects.

* Failures have, so far, often outnumbered successes.

Despite these arguments, many tangible and intangible benefits have clearly emerged as a result of experimentation with EIS. Further improvements in technology have also improved the ease of use of the interface of EIS and its capability in terms of access to information. As graphical user interface or GUIs become better and better and technologies, such as OLAP (on-line analytical processor), are introduced, the prospect looks good for the development of truly useful executive systems.

Box 4.1: British Airways.

The example of British Airways is worthy of interest for several reasons. It was one of the very early EIS, the project started in 1982. It was originally designed for the top managers of the company, but it now has more than 250 regular users. It provides a digest of key performance indicators that sums up the activities of the airline including graphs of performance on a 52-weeks rolling basis for marketing information (passenger and cargo traffic, etc.) and also competitor activities on different routes, share prices and so on.

The team in charge of the system took as a rule that, in order to encourage a continuous use of their system, they had to keep people's attention and, therefore, updates of the information occur every single day even though the calculation of most measurements is weekly. New versions of the system are developed periodically which incorporate the latest technologies. But the managers in charge of the system are aware that no technology will match the attractive power of the information content of their system. On top of their permanent efforts to make the interface look better and bring updated information every day, the team is trying to "give the system a competitive edge over alternative sources of information. . .most notably by providing data on the system which cannot be obtained elsewhere".

BENEFITS OF EIS

The main benefits to be expected from EIS are said to be the following.

1.   An increased span of control is made available on request from the keyboard (and not imposed as in the case of reports that pile up on worker's desk).

2.   A saving in time is achieved by the ability to get answers to specific questions more quickly because, not only is the data already in the corporate database (more and more companies have a large amount of well organised computer data available), but also because new software allow users to formulate their requests directly into English-like language or use simple point and click interfaces.

Box 4.2: Builders Square

At Builders Square, an American chain of warehouse home improvement centres, the EIS was designed and implemented in the shortest of times on the basis of a well-established information network. Their vice president for MIS explained: "We were able to put up our system as quickly as we did because the information network – a necessary ingredient and the hardest part to build – was already in place. . .executive information systems are easy if all the necessary information is available on a timely basis." In this context, all the team had to do was to search the market for the software that was going to provide the most suitable interface and build a prototype respecting the recipes that had been applied for years in the organisation. The system itself was broken down into three areas: internal information (static and trend lines available), external influences including the world situation, the weather (which is an important factor of turnover during certain times of the year) and some 'what-if' modelling facilities. Smith pointed out that the existence of a centralised collection of data prior to the design of an EIS was a great help since all issues of data ownership and integrity had already been dealt with. He claimed that his EIS, even though it is using information that was there before, gives a new view of the business to top management, a view that they are going to stick to because they really need it.

Many executives now enjoy an unlimited access into the corporate data resources guided by several levels of summary authorising them to 'drill down' through the data structure to the level of detail they need for each question they have and with easy to use access to external sources of information now.

A more complete list of potential benefits of EIS has been compiled by a recent survey of South African companies with executive systems[1]. In this survey, it was found that EIS helped managers in the following areas.

- **Responsiveness to organisational changes**: an EIS helps organisations adapt faster, helps to focus and direct changes, increases the speed of decision making and improves productivity and understanding of the business.

---

1. N Duffy, "EIS in Context" in Berkeley et al, *Context Sensitive DSS* (London: Chapman and Hall, 1988) Chapter 3.

- **Satisfaction of users' changing needs**: an EIS can be personalised and adapted to the ongoing evolution of needs and helps direct attention of users on critical success factors (CSF).

- **Problem identification and resolution**: an EIS helps identify problems more quickly and improves the quality of information.

- **Management co-ordination**: EIS helps co-ordinate the efforts of managers and employees, improves communication and control and can be used to share key information across functional areas.

- **Strategy formulation**: an EIS helps formulate future strategy and, by directing managerial action, also helps implement current strategy.

FEATURES OF EIS

Maybe the most useful way to describe EIS systems is to provide an indication of the kind of functionalities that they provide to their users in organisations where they have been implemented over the last decade. At this point in time, there is relative agreement regarding the different manipulations of the data that an EIS should enable. A synthesis of the capabilities of EIS that have been put forward by researchers and practitioners in information systems is presented below.

Access to Current Status and 'Drill Down' Facilities

The functions associated with the access to current status, namely drill down, exception reporting using colour indicators and graph based trends monitoring, are often described as the most important for executives. Surveys of existing EIS indicate that most respondents judged these functions necessary to an EIS and that the most desired goals for EIS implementation are improved management reporting and more timely data. Users of EIS claim that being aware of what is happening in their organisation is crucial to them. Numerous articles written about EIS focused on this same factor of success. In one company, the sales had been down by 5 per cent in a specific area over the previous month and management needed to know if it was the result of the action of a competitor, a real slowdown of the market or the failure of the distribution network. The task of determining such cause/effect relations is always difficult, if not impossible. This is the kind of question that an EIS is supposed to be able to answer, bringing sought-after information that would not otherwise be available because too much data would need to be put together (even though the model underlying the calculation might be relatively simple).

An indirect effect of EIS seems to be the improvement of reporting overall, although it is not certain that it is always the case. This uncertainty can be illustrated by the confrontation between the theory of EIS and the examples of systems presented by the literature. Researchers have claimed that, since it is based on a direct access to information, EIS has a potential for decreasing dramatically some of the filtering, distortion and omission problems caused by serial transmission because, with EIS, information is collected at its source into an information base. By contrast, the designers of the EIS at Rockwell (see Box 4.3) consciously decided that data ownership would be fundamental in their system, to reinforce accountability and facilitate integration (information is 'prepared' before being included into the system by aligning it to predetermined formats). Designers at Rockwell took the view that direct access was too threatening to the political structure of the organisation and that, even though the idea of being able to look directly into the production figures, etc. appealed to most executives, the preparation and the control of data by their owner was more important. They even found the advantages important enough to overcome the little extra delay required for this additional step to take place. As a consequence, the name and extension number of the provider of each page of information is available on the screens of their EIS.

EIS must also authorise 'drilling down' through the data to find problems that would have gone unnoticed, buried under levels and levels of data. Thus, EIS must enable managers to use information to manage more intelligently and effectively rather than just to make the same old mistakes with more speed. Using colour control, EIS reports must enable executives to find out where their attention is needed and to what degree.

Overall, these functionalities of the EIS aim at enhancing

the short-term planning and control systems of managers. With EIS, executives are supposed to be more in touch with their organisation and be rid of that feeling that they are isolated from the information. This 'watchdog' function of EIS is important for both internal and external information, although the access to external information used to raise additional difficulties of data collection. Alternative solutions have been put forward, including direct connection to a database or a systematic organisational collection, by a group whose specific task is to compile information on the environment. There again, the choice seems to be between a direct and an indirect access to the information, each system having its particular strengths and weaknesses. Nowadays, the development of the internet and, more specifically, of the World Wide Web (WWW) constitute a robust and cheap alternative to any kind of in-house data gathering. However, it would be risky to assume that managers can readily find the information they require on the Web: the volume of information and the lack of relevance of most of it are such that some information preparation may well be required as a filter between managers and the net (see Section 3 of this book).

Presentation of Documents and Reports

The presentation of documents and reports in an EIS is vital and must be interesting, memorable and understandable as well as being complemented by easy to use graphics facilities highlighting the trends of the main indicators used by executives. Many companies use the occasion of the design of their EIS to work on the presentation of their critical indicators. PepsiCo Inc. turned their weekly 'book' of market research – useless in the former 300 pages format – into a set of graphs that, could be investigated by executives and on the basis of which more informed decisions could be taken.

EIS as a Communication Tool

Under pressure from the environment, communication has often become a top priority of organisations. The potential of e-mail is considerable and its integration within EIS has proved very successful. Some companies have been experimenting with e-mail systems for years with more or less success. As early as 1974,

New England Telephone[2] reported the benefits that the company had gained from the general implementation of e-mail. New England Telephone, like most companies of its size had communication problems due to the top-down approach that was all too often adopted. The problem with top-down communication is that its efficiency is directed by the perception that subordinates have of their bosses' characters, personal motivations and styles. Items that appear to be important to the boss are given top priority, whereas the rest of the messages remain unanswered. Executives naturally have to be careful with the messages they send, but nothing replaces a good balance of two-way communication, which means improving upward communications as well. Upward communication has always been poorer, due to the lack of perception that top executives have of their subordinates and the filters of management levels that dilute messages. Acknowledging these failures, New England Telephone started a program called 'private lines', which allowed all employees to question or discuss anonymously any matter of concern, from corporate policies to job-related problems, with any manager of the company. The most typical messages were answered and published in the corporate newsletter. Later, co-ordinators were added to handle some of the requests that needed to find their exact target. In these cases, employees had the option to either preserve their anonymity or to forgo it. Overall, the program turned out to be a big success with nearly all the messages being serious and concerned with the welfare of the company and the satisfaction level being high on both side (source and target).

Another example of the use of e-mail for corporate communication is DEC. As early as 1982, e-mail had become an essential and highly effective interpersonal telecommunication medium in DEC. The company was then the only one to have a worldwide network connecting all the corporate functions and improving considerably all types of communication. The efficiency of e-mail appeared even to challenge the telephone due to the worrying number of calls that were lost or just not returned. Due to the spread of DEC's functions on the five continents, the effectiveness of no simultaneous communication was seen as irreplaceable. E-mail allowed managers to do things

2. B Harriman, "Up and Down the Communication Ladder" *Harvard Business Review* (September/October 1974).

that could simply not have been done otherwise, such as transmitting messages instantaneously to several people in very different locations. Overall, it resulted in wider communication than previously, especially for managers who felt it provided them with an alternative mode for their communication with their subordinates, less personal than telephone but more personal than a memo. Such as seamless communication network is naturally within reach of any organisation at this point in time, thanks to the availability of the internet.

As a conclusion, it must be pointed out that, if integrated into the overall communication system of the organisation, the benefits derived from e-mail can be maximised. E-mail has a great potential in terms of improving the communication within an organisation and should be integrated with an EIS interface if one is developed. In fact, it should be one of its core components.

ORGANISATIONAL EVOLUTION OF EIS

Another interesting way of assessing the reality of EIS is by studying the surveys that have been done within industry. These surveys are particularly interesting because they indicate how an EIS may evolve over time in an organisation as it gains expertise and experience with executive systems.

As early as 1984, surveys of EIS revealed that the number of users per EIS was increasing. The original idea of a tailor-made EIS dedicated to one individual only – typically the CEO – had already been discarded. Nowadays, systems with more than 100 users are commonplace. This indicates that not all users are senior executives and that the circle of EIS users has been opened to other categories of managers who can also benefit from EIS. This kind of evolution has resulted in the acronym EIS being re-interpreted as 'everybody's information system' or 'enterprise information system'.

Recent studies have also indicated that companies increasingly regard the development of the corporate databases underlying EIS as their highest priority. Corporate databases are often the primary source of internal information and companies are taking to develop data warehouses (or huge repository of more or less structured data) in order to provide the broadest possible access to information to their users.

On a different level, EIS are often found to be expensive systems limited to large firms. The latest developments in the area, such as data warehousing, aggravate this aspect of EIS as these vast repositories of data often turn out to require very large investments.

Box 4.3: Rockwell

The experience accumulated at the North American Aircraft Division of Rockwell led to emphasising the importance of the 'people factor' in the success of EIS, as opposed to any technological issue. In particular, the importance of the role of:

(1) *the data providers (who define source data for the application and determine where the information requested by the executives comes from);*

(2) *the data keepers (who manage and maintain source data and systems and use the EIS to update the files and generate the output reports);*

(3) *the EIS developers (who create and maintain the applications and organise the raw data transmitted by the other two groups and the desires of the executives into a structured database with menus, reports and graphs) was pointed out as paramount.*

Political issues involved in the transfer of power facilitated by EIS have also been potential threats to the success of such systems because information is the basis of corporate power and an EIS challenges traditional lines of communication. It makes information more readily available and, in some cases, changes the source of information. These issues have to be dealt with when designing an EIS-type system.

CONCLUSION

First of all, the extreme difficulties arising from the design of EIS should be noted. Executive use of computers has remained so subject to fashions that it is obvious that top executives are still not convinced by the usefulness of the technology and are not ready to invest unreasonable amounts of time in thinking about what could be done or how they should adapt to it. 'Keeping up with the kid' will never be the goal of their professional lives. Nevertheless, as evidence has been given that executives want to listen to the proponents of EIS, researchers and practitioners have worked hard and will have to work even harder to deliver useful information systems for executives.

On one side, executives increasingly feel the burden of their responsibilities as they try to steer their companies through difficult times in less and less stable environments. On the other side, technology has demonstrated its huge potential in many relevant areas, such as control, communication and environment scanning, but failed to become so specific as to be integrated into the world of the executives. What should the next step be?

In order to gain the credibility that is required for success, an EIS must bring something that was not there before, be it, for example, speed or accuracy, and must be totally integrated within the business functions it was designed to serve. That is why, the design of EIS must be the occasion of a careful process of analysis of the critical success factors (CSF) of the organisation. This part of the process is, however, not determined by the concept of EIS, it is determined by organisational characteristics, both internal and external and the degree of informational maturity of these organisations. Some companies will know more about their CSF than others, whereas some companies will need to take more time in determining which aspects of the management of their firm they have to focus upon. This analytical step, however lengthy, simply cannot be by-passed and no technology can even simplify it.

Eventually, if computers are to become the privileged intermediaries between executives and their information or even valuable alternative information providers, the relationship between them and the executive users has to be improved. Managers may not be convinced yet by the necessity to spend time getting familiar with computers. There are issues of trust and compatibility at stake. How much of a stumbling block are staff and managers going to raise if an EIS is generalised? By-passing this stumbling block will be absolutely vital for the overall success of an EIS because EISs need to be used by as many managers as possible to be optimally efficient. But bear in mind that managers always have the choice between alternative sources of information and will never be wholly dependant upon computers.

Section 2

Managing IT

This section is made up of the four chapters listed below.

5.   *Disaster Recovery Planning.*

6.   *Managing Staff for Better IT.*

7.   *Faster Information Systems Development with RAD and Other New Techniques.*

8.   *Realising the Benefits of CASE: Lessons from the Adoption and Use of I-CASE in a Large, Irish Organisation.*

Section 2 deals with specific issues related to the management of IT in organisations in a broad sense. The first three chapters examine issues that are at the core of a safe and efficient usage of IT in organisations and use the findings of recent surveys carried out by members of the Executive Systems Research Centre (ESRC). Disaster recovery planning is a much neglected aspect of IS management which can make the difference between organisations being wiped out within short periods or surviving unplanned events. The management of IS personnel is also becoming paramount to the well-being of companies because of the very high turnover of IT staff in some organisations and the difficulty in hiring leading-edge IT specialists in certain regions and industries that are considered less attractive. Finally, the efficient development of new information systems is an essential component for the success of any organisation and Chapter 7 examines how new systems development methods can enable organisations to use information systems to adapt more rapidly to changes in their environment.

Following on the same idea, the fourth chapter in this section gives readers unique insights into the experience of one of the largest Irish organisations with its implementation of computer-aided software engineering (CASE) tools in search of greater efficiency in the development of its information systems.

5
Disaster Recovery Planning

Joe Haslam and Frédéric Adam

INTRODUCTION

Disaster is a feature of almost every facet of life. The capacity of events from the simple to the most complex to end up in catastrophe has endured right from earliest times. As science has progressed in achieving a modicum of control over many of the worst causes of disaster, it has also presided over a parallel development of more and more human creations which, although useful, offer greater and more diverse sources of misery and misfortune. While Murphy's prediction that "anything that can go wrong will" is admittedly pessimistic, as advice to safeguard against disaster it can be quite useful.

The concern of most executives with disaster recovery has principally to do with the extent to which the data, which is stored on company disks, is the 'lifeblood' of the organisation. While information technology has made operations more cost effective and helped to improve the services provided, there are pitfalls associated with this development itself. In many industries computer data has reached a point where it has become the organisation, its loss being totally irreplaceable. The key word is dependency. How dependent are you on your data?

Pretend that at the very moment you are reading this book, one of the following has just happened to your computer system.

1. A power surge has blown the fuse in every PC on the network.

2. That new program, which has just gone live, is full of bugs and the payroll needs processing.

3. The builders upstairs have caused the computer room ceiling to collapse.

4. The local branch of a union has led a walk out, the IT staff cannot pass the picket.

4.   The mainframe installed today was incorrectly wired.

5.   Water has been leaking into your main systems room.

All of these have happened in Irish organisations and in others all over the world in the last five years. How would your organisation survive given that there is absolutely no reason why any of the above should not happen to you?

IMPORTANCE OF DISASTER RECOVERY PLANNING (DRP)

Although disaster has always been written about in the academic and trade press, interest has often been limited to specialised circles. Since most senior managers pay more attention to CNN than *PC Magazine*, this topic rarely receives consideration outside the IS domain. This has changed noticeably with the latest high profile cases of natural disasters (the Kobe earthquake, Hurricane Andrew, Mississippi floods) and terrorist attacks (World Trade Centre, Canary Wharf, Bishopsgate, Oklahoma). Slowly senior managers are beginning to realise that when critical information is lost, it is a problem for the organisation as a whole. Thus, managers are slowly accepting that they must become involved in the area of disaster recovery planning (DRP).

As recently as five years ago, the most popular method of drafting a disaster recovery plan was through analysis of 'a strategic case' which outlined the benefits of DRP and readers was urged to put them into operation in their organisation. Since then, however, disaster recovery planning has become 'operational', just another cost of doing business, a 'worst case insurance'. While the statistics presented in Table 5.1 clearly indicate both that some form of disaster is likely and that organisations without a plan won't cope as well as those who have one, this should not in itself be the only motivation for the drafting of a disaster plan. IS managers, must regard the responsibility for the adequate protection of electronic data as an important part of their job. DRP, then, should be undertaken because it simply makes good business sense.

Table 5.1: Survey of the Situation in Irish Organisations Regarding DRP

- 29% have had to deal with a disaster situation.

- 50% have a workable plan – 9% have no disaster plan.

- 37% test/update the plan every six months – 28% have never tested their plan.

- 40% of plans do not involve any external organisation.

- 45% have not formed a recovery team.

- 50% do not circulate details of the disaster plan internally.

- 53% have carried out a legal review of their obligations.

Yet, the extent to which organisations plan for ensuring the continued running of their information systems infrastructure following an interruption varies enormously. It is a classic security challenge: while excessive measures slow the business down, inadequate preparation leaves it ominously vulnerable. The optimum solution lies between mirrored real-time solutions, in which replica systems are updated simultaneously, and periodical back-up where data is downloaded to disks at specified intervals and stored off-site. The solution adopted between these two extremes is dictated by the resources allocated by senior management and the industrial sector in which the organisation operates.

Many organisations have formed a specialist division to monitor the threat daily, some have even set up a complete off-site replica of the main data centre. Others have largely ignored the issue or make only token back-ups, selecting this approach more in an effort to appease their fears rather than as a solution which has their confidence. This mentality is not an adequate response to the threat posed by the potential disasters which can affect organisations. You probably won't have to deal with the major bomb or flood scenario, but small human error or 'power out' disasters are too real a possibility to be ignored. Some examples of the types of threats to which companies are exposed are detailed in Box 5.1.

Box 5.1: Recent Disasters

London, March 1996: *"In the aftermath of the explosion at Canary Wharf, several companies have moved to set up replica dealing rooms. Deutsche Morgan Grenfell have an underground bunker with places for 1,100 staff. Merrill Lynch have a similar operation for 276 staff. They each cost about £2m a year to maintain."* The Sunday Tribune.

Paris, May 1996: *"Fire gutted the headquarters of the State-owned, French-owned bank Credit Lyonnais. The fire was caused by a short circuit in the cabling of the first floor dealing room which is filled with computer screens and electronics. The fire was unfortunate but was something which was planned for. All trading operations were backed up and no data was lost."* The Irish Times.

Manchester, July 1996: *"A team of specialist salvage experts had to be hired to retrieve personnel records from the wreckage of the Marks & Spencer building in the aftermath of the Arndale Centre bomb. It was a major cause of worry to management as there were no back-up copies. Many of the files were damaged and now have to be recreated by contacting the people themselves and merging this information with past documentation."* The Sunday Business Post.

WHAT CONSTITUTES A GOOD DISASTER RECOVERY PLAN?

A disaster has been described as any event which causes suffering and loss happening either suddenly or unexpectedly, generally through human fault, mechanical/structural failure or the forces of nature. In a business or computing context, therefore, it is sufficient to regard DRP simply in terms of the actions to be taken in advance of any event, which negatively effects the ability of the organisation to operate, in an attempt to ensure that the organisation limits the consequences of, and recovers from, a disaster, with the minimum loss of efficiency and effectiveness. A sample DRP, including the main sections which should be tackled by companies, is presented in Table 5.2.

Table 5.2: Categories of the Disaster Recovery Plan

I   Introduction
Description of Plan
Executive Endorsement
Purpose & Area of Operation
Events Which Trigger Implementation

II   The Disaster Team
Background - Aims & Structure
Personnel, Functions &
Responsibilities
Submissions of Department
Heads/Supervisors
Outlines of Major Disaster Strategies
Solutions to Possible Scenarios
Procedures For Support of Disaster
Team
Details of Departmental Disaster Plans

III   The Disaster Unit
Background - Aims & Structure
Personnel, Functions &
Responsibilities
Testing Procedures and
Responsibilities
Training Procedures and
Responsibilities
Maintenance Procedures and
Responsibilities
Details of Plan Circulation

IV   The Recovery Team
Background - Aims & Structure
Personnel, Functions &
Responsibilities
Mobilisation Framework For
Recovery Personnel
Immediate Emergency Measures &
Priorities
Lists of Special Skills For Specific
Hazards
Plan for Dealing with the Media
Interim Processing Procedures
Alternate Operating Procedures
Restoration Procedures
List of Automated Applications
On-line Computer System Access
Crisis Management
Recommendations

V   Appendices
List of Site Maps
Internal Telephone Numbers List
External Telephone Numbers List
Minutes of Past Disaster Meetings
Offsite Storage Facility Details
Inventory Lists of Equipment
Vendor Lists and Contracts

A properly considered disaster plan should cater for the requirements implied by each of the headings in Table 5.2. There seems, however, to be a trend in disaster plans to focus on the IT-related issues which are associated with potential disasters. This is as a result of the fact that most disaster plans are initiated, developed and maintained by the IS department, and consequently have very solid IT elements. Issues, such as processing requirements, telecommunication connections, end-user considerations, etc., are generally dealt with soundly. Conversely, the problems which occur outside the IT framework, such as sloppy reporting of requirements by other departments or inadequate support from an outside body, are not always handled so successfully.

Barriers to the Creation of a Useful Plan

From the issues detailed in Table 5.2, it is obvious that a disaster plan requires the co-operation of many departments in an organisation to ensure its completeness and optimise its usefulness to that organisation. Unfortunately, at present, many IS managers view the process of developing and maintaining a disaster plan as a weapon in the struggle for position with other departments. Armed with an executive order to 'do what is necessary', many IS managers do not involve other departments sufficiently as they are anxious to maintain their image as the organisation's potential saviour. This situation, however, may be changing as many non-IS managers are becoming more anxious to be involved in DRP, partly in the belief that it can help them to be seen as more mature executives, anxious to deal collectively with any threat to the organisation. It is important, however, that the support given by senior management in organisations to DRP involves more than a superficial interest. As a general rule executive support for DRP tends to be strong as it projects an image of control and organisational concern on their part. This is particularly true in larger organisations in which sizeable IT budgets can be secured by feeding the executive ego.

Often, however, senior management will seek to portray an image of concern over the DRPs of their organisation without being willing to invest the time and effort necessary to ensure that the plans meet the requirements of the organisation. Instead, security memos tend to be drafted by IS managers and signed as a matter of procedure by CEOs, with little other senior management involvement. This provides little incentive for IS managers to invest the necessary effort into pushing for the development of a comprehensive disaster plan.

In recent years, pressure to plan has increased from industry regulators, commercial auditors and partner organisations. In the case of the latter, it is certainly a legitimate concern that any organisation, on which you rely for a service, is capable of surviving a disaster. At the same time, however, there have been complaints that the issue of DRP is being abused by parties anxious to further their own interests, such as regulators keen to demonstrate their power and auditors attempting to promote additional services. Consequently, it appears that the renewed interest in disaster recovery planning has had mixed benefits for organisations attempting to develop safeguards for their own operations. For, while the upper management support which may have been previously lacking is becoming increasingly more forthcoming, the pan-departmental nature of disaster plans makes them a prominent target for the forces of organisational politics. Consequently, it is necessary to ensure that the quality of the plan is not subordinated to the interests of any parties during its creation.

DEVELOPMENTS IN DISASTER RECOVERY PLANNING IN IRISH ORGANISATIONS

In Ireland at present, there appears to be a far stronger perceived need for DRP among larger organisations. Smaller companies tend to have minimal, if any, preparations made, should disaster occur. Indeed, very few of these small organisations have even considered the issue of DRP in great depth. Furthermore, where the issue of disaster recovery planning has been discussed, many of these companies view planning for disasters as requiring the allocation of material, financial or human resources which they can ill afford.

Relationships with External Organisations

Even among large Irish organisations, however, many disaster plans remain incomplete or unrealistic. Furthermore, disaster plans of organisations of all sizes tend to be too IT focused, and lack a viewpoint broad enough to consider the opinions of all of the relevant parties. Consequently, there is a widespread need for disaster planners to recognise the importance of not only other departments within the organisation, but also the role of external parties in recovering from a potential catastrophe. There is a need for two-way communication with all parties involved in the drafting of a disaster plan. Indeed, bodies, such as Local Authorities and other public services, are keen to emphasise that if planners make them aware of what they would require in the event of a disaster situation, they in turn would be better capable of explaining what they can provide. It is vital that companies of all sizes seek the advice and assistance of the parties within these bodies to whom they will turn should events arise requiring the implementation of their plan: at present this is not being done by Irish companies.

One area which has been recognised as requiring important

consideration in the drafting of a disaster plan is that of legislation and standard practice guidelines, as laid down by the Irish government, as well as European and professional bodies. Many firms include detailed reference to the requirements of legislation, such as the Computer Security Act 1987 (US), the Data Protection Act 1988 (Ireland) and other recommendations of professional bodies relating to computerised information in their disaster plans. Yet, while organisations are willing to go to great lengths to conform to the requirements of this legislation, they fail to realise that similar attention to detail should be exercised in other aspects of their disaster strategy.

Consequently, little consideration is given to issues such as how contracts with customers would operate should disaster occur. Many contracts, for instance, include penalty clauses for non-delivery of goods, with no provision made for a disaster scenario. Irish organisations may be unprepared to handle the tasks which must be fulfilled for these safeguards to be put in place, and many admit to not even knowing where to begin in the implementation of such a complete DRP strategy. Yet, despite the regional, specialised and legal difficulties posed by DRP, organisations, particularly in Ireland, remain reluctant to involve the external sources of expertise, which consultants would provide. A number of advantages and disadvantages pertain to the use of consultants for this purpose, and these should be considered by companies before involving consultants in their disaster recovery planning as described in Box 5.2.

Box 5.2: Positive and Negative Aspects of Involving Consultants

Strengths of Consultants
- *Have good access to senior managers, which allows them to ask the awkward questions, which IS managers cannot.*
- *Impose an internal discipline on vital procedures, such as backups, testing, updating, plan circulation, etc.*
- *Provide specialised expertise and equipment which the company is unlikely to possess.*
- *Understand the urgency of situation if a disaster strikes and acknowledge the need to provide assistance.*

> **Criticisms of Consultants**
> - *Are outsiders, not as concerned about the survival of a company as its employees.*
> - *Provide generic solutions, not always compatible with individual organisations.*
> - *Tend to be excessively critical of existing operations and unable to appreciate organisational subtleties.*
> - *Too expensive, forcing companies to spend in excess of what they can afford.*

Internal Circulation of the Plans

Because the role of disaster plans is generally misunderstood by Irish organisations, the circulation of a disaster plan document within an organisation tends to be very poor. One of the most important requirements of a disaster plan is that it is widely disseminated, for without adequate insight into what they are expected to do according to the disaster plan, employees will be confused and disorganised should a disaster occur. The two main reasons why most Irish companies do not circulate their disaster plans are:

(a)   non-prioritisation of the plan among senior management;

(b)   a misplaced sense of secrecy relating to the knowledge contained in the plan.

Both of these viewpoints are flawed. In the first case, organisations may or may not have a plan, but view its dissemination as being of a low priority, reflecting a lack of interest or belief in the need for a DRP. Among organisations with this viewpoint, no matter how well conceived a disaster plan is, its benefit is limited due to a lack of knowledge of its contents among employees, hampering the speedy mobilisation of resources should a disaster occur. In the second case, managers may be paranoid about the potential for parties external to the organisation benefiting from the information contained in a disaster plan if it is widely circulated. However, the information contained in most disaster plans is relatively mundane and of very little value to competitors, etc. Furthermore, most of this information is usually quite easily available anyway.

Consequently, organisations should be willing to overlook

the potential circulation of useful information to a competitor if the contents of a disaster plan are widely disseminated, for choosing the alternative approach can be much more detrimental to a company. Not only will the plan created be of little value to the organisation, but attitudes to testing and maintenance will subsequently suffer due to a lack of understanding of what the plan is attempting to achieve. This is the situation faced by a large number of Irish companies with regard to their disaster recovery planning. Drills, in which every employee is instructed what to do in the case of certain scenarios, remain unusual, backup schedules are not maintained and DRPs tend to be simply done and left on a shelf, sometimes not even off-site!

Small organisations are particularly at risk. This is mainly because they either don't have an IT division to make senior managers aware of the threat or because they choose to overlook the poss-ibility that a disaster may happen to their company. Yet, if the issue of DRP is addressed even at a low level, some things can be achieved which could make a real difference. Relatively cheap and easily implemented measures of protection include imp-lementing a UPS (an uninterruptable power supply system) for the local area network, or off-site collection and the storage of back-up tapes. It is one of the great myths of disaster planning that it is always a big job. The components of a workable disaster plan are commercially available and competitively priced.

A FRAMEWORK FOR DEVELOPING A DISASTER RECOVERY PLAN

Most forms of planning are undertaken using a framework, model or methodology. One such model has been devised by the Executive Systems Research Centre (ESRC) at University College Cork, Ireland for use in developing disaster plans. Called the 'hopscotch' model, it uses the grid from the children's playground game to impose a structure on the planning process and illustrate some of its key aspects. This model is presented in Figure 5.1.

For reasons of history, expectation of others and expertise, the task of developing a disaster plan begins with the IS manager. This holds irrespective of organisation size, industry or location. While much of the actual work may be delegated to a network

Figure 5.1: The Hopscotch Model

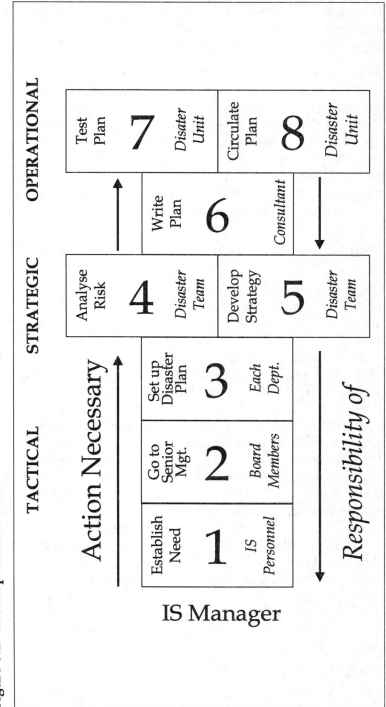

manager or driven by a project champion, it is important that IS managers understand and accept the challenge of developing a plan and protecting the organisation from disaster.

Stage 1: Establish the Need for Disaster Recovery Planning

The first step for the IS manager is the establishment of the needs of the organisation. This involves looking at the existing state of the organisation, in terms of disaster recovery planning, and deciding where the company should, ideally, be given the constraints imposed by the amount of human and financial resources available. This often results in an acknowledgement that a plan needs to be developed or the existing one improved, as organisations tend to discover inadequacies in their current level of protection which are too important to be ignored.

Stage 2: Present Case for Disaster Recovery Plan to Top Management

Stage 2 is the point at which the issue of disaster recovery planning first comes to the board's attention. Communication between IS and senior management on this issue tends to be poor. Senior management needs to become more aware of the threat posed by disasters and assemble the specialist skills that are needed to protect the organisation from them. IS managers should, at this stage, clearly indicate that DRPs should not exist solely within the brief of the IS department. Yet, many senior managers continue to believe that both the responsibility and control for DRP lies entirely with the IS manager.

IS managers, therefore, must be willing to inform senior management of the need for interdepartmental co-operation in the creation of the DRP. They must ensure that senior management understands that disaster recovery planning is best seen as a subset of corporate planning. It should, therefore, be funded separately within the planning budget at corporate level and should not interfere with the IS budget. IS managers should bear in mind at this stage that senior management's support for disaster recovery plan is the direct result of the IS manager's success in demonstrating that a credible threat exists. Commitment (human and financial) is the result of senior management appreciation and support for disaster initiative.

Stage 3: Establish a Disaster Team

The disaster team is made up of a senior representative from each department within an organisation. They present the requirements of their departments to the IS manager. The team collectively provides specific answers to straightforward questions such as:

- What are the critical functions for daily operation?

- What is the tolerable length of time to go from disaster to recovery?

- Which operations can you do without?

- Which personnel are absolutely essential?

- What is the minimum number of staff required?

- What work, done in one place, affects operations in other places?

- What external resources will be relied on to recover?

- What is specific about your organisation in comparison to the 'generic' case?

Many of the answers should be straightforward, but others will require investigation and should be debated over a suitable time period. The disaster team formally takes responsibility for the organisation's DRP from the IS manager at this stage. Consequently is responsible for ensuring that the DRP remains workable.

Stages 4 and 5: Analyse the Risk and Develop a Strategy

A thorough analysis and understanding of the risks associated with disasters is crucial to the preparation of any disaster plan. From the commencement of the DRP creation project, it is necessary that the organisation accepts the fact that there is no such thing as total security. All forms of security, therefore, involve the acceptance of a certain level of risk, the consideration of familiar factors such as luck, time, money and reduced efficiency and their application to find the elusive combination of optimum loss prevention and reasonable costs. The fourth stage of the framework then, attempts to assess the degree to which the organisation is vulnerable should a disaster occur, and is often developed in tandem with the fifth stage, in which a strategy is developed to overcome the threat posed by these potential disasters. Trade-offs must be resolved, however, between catering for unlikely but expensive disasters and more likely but less destructive disasters.

The result of these stages should be the identification of major risk areas to the organisation and very general guidelines on how to approach these risk scenarios. Detailed documents are not overly important at this stage and, if necessary, should be included in a sub-plan. A number of useful guidelines to be borne in mind while discussing and formulating the DRP were listed in Table 5.2, on page 77. These guidelines are based on lessons learned from previous disasters and provide a useful means of analysing risks to the organisation and its vulnerability to these risks.

If an organisation finds that it lacks the expertise required to complete a disaster plan, it will become apparent during these stages. Consequently it may be an excellent time to involve consultants who can advise the disaster team on all aspects which should be included in the DRP.

Stage 6: Write the Disaster Recovery Plan

The eventual outcome of this process should not be a 'Disaster Recovery Plan' stored away in a folder. If it exists at all, it is not so much a self-contained document as a collection of relevant material from other sources, such as contracts, inventory lists, personnel lists, the disaster sections from each departmental plan, sections from the security plan, etc. A disaster manual should then emerge with an index and a section on aim, executive support, confidentiality, etc. Any detailed documents should be included in a sub-plan and a reference made in the manual. A sample disaster manual was provided in Table 5.2, listing the sections commonly found in a disaster plan.

Stages 7 and 8: Test and Circulate the Plan

It is recommended that, for the final two stages of the framework, a disaster unit be formed, which is a different concept from a disaster team. A disaster team is a high-level body with the IS manager and the department heads, whereas a disaster unit is a highly motivated, cohesive, specialist group of 'designated worriers'. They carry out the operational tasks which, although not essentially complex, are nevertheless vital for the overall effectiveness of the DRP. The disaster unit is initially entrusted with testing the DRP in an effort to determine how workable and effective it would be should a disaster occur. Once a DRP has been adequately tested, it must be circulated to employees. Preferably these two stages should occur in tandem, so that, while the disaster tests are conducted, the employees gain an insight into the roles they are expected to fulfil as part of the DRP.

This methodology provides an example of what should be done in the creation of a disaster plan. It is not intended to be a means to the creation of a flawless plan, but instead a guide which provides some degree of rigour to the process of developing a DRP. Consequently, companies which follow these stages, though not guaranteed a perfect DRP, should end up with a satisfactory level of protection. This model is, however, not the only one which an organisation can choose to follow in developing a disaster plan, in particular, smaller organisations may skip some of the stages if they do not make sense in their particular case. At the end of the day, the aim is to obtain a reasonable, workable, realistic and effective plan.

TRENDS FOR THE FUTURE

Technology is providing an increasing variety of ways to solve business problems. It is also, however, generating new potential problems to solve. The 1990s is a decade of mobile telecommunications, international co-operation, flexi-time, laptops and home-based workers. As the organisation moves out of the office, one of the results is that the IS manager has substantially less control over the flow of company information especially as the traditional mainframe-terminal model is now being almost totally replaced by a client-server model.

Another outcome of the loss of control from the IS department, is that many solutions to data protection no longer exist on paper. The study of disasters after they have happened has become the only way in which disaster recovery planners learn new methods to safeguard their data. As a result, the main method now used to develop a plan is to buy a number of case studies of past disasters. Box 5.3 indicates the main lessons to be learnt from past disasters.

Box 5.3: Lessons from Previous Disasters

- It is better not to have any plan than to try and recover using a dubious plan.
- It is easier to recover if the disaster happens at a weekend.
- Suppliers of services vital to recovery need to be contacted in advance, plan expectations outlined and guaranteed by contract. Agreements with other organisations to share computing facilities are not reliable.
- A supply of standard office equipment, such as stationery, should be stored off-site.
- The location of recovery co-ordination HQ is critical to the success of the plan.
- Recovery plans need a substantial non-IT input.
- Organisations which need dealing facilities have to build and maintain an off-site replica.
- The personnel chosen to co-ordinate recovery should be good at handling crises.
- The whole plan needs to be tested together, not just parts of it in isolation.
- Organisations which are not concentrated in one site tend to recover more quickly.
- Expect not to be able to re-enter a disaster site for a considerable period.
- Clear chains of communication need to be established in advance of a disaster.
- A post-disaster chain of command needs to exist organisation-wide. Relying on insurance alone will not cover all losses.
- Most organisations tend not to spend enough on disaster recovery planning.
- No matter how good recovery is, there will still be other effects to deal with later.
- Ultimately, the success of every disaster plan relies to some degree on luck.

One result of this situation is the recognition that preparing correctly for disasters should not be aimed at the restoration of what was there before but at the resumption of business activities. This is termed a business continuity approach to disaster recovery planning and is becoming increasingly popular as organisations become more focused on the service they provide as opposed to the way their organisation operates. Consequently, there is a growing awareness that the most important criteria by which a disaster plan can be measured is the speed with which an organisation's business can be resumed, and organisations are aligning their DRPs more closely with this objective.

When viewed from a position of extremes, disaster recovery planning seems to involve a lot of trouble for what constitutes an hypothetical situation. This is perhaps responsible for the diversity of opinions which exist among IS managers. While some are obsessive about a workable plan, others are still prepared to take the gamble that everything will work out if it has to. Despite the uncertainties inherent in any planning process, organisations must ensure that they are prepared for as many of these uncertainties as possible. In the meantime, however, even with the industry of DRP becoming increasingly specialised, no disaster plan is good enough that its planners do not fear that one will strike.

FURTHER READING

R Bates, *Disaster Recovery Planning: Networks, Telecommunications and Data Communications* (New York: McGraw Hill) 1992.

M Smith, *Common-sense Computer Security: Your Practical Guide to Information Protection* (UK: McGraw-Hill) 1993.

The Safetynet Report, *After Bishopsgate* (UK: Safetynet PLC) 1993.

J Toigo, *Disaster Recovery Planning, Managing Risk and Catastrophe in Information Systems* (Englewood Cliffs, NJ: Yourdon Press) 1989.

L Wrobel, *Disaster Recovery Planning for Telecommunications* (Massachusetts: Artech House) 1990.

6

Managing IS Staff: The Key to Improved Systems Development?

Patrick Finnegan and John Murray

INTRODUCTION

Powerful programming languages and fast compilers do not produce good software. Advanced development methods and software engineering practices may help, but offer no guarantees. In the real world of software and applications development, even the most rapid of prototyping takes time and even mildly sophisticated systems need the contributions of multiple developers. Under these real circumstances, how the human resources of programming are organised and managed become the crucial factors in the success or failure of development projects. Only good people, well organised and well managed, can enhance productivity and produce good software.

LL Constantine

The international computer industry is, perhaps, the most competitive business of modern times, and the software component of that industry is rapidly becoming the driving force behind innovation in computing applications. Yet, software engineering project management (SEPM) has evolved as little more than a black art. For four decades the software industry has placed its hope for improved results on better languages (e.g. 4GLs), design methodologies (e.g. SSADM) and tools (e.g. CASE). However, studies have continually shown that improvements resulting from the introduction of these advances have been disappointing.

In 1968, the North Atlantic Treaty Organisation (NATO) convened a workshop under the heading of "Software Engineering" to assess the state and potential of software production. This term quickly captured the imagination of developers as they looked towards bringing new discipline into software development. A major concern of early software engineering conferences was the need to improve software engineering management. However, most of the suggestions for achieving such improvements were concerned with introducing new technologies.

More recently, it has been recognised that there are three components of software engineering: the technology, the process and the people. The first wave of evolution used technology as the means of driving progress in the field. Today, the second wave is concentrating on improving the process. This is where the field is attempting to formally define the process of software development and the best ways to continually improve it. By simple process of elimination, the remaining component is the people or the human resource, which has yet to receive the attention of the software engineering field.

HUMAN RESOURCE MANAGEMENT

Human resource management refers to the philosophy, policies, procedures and practices related to the management of people. The success of an organisation rests ultimately on how people are managed. However, many industries had been slow to recognise this before Japanese management styles became popular. Today, the management of the human resources is receiving improved status across the spectrum of industry; industrialists view their personnel as an investment rather than a cost. The bottom line is that success depends on quality and innovation; quality and innovation depend on people.

At present, the attention of many in the software engineering field is oriented towards improving the process – the *process maturity* movement. Much of the emphasis on human resource management and the human dimension of software engineering has been deflected to this maturity movement. However, process improvement has brought its own particular focus to software engineering, which, to some, will only prove to overshadow human resource management as a viable means of solving the traditional and perpetual problems of software engineering.

Nevertheless, the software industry is slowly shifting its

emphasis towards the human dimension, with the lead being taken by the US Army and the Office of the Secretary of Defence with sponsorship of people management projects at Carnegie-Mellon University. 'Peopleware', the singularly apt neologism introduced by Neumann in 1976 and permanently ensconced in the lexicon of the software engineering field by DeMarco and Lister in 1987, is seen as central. The *American Programmer* devotes an issue a year to peopleware.

The Executive Systems Research Centre (ESRC) carried out a survey of software organisations in order to determine the nature of human resource management in this industrial sector. The results of this survey are reported in this chapter.

SOFTWARE DEVELOPMENT STRUCTURES

Software organisations have been identified as being far more complex that their size would initially indicate. Many of the problems readily identifiable with software engineering project management emerge directly from existing IS development structures. These structures are most recognisable in the form of the software manager and the software development team. The role of these structures in human resource management is illustrated in Figure 6.1 and is discussed in the following sections.

Software managers have been identified as having a pivotal role to play in the management of human resources. It is the software managers who are in close contact on an ongoing basis with software engineers. Thus, the software manager has enormous responsibility to his/her subordinates to manage the human relations of the software team well. However, much research has highlighted the fact that software managers are for the most part, not adept at managing human relations due to their technical backgrounds and because the emphasis of the software engineering discipline is the technical demands of the software manager's job, rather than the 'softer' dimensions of the job (e.g. human resource management). Software managers consequently focus on technology and process management.

The majority of software organisations in our survey place the responsibility for human resource management with software managers. The educational background of those responsible for

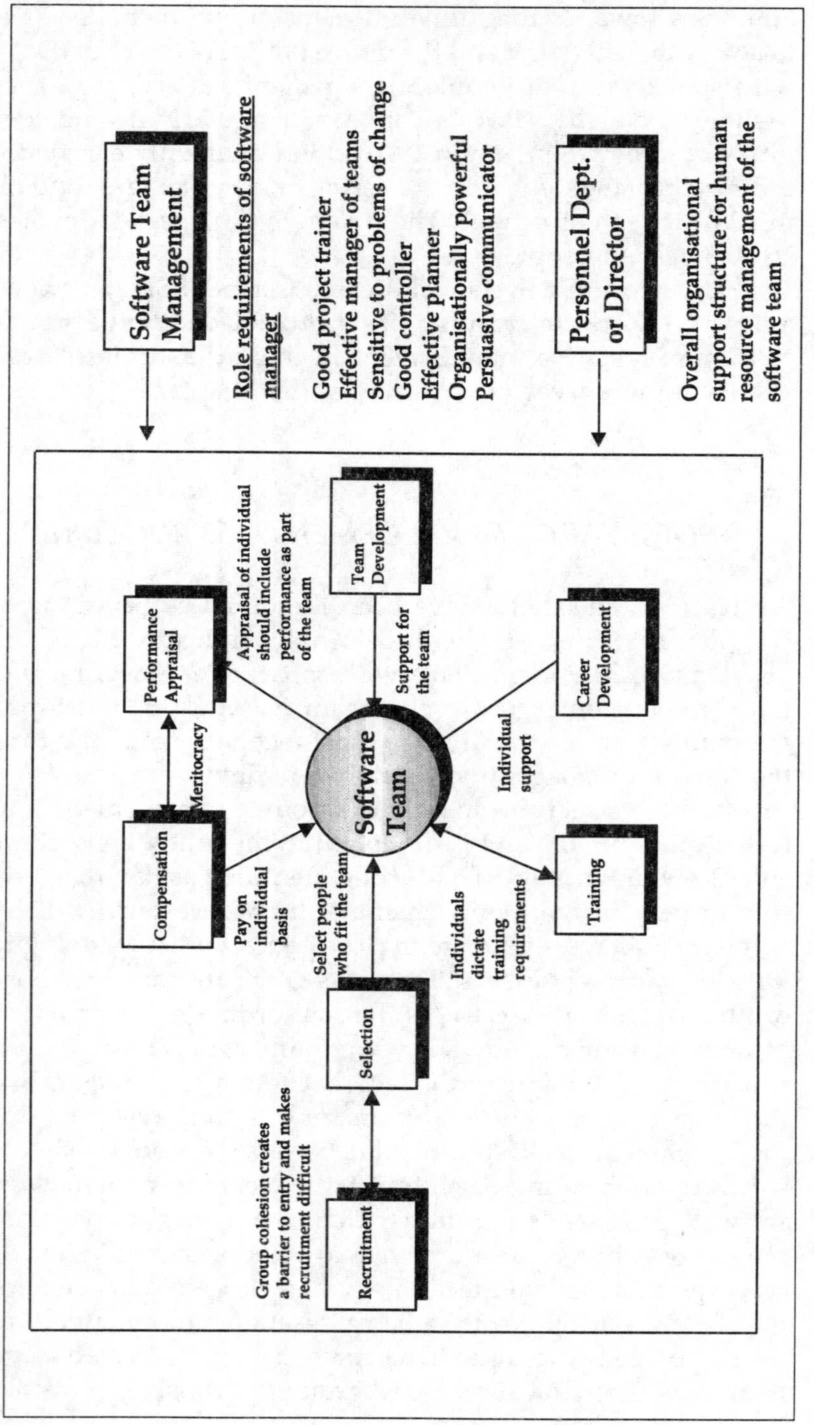

Figure 6.1: Software Structures and Human Resource Management

human resource management in software organisations is primarily engineering, rather than computer science. This is interesting because computer science graduates do not occupy the more senior positions in software organisations. Obviously, the lack of emphasis in computer science degrees and diplomas on management and human factors theory as opposed to their engineering counterparts means that computer science graduates are less likely to be promoted to top management positions in software organisations. This is compounded by the fact that the majority of those who have computer science backgrounds tend to have a relatively lower standard of education, which reduces their chances of gaining managerial positions in software organisations.

Box 6.1: Key Facts in our Survey

To a large extent, software engineering takes place in a team environment. Ninety-eight per cent of organisations have more than 75 per cent of their software development performed in teams. These teams are volatile as the rate of staff turnover is a significant problem in the majority of organisations surveyed. Sixty per cent of organisations have an annual staff turnover rate which is greater than 10 per cent.

Amongst the organisations that had the highest percentage of software being produced in teams, a large majority (65 per cent) believed that their organisation does not give sufficient resources to teams. The majority of those organisations who had the highest staff turnover rates also do not provide enough resources for software teams.

On the other hand, 72 per cent of those organisations that had low staff turnover rates (less than 5 per cent), believed that the organisation provided sufficient resources for software teams. Those organisations who were seen to be providing sufficient resources to software teams had lower staff turnover rates than those that were seen to provide insufficient resources to software teams.

Software teams are a fundamental concern of SEPM and more especially of the management of the human resource component of software engineering projects. Such teams have been described as the 'ferraris' of work design: they offer high performance, but are expensive and require high maintenance. The objective of supporting the software team should drive the management of software projects. It is generally accepted that a software engineering team needs to be more than a mere collection of individuals if it is to be truly effective. Thus, the problem for software teams resides in the fact that:

(a)   few organisations institute an organisation-wide programme to ensure team effectiveness;

(b)   little, if any, resources are allocated by organisations to team development.

HUMAN RESOURCE PRACTICES

Human resource practices cover issues of recruitment, team building, compensation, performance appraisals and career development. These practices are tangible evidence of the human resource strategy used by a software organisation. The human resource practices of the software organisation should be made to fit the unique characteristics of the software engineering profession. In practice, this generally does not happen.

Recruitment and Selection Practices

One of the most important duties of the person responsible for human resource management is the recruitment and selection of software team members. The quality of the software products the organisation produces, relies substantially on the quality of the people in the software team. In general, software managers determine that a software engineering position exists and also decide the characteristics and qualifications necessary for the job, which is in line with their responsibility for the human resource management of software engineers. However, even though software managers have responsibility for human resource management, the directors of the organisation often make the majority of final selection decisions for new recruits. These decisions are generally taken in isolation the teams into which the recruits are placed, as directors generally do not personally know the team into which the recruit is being selected. It is interesting to note that when an organisation has a personnel department, software managers make final selection decisions. This may be because the organisation recognises that software managers are the closest to software team members. They know the team processes and culture, and are able to make a more informed decision about who may be suitable for the job. The danger occurs when this decision is removed from software managers and placed in the hands of a director of the organisation who may not be as well informed of the human qualities and attributes necessary for the new recruit to fit into the existing team structure.

Box 6.2: Key Facts in our Survey

Seventy-four per cent of organisations who had directors making the final selection decisions believed that human attributes did not enter into the selection decision process. This contrasts with 82 per cent of organisations that had software managers making the final selection decision stating that human attributes and human qualities were very important in the final selection decision.

TEAM BUILDING AND TRAINING

Building teams and improving the work climate is one method of tackling the problem of staff turnover. Thus, one would expect that organisations which have high rates of staff turnover would do everything possible to reduce this by, for example, improving the work climate. Sixty per cent of software organisations surveyed revealed that they had never used team building exercises, even on an experimental basis.

The apparent irony was that the majority (i.e. 65 per cent) of those organisations that had never practised team building also had the highest percentage of software being produced in teams. Ninety-five per cent of organisations that had employed team building exercises believed that it had improved team cohesiveness and in general expressed a favourable response to such an investment.

Software engineers have the highest individual growth needs of any other job type ever studied. Thus, a software engineer's ability to improve his or her set of skills is central to job satisfaction and performance. Research on software engineering projects has shown that a common factor which is attributed to problems in software engineering is that the software engineering project has not planned or funded adequate training of the software team.

Box 6.3: Key Facts in our Survey

Sixty-five per cent of those organisations that ranked or rated people as the most important component in terms of software engineering, engaged in career development. Organisations that held people factors important to the software engineering effort supported the software engineers by mapping and planning career paths for their staff. It is noteworthy that 70 per cent of those organisations that did not engage in career development ranked people as being of little importance to the software engineering effort.

The findings of the survey show that 40 per cent of organisations had no training schemes at all. This was one of the more striking results of the study. Seventy-five per cent of those organisations who had no training schemes for software engineers had very high staff turnover rates. Low staff turnover rates were found to be related to the existence of training schemes. It was also noted that organisations, which had a personnel department, had a formal training policy which was jointly formulated by the personnel department and software managers.

An important motivational factor of software engineers is that they are able to dictate their training requirements. Eighty-six per cent of organisations said that software engineers in the organisation had some element of control over their training. However, 70 per cent of organisations who had training schemes did not allow individual software engineers to dictate their own training requirements. In other words, there was not a definite link between what the software engineer thought he or she needed and what he or she received. It was also found that software engineer input into training and staff turnover were inversely related, i.e. the higher the input the lower the staff turnover rate. Sixty per cent of all the training methods used by organisations surveyed was on-the-job. This figure means that the majority of training was not planned and, arguably, haphazard. Seventy-two per cent of organisations that employed on-the-job as the primary training method also indicated that the organisation did not provide sufficient resources for teams.

There is a remarkable indifference towards the motivating potential of career development. Eighty-four per cent of organisations surveyed dismissed the practice of career development. The message is clear, the majority of organisations did not engage or recognise the potential, motivating aspect of career development. This was not withstanding the fact that 72 per cent of those organisations that had low staff turnover rates engaged in career development. On the other hand, 63 per cent of organisations that had high staff turnover rates did not engage in career development at all.

PAY AND PERFORMANCE APPRAISALS

Compensation should be visibly tied to performance in a way that creates a sense of reward for good performance. It has been proven empirically that salary provides security but is not the most important motivator for computer personnel. Despite this, compensation must be seen to be 'visibly' tied to performance or else it might have a negative effect on performance.

It is generally accepted that performance appraisals should be conducted at regular intervals and should concentrate on specific performance as opposed to overall global judgements. They should assess all facets of the job, not only those directly related to goal attainment.

The research revealed that the frequency of performance appraisals in the organisations surveyed was very low. Seventy-eight per cent of organisations indicated that software engineers were appraised once or twice a year. A mere 22 per cent of organisations attested that performance appraisals were carried out on a monthly basis. This is low considering that performance appraisals are crucial to many of the other human resource practices including training, compensation, career development and team development. Without regular information about individual performance, the individual software engineer cannot be given the proper support in order to ensure team effectiveness.

Ninety-seven per cent of the performance appraisals are conducted by software management. This seems paradoxical in that they only make 26 per cent of the final selection decisions.

In comparison, directors do not conduct any performance appraisals, yet make 72 per cent of the final selection decisions. It must be questioned if the company directors are best at making the final selection decisions, then surely they ought to be involved in the appraisal process. If directors are the most informed of the needs of the software team and the manner in which it operates, then surely they are equally as qualified to be involved in the performance appraisal process. Ninety-four per cent of the organisations surveyed verified that they used a standard performance appraisal form to assess software engineers' performance. There is a danger when using a standard performance appraisal form that all aspects of the software engineers' job would not be taken into account in the performance appraisal, because standard performance appraisal forms usually concentrate on individual performance not on performance as part of a team. Seventy-five per cent of organisations did not include the software engineers' support of team processes in the performance appraisal. In effect the majority of software engineers are not appraised on how well they support their team and how well they function as part of the team.

In our study, 74 per cent of organisations claimed that pay was related to performance. However, this seemed peculiar as the majority of organisations studied, appraised software engineers only once or twice a year. Seventy per cent of those organisations testifying that pay was related to performance, appraised software engineers on an irregular basis, and so, those organisations were basing their compensation of staff on one or two performance appraisals a year. Only 30 per cent of organisations considered that they paid for performance and appraised staff on a monthly basis. In real terms compensation was not visibly tied to performance in the majority of organisations.

Box 6.4: Key Facts in our Survey

Sixty per cent of organisations that revealed that most of their software engineering is done in teams do not assess their software engineers' performance as part of the team. The result is clear, organisations implement teams and expect software engineers to work as part of a team, but do not recognise that their performance has anything to do with their involvement with the team.

CONCLUSION

It is clear from the study that for most organisations human resource management and people issues take second place to more technical matters concerning software project management. Human resource management is not seen as being an important component of software engineering by most software organisations. Yet, a wide variety of potential improvements exist, including training schemes, frequent performance appraisals inclusive of software engineers' support to the team, team development and team building programmes, career development, performance related pay and more involvement of software managers in the selection decision.

The software team is not given the proper support and resources in the organisations we studied. The organisations do not recognise that for a software team to be effective, it requires a consistent supply of resources. The individual is the unit of project management in most of the organisations studied as opposed to the software team. The typical software engineer working in the organisations surveyed, spends most of his or her time working in pseudo-teams, and yet does not get appraised for his or her involvement with this team, does not get paid based on this performance, does not participate in training programmes and does not become involved in any team development exercises or career development. This adds to the already high staff turnover rate in such organisations. The organisations surveyed promote conditions of work which lead to:

(a)   the software engineer not working as a member of a team but as an individual with his or her own goals;

(b)   high staff turnover;

(c)   a very unrewarding work environment.

One possibility for software organisations who wish to improve their human resource position is to work from the People Management Capability Maturity Model (PM-CMM) as proposed by B Curtis.[1] This model is a statement of best practice in relation to the management of human resources in the software engineering field. The 5-level model is based on the capability to

---

1.   Curtis, "Increasing Software Talent" *American Programmer* (1994) 7(9) pp. 14-20.

Figure 6.2: The People Management Capability Maturity Model (PM-CMM)

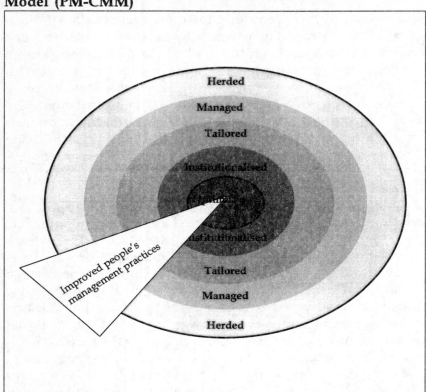

achieve better people management and to improve software development. The stages are:

1.   **Herded**. The development of software human resources is left to the intuition of individual managers. Since human resource work is seen as meeting regulations involving legal and administrative aspects of handling employees, there is no recognition of how human resource work should be intimately integrated into the management of software development.

2.   **Managed**. The first step in improving the human capability of a software development organisation is to install a plan that has senior management approval and commitment. This level of capability is primarily concerned with establishing a basic human resource practice as a normal course of business.

3.   **Tailored**. At level 3, the organisation takes the base of human resource practices it established in level two and tailors it specifically for the software engineering profession. Level three is attained when human resource practices are made to fit more closely with the special characteristics of a software development activity.

4.   **Institutionalised**. At level 4, the steps taken to tailor human resource practices to the software engineering project teams should be expanded to impact performance at the division or company level. That is, these practices are institutionalised in a way that makes them part of a working culture and their impact is at the organisational level rather than at the project level.

5.   **Optimised**. At level 5, the successful integration of the entire staff has taken place into an effective software development team. This means the active collaboration of a software management team that has knowledge of the software engineering job, with the human resource staff that has the knowledge of how to organise the work required to advance up the maturity ladder.

FURTHER READING

B Curtis, "Increasing Software Talent" *American Programmer* (1994) 7(9) pp. 14-20.

A Dyer, *Team Building* (Reading Massachusetts: Addison Wesley) 1987.

C Jones, *The Human Factor* (New York: McGraw-Hill) 1992.

Mankin, Cohen & Bikson, *Teams and Technology* (Boston: Harvard Business School Press) 1996.

O'Reilly, "Getting the Right People" *American Programmer*, (1995) Issue 1, pp. 6-10.

Note: The *American Programmer* has featured a number of very interesting articles relevant to the issue of software development. There are too many of them to provide all references, but it is worth noting that this magazine provides quite a lot of sound information on IS development.

7

Faster Information Systems Development with RAD and Other New Techniques

Brian Fitzgerald

INTRODUCTION

The term 'rapid application development' (RAD) was introduced to the literature by James Martin in his 1991 book.[1] However, Martin drew on the development experiences of Scott Shultz at the Dupont Corporation in 1984. Shultz described a particular development approach, 'rapid interactive production proto-typing' (RIPP), which was clearly the forerunner to the RAD approach proposed by Martin. Earlier antecedents in the literature include that of Gane.[2] However, as illustrated by its emergence in actual development practice, it is a concept which has resonance for practitioners. Indeed, the Dynamic Systems Development Method (DSDM) Consortium, who are elaborating their own RAD method,[4] currently has around 200 affiliated organisations in the UK and Ireland.

This chapter discusses the rationale behind the emergence and current popularity of the RAD concept. The difficulty of defining RAD is discussed and, in light of this, the fundamental principles that characterise the RAD approach are identified and discussed. Following this, the results of a field study which invest-igated the application of RAD in practice are briefly presented.

---

1. Martin, Rapid Application Development (1991).
2. Gane, *Rapid Systems Development* (1989).
3. DSDM, *Dynamic Systems Development Method* (1995).

RATIONALE FOR RAD

Early efforts at software development in the 1950s and 1960s often relied on unsystematic and random methods. However, at a conference in 1968, the term 'software crisis' was coined to refer to a number of fundamental development problems which were universally acknowledged by conference participants. Simply stated, the software crisis referred to the fact that systems took too long to develop, cost too much and did not work very well. As the complexity of the systems which needed to be developed was actually on the increase, the situation would inevitably be further exacerbated.

The initial response to the software crisis was to endeavour to introduce engineering principles to software development. Over the last 30 years or so, these engineering principles have been enshrined in the many software development methodologies that have been proposed. Indeed, recent estimates suggest that more than a thousand such methodologies are in existence.[4]

However, the software crisis has not abated. In relation to development timescales, different estimates have been made as to completion times for systems development. For example, some estimate development time to be about eighteen months on average[5] – a conservative figure given that other estimates put the figure at about three years[6] or even up to five years.[7] Also, a recent IBM survey estimated that 68 per cent of projects overrun schedules.[8] In relation to cost, the IBM study suggested that development projects were as much as 65 per cent over budget,[9] while a Price Waterhouse study in the UK in 1988, concluded that £500 million was being lost per year through ineffective development. Finally, in relation to performance, the IBM study

---

4. Jayaratna, *Understanding and Evaluating Methodologies* (1994).
5. Flaatten, McCubbrey, O'Riordan & Burgess, *Foundations of Business Systems* (1989).
6. "The Software Trap: Automate – or else" *Business Week* (9 May 1988) pp. 142-154.
7. Taylor & Standish, "Initial Thoughts on Rapid Prototyping Techniques" ACM SIGSOFT *Software Engineering Notes* (1982) 7, 5 pp. 160-166.
8. Bowen, "Rapid Application Development: Concepts and Principles" *IBM Document No. 94283UKT0829* (1994).
9. *Ibid.*

found that 88 per cent of systems had to be radically redesigned following implementation.[10] Similarly, a UK study found that 75 per cent of systems delivered failed to meet users expectations.[11] This has led to the coining of the term 'shelfware' to refer to those systems which are delivered but never used. Thus, the problem has not been solved. However, given the increasingly complex nature of systems that are being developed and the rapid pace of change characteristic of today's organisational environment, traditional monolithic development approaches are clearly inappropriate. Indeed, it has been estimated that development productivity needs to increase tenfold to satisfy demand.[12]

Box 7.1: Evidence of the Software Crisis[13]

- Average completion times for systems development projects range from eighteen months to five years.
- Sixty-eight per cent of projects overrun schedules.
- Sixty-five per cent of budgets exceed budget estimates.
- Seventy-five per cent of projects face major redesign following initial implementation.
- Development productivity needs to increase 10-fold to keep up with demand.
- Productivity differences of 10-to-1 have been reported among individual developers with same level of experience.
- Productivity differences of up to 5-to-1 have been found among different development teams.
- Average developer in the US works 48 to 50 hours per week.
- Seventy-five per cent of development organisations have inadequate project management practices.
- Requirements errors cost 200 times as much to fix if not discovered prior to implementation.

---

10. Bowen, *op. cit.*
11. Bates & Stephens, "Rapid Application Development – Concept, Methodology or What?" *NDISD RAD* (April 1995).
12. Verity, "The OOPS Revolution" *Datamation* (1 May 1987) pp. 73-78.
13. McConnell, *Rapid Development* (Microsoft Press: US, 1996).

- Fewer than 3 per cent of developer interviewees at Microsoft could accurately explain the fundamental design concepts of modularity and information hiding.
- Development projects which have experienced excessive pressure to complete on schedule have been found to have four times the normal number of defects.
- Thirty-five per cent of companies have at least one runaway development project.
- Based on a comprehensive study (4,000 projects), the overall rate of efficiency for the software industry is estimated to be 35 per cent.

RAD: GREAT HOPE OR GREAT HYPE?

As already mentioned, over the past 30 years various solutions have been proposed, ranging from tools and techniques to overall methodologies. Brooks[14] suggests that these have often been offered as 'silver bullet' solutions, and concludes that they typically do not address the essential and inherent difficulties of software development. At first glance, RAD might be dismissed since it does not offer anything radically new in terms of tools or techniques. However, the real potential of RAD arises from the synthesis of currently available tools and techniques, coupled with fundamentally different management principles that serve to overcome bureaucratic obstacles to faster development. Thus, the mission of RAD is the simple but powerful one of increasing development speed at a reduced cost without sacrificing quality.

FUNDAMENTAL PRINCIPLES UNDERPINNING RAD

It is probably inevitable with any emerging concept, which is being shaped through practical experiences, that definitions are elusive and RAD is no exception. Definitions of RAD vary in

---

14. Brooks, "No Silver Bullet: Essence and Accidents of Sofware Engineering" *IEEE Computer Magazine* (April 1987) pp. 10-19.

terms of it being characterised as a tool, methodology or life cycle. Given this definitional quagmire, the approach taken here is to document the fundamental principles underpinning RAD, thus allowing a clearer picture of the concept to coalesce. These principles include active user involvement, small empowered teams, frequent delivery of products (which focus primarily on satisfaction of business functionality), iterative incremental development, the top-down approach and the use of integrated CASE wherever possible. These principles are complementary in many respects and, as a whole, are extremely powerful. They are discussed in turn below.

Active User Involvement

The schism between users and developers in traditional development approaches has rightly been condemned – indeed, it is almost an axiom that user involvement is necessary for successful development. However, several studies have found that user involvement is not a simple issue, and the link between involvement and success is not a simple one. The RAD approach recognises that user involvement is necessary for intellectual reasons (for example, to reduce costly requirements elicitation problems) and for political reasons (users may reject systems outright if they have not been sufficiently involved in development). However, the RAD operationalisation of the user involvement concept is a very rich one. At the heart of the RAD approach are joint application design (JAD) and joint requirements planning (JRP) workshops. These are extremely intensive sessions of short duration which serve to identify more completely problematic requirements analysis and systems design issues. All relevant parties are co-located, which leads to synchronisation in the communication process. Also, RAD recognises that users are not homogeneous and identifies a number of different roles that users may play.

Small Empowered Teams

Again, the concept of development teams is not a new one. However, focusing on each of the words 'small', 'empowered' and 'teams' in turn, the advantages which accrue can be seen to be considerable. Firstly, communication channels increase exponentially in relation to team size. Thus, small team size ensures that the potential for communication distortion and conflict is kept to a minimum. Secondly, the empowerment element helps ensure that bureaucratic delays and shirking of decision making responsibility, so inherently characteristic of the traditional requirements sign off, are minimised. Teams are empowered to make vital design decisions (although changes are reversible, an issue which is discussed again below). Finally, the team aspect serves to ensure that all the vital skills for successful development are present. As has already been mentioned, the team issue has already proven useful. For example, the Chief Programmer Team (CPT) under Harlan Mills which developed *The New York Times'* system achieved incredible results: 83,000 lines of code written in 22 months; after implementation, the system ran for twenty months before the first error occurred.[15] Successful development requires that many varied roles be accommodated, e.g. project manager, technical co-ordinator, developer, tester, scribe, user, executive sponsor. The fulfilment of these roles is facilitated by team composition, and their importance has been acknowledged by Microsoft which organise their software development around various development roles in a similar manner.[16]

Frequent Delivery of Products

As mentioned, traditional development projects can take from eighteen months to five years to complete – an issue increasingly problematic given the rapidly changing nature of today's competitive marketplace. RAD, by definition, seeks to reduce development timespans. Thus, shorter time-boxes for development (typically 90 days) are an important feature. These shorter time-boxes make project management more straight-forward in that it is easier to focus on necessary activities, and be more accurate in what can be achieved. Also, this principle is concerned with delivery of products. Rather than being focused on process, RAD is premised on delivering products which satisfy the essential criterion of addressing some business function.

Iterative Incremental Development

Another fundamental principle of RAD is that systems evolve incrementally and are never complete. Rather, new requirements emerge which are then built into the system. Thus, systems emerge through iterative prototyping, with iteration seen as useful

---

15. Yourdon, *Classics in Software Engineering* (1979).
16. Sinha, "Development Practices at Microsoft" Seminar given at the 6th International Conference on IS Development, Boise, Idaho (11-14 August 1997).

and necessary, not as rework delaying development.

It is recognised that requirements specification is a heuristic or learning process which greatly benefits from the deeper insight that both developers and users get from realistic experience with an actual prototype system. Users may not be able to specify in advance exactly what they want in a system but are able to recognise it when they see it – an example of a well-known psychological phenomenon, namely, that recognition is a far easier process than recall. In traditional development, errors in requirements which are not identified before coding or implementation are extremely costly to correct.[17] In fact, it is now commonly accepted that since the system produced by the traditional life cycle undergoes a significant maintenance phase, it may be more properly viewed as a prototype anyway.

Top-Down Approach

As already mentioned, the RAD philosophy accepts that requirements cannot be completely specified in advance. Rather, they are specified at a level appropriate to the knowledge available at the given time. These are then elaborated through incremental prototyping. Similarly, products fit for business purpose are produced according to an application of the Pareto Principle – i.e. approximately 80 per cent of the functionality may be delivered in 20 per cent of the time. Systems are then elaborated and finessed as knowledge grows, from broad outline to precise detail. Also, being a top-down approach characterised by short timeboxing, all decisions are assumed to be fairly quickly reversible. This also contributes to developers feeling more empowered to assume responsibility and being less likely to shirk decision making.

Integrated Computer Assisted Software Engineering (I-CASE)

If dramatic increases in development productivity are to be achieved, it is vital that the more routine and time-consuming aspects of development be automated, for example, code generation and documentation. The automation of these tasks may be achieved through the use of I-CASE. The latter provides a single electronic repository for project-related data. Change

---

17. Boehm, *Software Engineering Economics* (1981) and DeMarco, *Structured Analysis and System Specification* (1978).

control and configuration management features – vital in an environment of iterative prototyping – are also provided. Additionally, I-CASE facilitates re-use by providing access to previously designed and tested elements. Thus, by increasing the granularity of the development building block, productivity improvement is further enhanced (see also Chapter 8).

RAD IN PRACTICE

This section reports the results of a two-stage field study conducted during 1996 and 1997 which investigated the RAD phenomenon in practice.[18] The first stage involved a postal survey of 100 leading organisations in the UK and Ireland. Following this, personal interviews were conducted with experienced RAD practitioners in eight companies (seven Irish and one UK). Among the main findings were the following.

Use of RAD

The survey found that 43 per cent of respondents were knowledgeable about RAD and using it for development in some manner, whereas 57 per cent were not using a RAD approach for systems development. The newness of the concept can be gauged from the fact that only 14 per cent of respondents had been using RAD for more than two years.

In terms of predicting use of RAD, no clear pattern emerged. Industry sector, for example, was not found to be significant. Organisation size proved to be interesting insofar as RAD was equally likely in both small (less than 100 employees) and large organisations (more than 500 employees). However, it was less common in medium-sized organisations (100-500 employees). One possible explanation for this is that small organisations are less bureaucratic and have less administrative overheads and thus may be more willing to practice a RAD approach. On the other hand, large organisations are likely to have large IS departments, and thus are more capable of establishing small teams which can pioneer the use of new concepts, such as RAD.

18. O'Connor, "An Empirical Investigation of the Implementation of the Rapid Application Development Approach" (Unpublished MSc thesis, University College Cork, 1996).

Suitability of RAD

A number of criteria were identified as rendering an application suitable for RAD. However, it should be noted that there was by no means widespread agreement on these issues. The factors are summarised in Table 7.1 and are briefly explained here. Firstly, application size was frequently cited with RAD seen as better suited to small projects with few developers and a small user base. By contrast, large projects with a large user base, and thus more complex requirements, were not viewed as suitable. Similarly, RAD was typically adopted in less complex applications which were perhaps targeted at a single department, and perhaps an interim solution, rather than for enterprise-wide applications which were expected to have a longer service life. Additionally, mission-critical systems were not seen as suited to a RAD development approach; rather RAD tended to be used in novel application areas where the emphasis was on discovering and surfacing user requirements. Finally, RAD projects differed in relation to the languages being used (typically 4GLs), the amount of documentation (less in RAD, with responsibility for producing it delegated to users).

Table 7.1: Suitability Criteria for a RAD Approach

Suitable for RAD	Unsuitable for RAD
Small project. Few developers. Small user base.	Large project. Many developers. Large user base with complex requirements.
System for a single department. Interim or temporary solution. Not mission critical.	Enterprise-wide application. Long service-life expected. Mission critical.
4GLs used. Emphasis on user interface, information presentation. Less formalised documentation. Responsibility for it delegated to users.	3GLs. Application area more algorithmically complex. Traditional formalised documentation pattern.
Novel application area. Emphasis on surfacing user requirements.	Traditional application areas.

CONCLUSION

RAD methodologies are now beginning to emerge, prominent examples being a variant of information engineering[19] and the DSM methodology.[20] However, much needs to be done to elaborate the concept. Problems may be anticipated in the areas of management and control, raised user expectations, half-hearted implementation of the concept, and so on. Also, the issue of RAD suitability – is it appropriate for use in the development of safety-critical systems – needs to be investigated. Indeed, it may be the case that traditional development approaches may be more appropriate in some circumstances.

The question also arises as to the extent to which RAD is a fad. For example, 'productivity' was the buzz word in the 1970s, with 'quality' being perhaps that of the 1980s. Both are incorporated into the RAD concept. However, the issue of whether development speed and quality can be increased and cost reduced has yet to be proven. Certainly, there is no royal road to RAD and companies will not find it to be the 'silver bullet' solution. Rather, as much work needs to be done in changing traditional mindsets as overcoming technical issues.

---

19. Gane, *op. cit.*
20 DSDM, *op cit.*

SOURCES

D Avison & G Fitzgerald, *Information Systems Development: Methodologies, Techniques and Tools* (UK: McGraw-Hill) 1995, 2nd edn.

P Bates & M Stephens, "Rapid Application Development – Concept, Methodology or What?" *NDISD RAD* (April 1995).

B Boehm, *Software Engineering Economics* (Englewood Cliffs, New Jersey: Prentice Hall) 1981.

P Bowen, "Rapid Application Development: Concepts and Principles" *IBM Document No. 94283UKT0829* (1994).

Brooks, "No Silver Bullet: Essence and Accidents of Software Engineering" *IEEE Computer Magazine* (April 1987) pp. 10-19.

T DeMarco, *Structured Analysis and System Specification* (New Jersey: Yourdon Press) 1978.

DSDM, *Dynamic Systems Development Method* (UK: Tesseract Publishing) 1995.

B Fitzgerald, "Systems Development Methodologies: Time to Advance the Clock" in G Wojtowski, (ed.) *Systems Development Methods for the Next Century* (New York: Plenum Press) 1997.

P Flaatten, D McCubbrey, P O'Riordan & K Burgess, *Foundations of Business Systems* (Chicago: Dryden Press) 1989.

C Gane, *Rapid Systems Development* (Englewood Cliffs, New Jersey: Prentice-Hall) 1989.

N Jayaratna, *Understanding and Evaluating Methodologies* (McGraw-Hill: London, 1994).

J Martin, *Rapid Application Development* (USA: Macmillan) 1991.

S McConnell, *Rapid Development* (USA: Microsoft Press) 1996.

A O'Connor, "An Empirical Investigation of the Implementation of the Rapid Application Development Approach" (Unpublished MSc thesis, University College Cork, 1996).

M Sinha, "Development Practices at Microsoft" Seminar given at the 6th International Conference on IS Development, Boise, Idaho (11-14 August 1997).

T Taylor & T Standish, "Initial Thoughts on Rapid Prototyping Techniques" ACM SIGSOFT *Software Engineering Notes* (1982) 7, 5 pp. 160-166.

J Verity, "The OOPS Revolution" *Datamation* (1 May 1987) pp. 73-78.

E Yourdon, *Classics in Software Engineering* (New Jersey: Yourdon Press) 1979.

"The Software Trap: Automate – or else" *Business Week* (9 May 1988) pp. 142-154.

8

Realising the Benefits of CASE: Lessons from the Adoption and Use of I-CASE in a Large, Irish Organisation

Tom Butler

INTRODUCTION

Systems developers face the dawn of a new millennium with many of the problems that have beset the field of information systems development since its inception still with them. Many of these problems are traceable to the 'software crisis' of the 1960s and 1970s – for example, the year 2000 dilemma is one hangover from this era – however, the bulk of today's problems present their own unique challenges for organisations endeavouring to develop new and evermore complex information systems. Radical improvements in developer productivity and the quality of the systems development process are required if these challenges are to be met effectively. In the face of an increasing scarcity of developers, computer aided software/systems engineering (CASE) is considered by many to be the 'silver bullet' that will help resolve the new 'software crisis'.

Designing large-scale, complex information systems demands a systematic approach. An information systems development methodology (ISDM) is said to offer just such an approach because it presents a set of methods and techniques for developers to use in the planning, analysis, design and implementation of information systems. Box 8.1 provides an overview of the benefits of an ISDM. Over the past two decades, academic researchers and vendors alike have argued that information systems development methodologies help practitioners improve both the process and product of systems development; however, doubt has been raised as to whether the methodology movement has achieved these goals. CASE tools provide automated support for systems development methodologies. As with the development methods they automate, arguments have been made that CASE tools increase developer productivity and bring efficiency and quality improvements to the development process and its product. It is, nevertheless, worth noting that these claims have not been entirely vindicated in either research or practice and questions have been raised as to the benefits that accrue from the adoption of CASE for systems development in organisations. The issues surrounding the adoption, implementation and use of CASE, therefore, merit closer scrutiny if IS managers are to assess CASE and the contribution it can make to their organisations properly.

Box 8.1: Benefits of ISDM Use

- Improved communication between users and analysts.
- Improved system structure.
- Improved system documentation.
- Increased importance of early development stages.
- Richer definition of system functions.
- Sequenced tasks and defined intermediate results.

COMPUTER AIDED SYSTEMS ENGINEERING: SETTING THE SCENE

The route from the identification of the need for an information system to its ultimate implementation and eventual use usually follows the general steps shown in Box 8.2. While the systems development life cycle (SDLC) provides a typical representation of the process by which information systems applications are developed, it must be noted that there are many variations on this basic theme.

Box 8.2: The Systems Development Life Cycle (SDLC)

- **Statement of requirements**: what the business needs in terms of IT.
- **Specification**: what requirements will be met.

- **Design**: comprehensive modelling and description of the requirements specification, including prototyping.

- **Detailed design and build**: building on the design, how programs are developed to meet design specifications.

- **Test**: ensuring that the system, as constructed, meets the initial requirements and agreed quality standards.

- **Implementation**: rolling out the completed system across the organisation.

- **Maintenance**: evolving the system to meets changing requirements and business needs.

In the past the terms 'computer aided software engineering' and 'computer aided systems engineering' have been used interchangeably, however, it is fair to say that computer aided software engineering refers only to those technologies that help automate and support systems development activities, such as detailed design and build, etc. Systems engineering, on the other hand, encompasses the whole of the development life cycle. Typically, each stage of the SDLC may be supported by a particular development method or technique, and automated by a computer-based solution that helps implement the particular method or technique. CASE-enabled systems information engineering approaches provide a set of methods-based tools that cover the entire development life cycle, including, for example, the pre-development planning stage. CASE tools, therefore, are of a wide variety of type and function, and because of the multiplicity of methodologies and CASE vendors in the marketplace, achieve their purpose in a wide variety of ways. The tools themselves have been classified according to the phase(s) of the SDLC targeted by them. Upper CASE tools are those that provide support for specification and high-level design activities. Lower CASE tools provide support for programming, test/debug and maintenance activities – i.e. software engineering activities. Integrated CASE (I-CASE) tools provide a consistent development environment that spans all stages. I-CASE tool-sets are usually referred to as workbenches or development environments and many of the current products on the market are based on the information engineering (IE) methodology. Commercially available CASE tools or workbenches range from those based on single-user PC packages to client/server and mainframe-based applications. The more popular I-CASE tool-sets include sophisticated prototyping and code generation tools: the latter tools usually provide extensive support for multiple programming languages, network protocols and database platforms. The cost of these applications typically ranges from $100 to $250,000, depending on the particular vendor application and the number of licenced users.

Table 8.1: Cost Breakdown of Systems Development and Maintenance Activities

Analysis	12%	
Specification and design	18%	
Detailed design	15%	
Code and debug	20%	
Testing	35%	
		100%
Systems development as a percentage of total system costs	34%	
Maintenance	66%	
		100%

If the breakdown of costs associated with a typical development project are viewed (see Table 8.1), it is clear that the development activities which CASE best automates also incur the greatest share of the production costs *viz.* detailed design, code and debug and testing. Given the significant costs associated with systems maintenance – e.g. such activities account for up to 66 per cent of the total costs associated with the introduction and use of information systems – there are also potential savings to be realised in post-development activities as a result of CASE use.

Another problem here, of course, is that the eventual success of information systems development within an organisational context chiefly depends on the analysis and design phases where CASE is said to be least effective. Thus, CASE has the potential to reduce development-related costs; however, developers must be realistic and focus on those activities where CASE use will give the greatest returns and, more importantly, recognise that the really significant savings will accrue after the system is developed and implemented.

A REVIEW OF THE PERFORMANCE OF CASE IN THE DEVELOPMENT OF INFORMATION SYSTEMS

CASE tools have long been considered to be a potential vehicle for easing systems development-related problems and bottlenecks. The following brief review of research on CASE offers mixed results and suggests that such claims for its utility have little basis in fact.

Box 8.3: Reported Benefits of CASE

- Provides a formal and standardised approach to systems development.

- Provides an adaptable and consistent development platform.

- More efficient development procedures.

- Improved development process and systems quality.

- Improved developer productivity.

- Facilitates software re-engineering and re-use.

- Reduces development costs.

Many researchers and practitioners argue that the systematic analysis and design of an information system requires a systems development methodology. The role of CASE is to give automated support to a methodology. Over a 1,000 brand name methodologies are in use all over the world. Correspondingly, since the introduction of CASE in the mid-1980s, the number of CASE tools has proliferated: in 1990, for example, it was estimated that there were in excess of 1,000 in existence. As with claims for the methodologies that they automate, improved standardisation, more efficient systems development procedures and improved systems quality are argued to result from CASE use. That CASE tools have the potential to increase developer productivity is not disputed; however, this takes time. In addition, CASE use is reported to have a positive influence on both the development function within organisations – by providing productivity and quality enhancements to the development process, and on individual developers, by increasing their effectiveness and engendering positive attitudes toward their work. Other touted benefits of CASE include its ability to facilitate software re-engineering and re-use and in its provision of an adaptable and consistent development platform for developers. Box 8.3 presents an account of the positive effects of CASE use.

While CASE has promised much, research has shown that it has failed to deliver on its promises. The reported benefits of CASE are not being realised, it is argued: the Butler Cox Report, for example, supports an argument that the introduction of CASE in organisations has led to a reduction in the quality of systems produced. Recent research also lends support to the view that practitioners are disillusioned with CASE *viz.* 70 per cent of CASE tools are not used one year after their introduction and only 5 per cent are widely used, but not to their full capacity.

However, more recent studies indicate that the situation may not be so serious, nevertheless, this body of research indicates that about one third of all organisations which adopt CASE abandon its use within two years of acquiring it.

> *70 per cent of CASE tools are not used one year after their introduction, and only 5 per cent are widely used, but not to their full capacity.*

Possible reasons for this are that development activities, such as logical modelling, prototyping, generating design document-ation, creating modular program design specifications, and design training, are not made easier by the use of CASE tools. Negative comments by practitioners who have used CASE has led researchers to suggest that: "CASE is simply another technology which automates a series of isolated systems design tasks, without addressing the underlying need for improving the systems design process."

Integration or tight coupling between the various tools em-ployed, e.g. between data modelling, process modelling, proto-typing, and software engineering tools, seems to be the critical issue here. Hence, if the right set of integrated CASE tools are chosen, and organisations commit to their use, then the benefits will eventually materialise. However, that said, there is a fairly steep learning curve associated with CASE use. For example, it often takes up to three years for the productivity improvements associated with upper CASE to materialise; however, significant improvements accrue thereafter. On the other hand, lower CASE tools typically see improvements filtering through in under eight-een months. Again, the difficulties experienced by practitioners in scaling the learning curve associated with a combination of upper and lower CASE, i.e. with integrated CASE platforms, means that productivity improvements with I-CASE take up to two and a half years to materialise. The major mitigating factor here is that productivity improvements of up to 30 per cent or more can be realised with I-CASE in under three years. Hence, one of the major problems with CASE is the significant time it takes for financial paybacks and productivity improvements to accrue. This poses a significant problem for many IS managers who may not be able to wait for the long-term benefits associated with CASE.

Box 8.4: Adoption and Implementation Issues Associated with CASE.

- No proof of payback.
- Multiple CASE products and confusion of alternatives, e.g. different technologies/methodologies.
- Steep learning curves.
- Non-scalability of tools.
- Non-integration of tools.
- Training.
- Cultural resistance:
  - existing practices;
  - existing tools.
- Organisation variables:
  - user/developer relations;
  - up-front costs;
  - pilot project requirements.
- Suitable project size.
- Primacy of design quality.

What are the implications of these issues for IS managers? It is clear that CASE is no 'silver bullet', it can be the source of additional development-related headaches to IS managers and developers. Box 8.4 illustrates several of the critical issues that need to be recognised and considered by IS managers when attempting to adopt and use CASE tools. However, previous experience has shown that problems which the adoption and use of CASE brings can be minimised through proper training, choosing the right project size, focusing on design quality and by using an integrated set of CASE tools. An in-depth description of these issues can, therefore, be of practical benefit to IS managers interested in adopting CASE. This is undertaken in the following sections.

A CASE STUDY OF THE INTRODUCTION OF CASE FOR SYSTEMS DEVELOPMENT IN TELECOM ÉIREANN

Telecom Éireann is the Republic of Ireland's national telecommunications company (telco). The Irish government is Telecom's major shareholder and holds 65 per cent of its equity there are three minority shareholders: Telia, a Swedish telco and KPN, a Dutch telco, which jointly own 20 per cent of the company, and the employee group who have a 15 per cent stake in the organisation. Telecom Éireann provides a universal telecommunications service within Ireland and presently enjoys a monopoly in many of its service areas. There are ten companies in the Telecom Group, the majority of which are wholly owned subsidiaries. At present, it employs in excess of 11,000 staff. Being a large company, in a highly competitive national and international environment, it has dynamic information systems needs; these needs are met chiefly by its in-house information systems development function – the Information Technology Directorate (ITD). The ITD is a centralised functional unit whose chief responsibility is the development, maintenance and support of all corporate information systems.

In 1994 Telecom Éireann's IS function faced a considerable backlog in its systems development portfolio. The function's previous experience with CASE products was with SSADM, a popular upper CASE tool-set; the IS function abandoned SSADM within one year due to:

(a)   difficulties associated with the steep learning curve for developers;

(b)   the concomitant decrease in developer productivity;

(c)   the absence of an early payback.

Senior IS management decided that a strategy of outsourcing and the integration of 'off the shelf' software packages might address some of their development problems, however, there was still a considerable number of organisational information systems that could only be developed in-house. Undeterred by their experiences with SSADM, they have cautiously set about selecting and implementing what they considered to be the optimal solution to their problems. This involved the introduction of an I-CASE workbench in a pilot setting of their choosing with clear objectives being set in terms of targets in budgeted time and financial and human resources for the project. The following sections describe Telecom Éireann's initial and subsequent experience with CASE.

An Overview of the Development Product

The Generic Appointment System (GAS) grew out of a business need in one essential area of the Telecom Éireann's operations – its telephone repair service. Business managers across the organisation recognised the need to introduce efficiencies into the manner in which repair service workloads were managed and associated service appointments made with customers. It was hoped that the introduction of this information system would eliminate the occurrence of unproductive visits by operational staff to customer premises when customers were absent.

The GAS would also assist supervisors in their task of allocating workloads to their repair teams, which consist of operational staff. Both groups, therefore, had a keen interest in the development and implementation of this system as it impacted on some of their basic functions.

> *The development of the GAS was budgeted to take place within a 3-month time period, this included three weeks of intensive vendor training for all team members in the I-CASE product.*

The GAS also supports the operation of the company's ten fault-handling and repair centres.

A development team, which consisted of a development project manager, a user project manager, two analysts, a consultant provided by the CASE vendor, a programmer, a user representative, and three user groups, as well as a range of individual users, all participated in the development of the GAS. The development approach adopted was consistent with extant radical application development (RAD) approaches, described in Chapter 7 of this book. The development of the GAS was budgeted to take place within a 3-month time period, this included three weeks of intensive vendor training for all team members in the I-CASE product selected for the development of the GAS and pilot study of the I-CASE platform.

The CASE-supported RAD approach saw development take place within the 3-month time period set for the project: however, the implementation of the first phase of the GAS took a further six months. As a distributed IS, the GAS is client/server app-lication using 8 Oracle®-relational databases that serve up to 180 Windows®-based PC terminals in fault-handling centres around Ireland and a further 400 terminals in operational depots nationwide. The GAS project came in on time and within budget.

The Issues Surrounding the GAS Development

Although business managers within the company had articulated a need for a customer appointments system, the chief stimulus for the development of the GAS arose out of an internal need within the IS function. Senior IS managers recognised that dev-elopment teams needed to produce modular, maintainable systems in a rapid manner. IS management also wanted to max-imise the productivity of a fixed developer resource and skillset and maintain product quality. Although the IS function had a brief, but unproductive, experience with SSADM, the return to ad hoc development practices was equally unsatisfactory. That said, the GAS project manager reported that, due to a range of development-related issues, support grew for the acquisition and use of a "common/generic development environment that we could use, cradle to grave, to give a total life cycle coverage".

Subsequent to a rigorous vetting procedure by the IS function's quality team, a computer-aided systems engineering workbench, called information engineering facility (IEF), was acquired from Texas Instruments. IEF is an integrated CASE workbench that operationalises and automates the associated information engineering methodology using a set of tightly integrated tools; essentially, it provides architectural (planning), conceptual (structured design modelling), external (prototyping), implementation (procedure writing, code generation and hard-ware) and execution (integration of the product into hardware, target databases, existing applications and data networks) layers that map onto the IE methodology. Besides the productivity imp-rovements promised by IEF, IS managers also viewed the intro-duction of IEF as a means to improve the quality of the development process and product and to quickly re-engineer and maintain development applications.

Although initial tests of IEF were favourable, IS managers were mindful of the function's previous experience with SSADM; a rigorous test of IEF's capabilities and suitability to purpose was deemed necessary in order to assess its potential fully. Therefore, a decision was made to employ IEF to develop rapidly an inform-ation system from the existing backlog of projects. A senior IS manager, who was responsible for the bulk of systems develop-ment at the time and who championed CASE use, selected "a small, non-critical project", the Generic Appointments System, to test fully the systems development capabilities of IEF (from conceptual to execution layers) within a real development environment. A 3-month deadline was set for the development of the project's core requirements and their implementation as a generic appointments system in one of the company's operational areas. The full implementation of the system was to be effected subsequently.

Selection of the GAS/IEF Development Team

A development project team was chosen with the special needs in mind: that is, team members were selected on the basis of perceived attitudes toward issues of demarcation of the CASE-enabled GAS development project and on their commitment to conflict avoidance. As the GAS was to be integrated with the existing fault handling system (FHS), two experienced analysts with prior experience in development of the FHS were chosen, along with a programmer who had worked on a related project. Both analysts possessed experience and skills in such diverse areas as traditional systems analysis and design, programming, com-puter hardware and technical aspects of network comm-unications. As with all IS development within the organisation, a user project manager and a user representative were appointed to participate in the development of the GAS; these individuals had a wide-range of experience in the operational areas en-compassed by the proposed system. User groups provided pools of experienced users, from the operational areas of interest, to participate with the development team to generate, refine, and validate the user requirements and system prototypes. The impact of this participative approach to development, which involved a combination of both joint application development (JAD) and participatory design (PD), was commented on by the development project manager who stated that "the appointments system development was really driven by the user group".

On the Systems Development Approach Employed

The IEF development environment supports a structured approach to development built around the SDLC. However, the GAS project team adopted a customised prototyping-enabled, rapid application development approach (RAD) for the development of the appointments system that saw developers omitting certain design procedures embodied within IEF deemed to be not relevant. The prototyping tool within IEF was the primary mechanism used to refine user requirements and to design system functionality. This prototyping approach worked well with IEF, and was approved of by the IEF consultant who was a member of the project team. However, the project manager had difficulty in estimating and managing development activities that were evolutionary and creative in nature and which were centred on user-led prototyping. A consultant from Texas Instruments was on-site during the initial stages (data and process modelling etc.) to assist with the CASE-enabled element of the RAD approach – subsequently, this individual operated in a support capacity for the development team.

The Development of a Consensus Approach to CASE Use

The project was well managed, co-ordinated and controlled; a strong positive relationship was in evidence between the development project manager and the development team. The project manager realised that, because existing development-related roles were heavily demarcated within the IS function, there was the potential for intra-team conflict to develop between analysts and programmers on the one hand and between the participating user and developers on the other. Prior to commencement of training on IEF, the project manager met with the proposed team to develop a consensus approach to CASE use. Whereas the analysts and programmers had their own areas of speciality, and were expected to contribute accordingly, there was to be no specialisation in development-related activities associated with the use of IEF – this applied to the user representative also, as he was a highly experienced technician and was, therefore, expected to participate fully with the developers in almost all aspects of systems development. In fact, it was he who was responsible for the technical implementation of the GAS.

It was clear that the consensus approach adopted by the development project manager and his team created a development climate that effectively mitigated any problems that may have arisen due to 'demarcation' issues between analysts and programmers when using IEF.

SOME LESSONS AND RECOMMENDATIONS FOR IS MANGERS FACING THE CHALLENGE OF I-CASE ADOPTION

The adoption and implementation of I-CASE in Telecom Éireann was a success; however, it is clear that the reasons for this centred chiefly on the foresight and capabilities of IS management in first selecting an appropriate system with which to pilot IEF, and in then selecting a project manager and development team who possessed the right mix of attributes and skills that would maximise the return from the exercise in order to reap the benefits associated with CASE. Only then could a serious argument be made for its adoption for all large-scale systems development within the organisation. What follows is a brief outline of the post-implementation issues that arose in relation to the rollout of IEF in Telecom Éireann and a short discussion of the benefits that this technology brought to this organisation. This chapter then concludes by offering some concrete lessons and recommendations for IS managers planning to adopt and implement I-CASE technologies.

Box 8.5: Suggested Benefits of I-CASE

- Significant productivity gains within a 3-month period.

- Development time radically reduced.

- Development-related costs reduced.

- Maintenance costs slashed.

- Improved user/developer communication.

- Higher quality and better maintained product.

- Allows systems to evolve and be re-engineered to meet changing business needs.

Some two years after the initial pilot project, IEF had been adopted as the IS function's application development environment (ADE) of choice for in-house, bespoke systems development. Thus, the initial management goal of introducing a function-wide development environment was realised. IS managers stated that the subsequent rollout across the IS function was facilitated by the lessons learned from the adoption and use of IEF on the GAS project. This allowed potential problem areas, particularly in developer training and project management, to be addressed and enabled the benefits associated with CASE use to be achieved in other development projects. Of particular note here was that the two analysts on the GAS/IEF project were promoted to the position of project managers as part of a strategy to integrate their knowledge and experience from the use of IEF in the pilot project to the development of new systems within the organisation.

It must pointed out here that only the conceptual, external, implementation and execution layers of IEF were employed in the pilot and subsequent projects: that is, the design (data and process modelling, prototyping), detailed design and implementation aspects of the systems development process. As was noted earlier, it is here that the bulk of development costs and problems lie – these have now been significantly reduced. Furthermore, the tight integration of IEF means that maintenance costs have been slashed due to the capabilities of IEF to cascade changes made at early stages of the development life cycle through to the finished product; the test features also add greatly to the relative ease with which post-development changes have been made to systems. This has also been shown to have a significant impact on post development costs. Box 8.5 provides a synopsis of the benefits that can accrue from I-CASE platforms, such as IEF.

IT vendors no longer refer to their products as CASE; instead, the term 'application development environment' (ADE) is employed. Vendors are of the opinion that the benefits of CASE were never fully realised and, as such, it has not been universally successful or popular with practitioners. Accordingly, they have focused on providing an integrated solution, a so-called development environment that is basically a well-integrated set of CASE tools such as that described in this chapter. This approach, it is argued, places emphasis on the strengths of CASE, and underlines the contribution it can make to the development process and its product. It, therefore, answers some of the major criticisms made, and, as we have seen, has provided a valuable development platform for organisations.

Box 8.6: A Management Checklist for CASE Adoption, Implementation and Use

- Adopt an open, participatory style of project management.

- Carefully select project team members.

- Facilitate developer and user commitment to the use of the I-CASE and to the development project.

- Develop a consensus among developers by the project team.

- Use a pilot project to test the suitability of the I-CASE platform.

- Ensure that the CASE tool-set is easy to use, customisable, well-integrated and includes prototyping and code generation tools as standard.

- Adopt a participate approach to development incorporating both JAD and PD.

- Ensure that comprehensive vendor training and post-training support for all project team members.

- Develop and maintain a strong relationship with the vendor at both IS function management and project team level.

The take-home message of this brief analysis of adoption and implementation of I-CASE platforms for systems development has been that a multitude of contextual factors exerts both positive and negative influences on the ability of IS managers and developers to realise the benefits associated with technologies such as IEF. Box 8.6 illustrates what one could call a set of recommendations or a checklist for IS managers when attempting to adopt and implement CASE in their organisations. Building on the experiences of IS managers and developers described herein, we can see that positive developer attitudes toward and high levels of commitment to the use of the I-CASE platform were chiefly determined by the project management style used. Here, the project manager *deliberately* employed a consensus approach to I-CASE use that saw analysts, programmers and user representatives agreed, up front that development-related demarcation –

i.e. between the respective roles of analysts, programmers and users – was not going to be an issue. His open style of project management enabled developers to become heavily involved in decision making and problem solving, this also had the effect of heightening developer commitment to the use of IEF. The adoption and use of a participative policy to systems development, by both business and IS management, that included the use of both JAD and PD approaches – i.e. joint development-related meetings to elicit requirements, develop prototypes, etc. – engendered high levels of commitment from users. The training, support and advice obtained from the I-CASE vendor also proved to be vital. Here, the input of an on-site vendor consultant ensured that the steep learning curve normally associated with I-CASE was rapidly negotiated.

In relation to the I-CASE tool-set itself, it was clear that the use of prototyping tools were central to IEF's success in enabling the project's RAD approach. It must also be noted that the ability to prototype enhanced significantly developer/user communication and was instrumental in heightening user commitment to the development process and product. Developers found that the tools provided to implement the IE-based data and process modelling techniques were easy to use and well integrated with the other CASE tools in the workbench. The flexibility and ease of use of the scripting tool and code generator drew special praise from developers and end-users alike: so too did the testing and trace tool. However, on the down side, developers found translating the analysis findings to CASE modelling conventions problematic, and would have preferred CASE support in this area also. Finally, there were several technical issues with the CASE-developed end product that required significant problem solving on behalf of both analysts and CASE vendor alike.

In conclusion, then, the lessons learned from this organisation provides a useful point of reference for IS mangers who are considering adopting I-CASE platforms for systems development. The CASE adoption and implementation process is not, as we have seen, straightforward or easy and the stakes are high for IS managers, especially if things go wrong. It is, then, all the more important for managers to learn from the experience of others, be it good or bad. This chapter will be of benefit in this regard as it is grounded in the experience of IT professionals and thereby provides a vicariously acquired know-how for all would-be adopters of I-CASE development platforms.

SUGGESTED READING

S Folkes & S Stubenvoll, *Accelerated Systems Development* (Englewood Cliffs, New Jersey: Prentice Hall) 1994.

P J Guinan, J Cooprider & S Sawyer, "The Effective Use of Automated Application Development Tools" *IBM Systems Journal* (1997) 36(1), pp. 124-139.

J Gyorkos & I Rozman, "Assessment and Control of the Requirements Elicitation Process in an CASE Environment" in N Prakash, C Rolland & B Pernici (eds), *Information System Development Process; Proceedings of the IFIP WG8.1 Working Conference on the Information Systems Development Process* (North Holland: Elsevier Science Publications) 1993, pp. 135-227.

H Lorin, *Doing IT Right: Technology, Business, and the Risk of Computing* (Greenwich, Conneticut: Manning) 1996.

O Orlikowski, "CASE Tools as Organisational Change: Investigating Incremental and Radical Changes in Systems Development" *MIS Quarterly* (1993) 17(3) pp. 309-340.

Section 3

The Electronic Revolution of Business

This section is made up of the four chapters listed below.

Section 3 deals with a much debated topic: the electronic revolution that has taken place in business over the last few years as a result of the take-off of global networking. Many organisations have been involved in large webs of relationships with their suppliers, partners and customers for a number of years. Inter-organisational systems, such as those using electronic data interchange (EDI) and electronic mail, are embedded into their operations. But now, everyone has begun to discover that they can belong to the 'global village' by connecting to the 'net' – meant to refer to the internet and its latest, more sophisticated manifestation: the World Wide Web, which anyone can browse endlessly given the availability of an up-to-date personal computer.

The chapters presented in this section look first at the internet/World Wide Web phenomenon from a general point of view, then to the more commercial developments that have taken place under the label of 'electronic commerce'. Some of the less well-known potential usage of internet technologies, such as for educational purposes, are also presented and their potential for both mainstream education and in-company training are discussed. Finally, the quieter 'intranet' revolution, which sees organisations developing internet-like sites that are designed to address the needs of their staff, as opposed to being externally oriented is presented as an avenue that organisations can follow when they feel the need to develop and strengthen their internal communication.

9

The World Wide Web: Implications for Business?

Frédéric Adam and Valérie Coatnoan

INTRODUCTION

Even though it was created as long ago as 1969, to provide the US military with a communication system that would be very difficult to destroy in case of a nuclear attack, the internet has only recently taken off as a worldwide communication medium. The last ten years have seen the number of computers connected to the internet grow from 2,000 (1986) to more than 10 million (1997). This growth has been especially fast since 1992 when the number of connected host computers broke through the 1 million barrier.

Up to 1994, the traffic on the internet was dominated by file transfer protocol (FTP) type of applications which provided very limited functionality to their users – i.e. they only provided access to large libraries of various types of documents, pictures, abstracts, videos, etc. The most interesting development on the internet from a commercial point of view has been the launch of the World Wide Web (WWW) in 1992. The WWW enables site owners to deliver a wide variety of services to users who log on to their servers. As early as 1994, the first shopping malls appeared on the WWW as the number of servers jumped from 50 in January 1993 to more than 100,000 in 1996 and probably in exess of 2 million in 1998.

The WWW is accessed using special navigation software; initially *Mosaic* and more recently *Netscape* and *Internet Explorer*. It can be used by anyone with a PC and the proper connections. In Ireland alone, close to twenty internet service providers (ISPs) are competing fiercely to provide internet access to Irish users. This competitive situation is very favourable for the users who can, initially at least, expect low prices and dynamic services. This has resulted in Ireland finding itself at the forefront of the internet/WWW phenomenon.

Internet – the Key to Wonderland?

There has always been a tendency for authors in fields related to technology (and especially to information technologies) to over-emphasise the importance, the scope and/or the potential of new technological discoveries. The areas of expert systems, artificial intelligence, executive information systems have all suffered from the excessive enthusiasm of their proponents at some point or another.

Although the success of the internet as a general comm-unication device can no longer be denied, there is a chance that its commercial potential has been overstated at a time when very optimistic claims are being made about its potential effect on business. The internet – the network of networks – has been widely tipped to become "an information superhighway" in the 21st century, making vast quantities of information universally available. The diversity of information available on the 'net' has humorously been described as ranging from a Dan Quayle fan club for political satire to a consumer's guide to handcuffs.

In the business arena, Bill Gates has warned that "only some of the companies laying bets on the internet will be winners. But companies that bet against the internet will be losers". Another author has predicted that "every business will be unrecognisable in a decade" and gave the example of the health care industry where it is envisaged that medical consultants will be able to access a patient's home medical record irrespective of their location and send e-mail queries to the patient's family doctor to obtain im-portant first-hand details, such as allergies to common drugs or information on previous surgery.

Up to now, European companies have been comparatively shy in comparison to their US competitors and there is a real risk that they are allowing competitors that they don't even know about invade their markets by not responding fast enough. Thus, the 'net' phenomenon and its consequences for business practices cannot be ignored by anyone. Indeed, the World Wide Web has been compared to the gold rush of 1849, "the best business opportunity that most business people are likely to find in a lifetime".

The new ways of making business enabled by the internet and the WWW have been labelled under the general heading of virtual business. Important businesses seem to emerge from nothing, without facilities, shop widows or any of the resources considered necessary to run a business in the past. Telemarketing, for instance, which consists of "a shop in 0.5 m²" enables the sale of any kind of product to millions of customers through the endorsement of famous entertainment figures, with the minimum requirement of a telephone number and a few contacts in suppliers' organisations.

The result can be astonishing. Organisations can establish themselves on a global scale at an accelerated pace through effective use of the internet. Instead of setting up distribution channels and establishing brand names over periods of months and years, the internet can be used as a high profile means of selling goods to a global market with immediate results. This is particularly true for technology and computer-oriented companies for which a WWW presence is perceived as a sign of dynamism. Thus, the internet becomes similar to a set of crossroads where petrol stations fight a tough price war; except that, with the internet, all companies are at the same crossroad.

The advertising area also provides us with a convincing example of how significant an effect new communication media such as the WWW can have on traditionally accepted wisdom. Advertising agencies have always charged their fees as a percentage of the amounts spent on the campaign they design, and with television commercials costing up to $500,000, a 15 per cent commission generates quite an attractive margin.

On the WWW, however, the cost of implementing a campaign becomes completely trivial, and the old methods of costing advertising services become obsolete. In fact, there is a strong possibility that some types of companies will no longer require traditional advertising agencies to the same degree as before as they can create and implement their own advertising on the WWW.

The WWW also enables a new form of advertising: interactive advertising. A recent Fiat car advertisement on European television provided a demonstration of such interactive advertising. In this commercial, two customers log into Fiat's WWW server and use the browser provided to investigate exclusively the features of the car of interest to them as opposed to being limited to viewing the features selected by the car maker as is the case in a traditional advertising campaign.

Up to now, car makers had to attempt to isolate the attributes of their products which most appealed to their target groups, an impossible task given the complexity of some of the market segments. They can now develop a WWW site which enables

customers to look at products from the angle they choose –
whatever that may be. This constitutes a mini-revolution from
traditional advertising because what used to be a "one feature –
many customers" message can become a "many features – one
customer" message, with a resulting increase in the effectiveness
of advertising campaigns. Overall, the Web gives commercial
organisations the opportunity to deliver new services and products
to a worldwide customer base without any major investment
(setting up a website is relatively trivial).

There is great belief amongst researchers and practitioners
that the internet, and in particular the World Wide Web, can
bring about radical changes in the way we live, work and learn.
However, a feature of the views of researchers and commentators
is that they are not based on solid empirical evidence but rather
on hopeful predictions. The danger with this approach is that it
results in a lot of hype which can mislead researchers and
business people.

Box 9.1: *International Herald Tribune*

- *This site is the on-line version of the newspaper.*
- *The issues of the week are available, a click on the required day will provide access to abstracts of selected articles. For more information, or for the complete article, virtual visitors can click on the article of their choice to download it. Specific subjects, such as 'technology index' or 'feature' and 'dispatches' can be researched using the search index provided in the site.*
- *It is also possible to subscribe to the newspaper via e-mail (but the newspaper is still delivered on paper!).*
- *Companies which want to advertise in the next issue of the newspaper can type the text of their ad in a special form and send it via e-mail. In order to support the decision making of these companies, the site indicates statistical analysis and surveys of the people who read the* International Herald Tribune *and its circulation.*
- *A connection to financial market related sites is also provided.*
- *Finally, the server provides the list of the firms which have advertised in the newspaper and a HTML link to some of those companies that have an internet site.*

In order to separate the hype from the reality of internet usage,
we studied a large number of WWW sites selected from ads that

we found in well-known international and national magazines of various origins. We focused on a European, an international, an Irish and a French magazine in order to determine the extent to which the World Wide Web is used by commercial organisations and, more importantly, to examine the degree of functionality that is provided on their homepages.

THE STUDY

The study was based on advertisements collected systematically in four magazines of diverse origins, published between January and April 1997. A list of the magazines used is presented below.

- *Time Europe*: the European issue of the American *Time* (6 January-10 March).

- *Business and Finance*: an Irish magazine (2 January-13 March).

- *L'Express*: a French Magazine (16 January-17 April).

- *The Economist*: an international magazine (4 January-1 March).

For the purpose of evaluation of these sites, we classified companies' internet presence in the following categories.

1. Internet server with no WWW access or facilities.

2. Site under construction.

3. Simple advertising and textual information with no service or navigation support.

4. Detailed information (products/services, company, etc.) with multiple pages and navigation tools.

5. Interactive exchanges enabled by special features, such as ready-made forms for electronic submissions (job opportunities, customers' services, etc.).

6. On-line shopping with products on display and special delivery services.

7. Visit a virtual place (shop, museum, etc.).

CLASSIFICATION OF THE SITES STUDIED

Figure 9.1 indicates the geographical distribution of the sites we looked at. The particular focus on Europe we adopted, in terms of the magazines we selected, is reflected in that the majority of sites studied belong to European organisations. American sites nevertheless represent more than a third of all sites because many of them are US-based companies which have subsidiaries in Europe, but maintain their sites from their American head-quarters.

Figure 9.1: Geographical Distribution of the Sites Visited

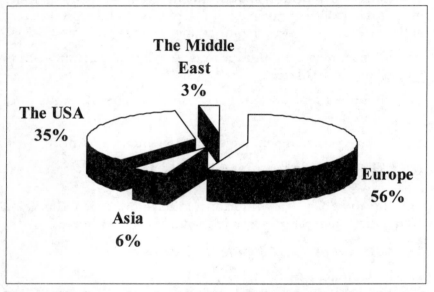

Figure 9.2 shows the classification of the sites we visited based on the level of functionality they offered. This diagram uses our classification in seven levels, as described in the previous section. It indicates that most companies now look at the WWW as a serious complement to their traditional advertising strategies and provide real services on their homepages. The typical pages with a logo or picture plus a few lines of text, which we found in so many sites in our previous study in 1996, have nearly disappeared and have been replaced by sophisticated pages with animations and many sophisticated Java Applets. On-line sales of goods have become common (nearly 20 per cent of the sites).

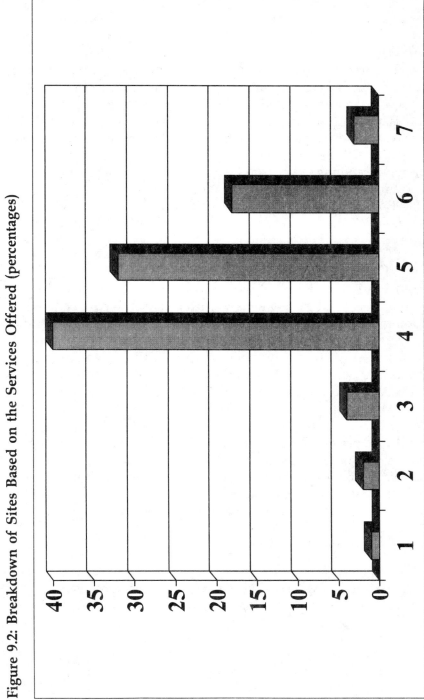

Figure 9.2: Breakdown of Sites Based on the Services Offered (percentages)

THE RESULTS

Language

As our sample contained European and international magazines, we investigated advertisements from different countries. But most sites were in English, thereby confirming the status of English as the major, international, business language. Most of the foreign sites we visited were both in the national language and in English.

Nevertheless, some of them were only available in the national language concerned, such as *Stet*, the site of the Italian Telecommunication Company, which was, of course, in Italian (the English version was under construction). At the other end of the spectrum, a Korean site could be visited in English, Spanish, Chinese, Japanese or French!

Homepage

We found that the sites have, on average, very similar pre-sentations. Most homepages are used as some sort of table of contents which allows visitors to get to the required information, without having to visit the whole site. Nevertheless, differences exist because a few companies, such as CNN, have advertising inserts for other firms. Some organisations are obviously betting on the net more than others as they can be found everywhere (e.g. Microsoft)!

In order to make navigation of the site easier for visitors, most sites provided maps. This is useful because many companies had areas in their sites that were "not yet available". Thus, many sites are expanding and are being continually updated. When it was the case, developers used 'new' and 'now open' labels to attract the attention of their regular visitors.

Box 9.2: Autovantage

This site, which is only operational for Americans, allows virtual shoppers to buy cars via their computers. Despite being so original, the site is technically very simple to the extent that it does not even provide links to other sites.

The site offers two possibilities for searching for a suitable car; whether potential customers are looking for a new or second-hand car.

If a new car is required, a list appears, based on the chosen model or make. Then, the technical specifications are presented. To go further, more information is requested about the body style, colour, engine, transmission and other available options. After having filled and submitted the application form, clients will receive an e-mail message to let them know when the car is ready.

In the case of a second-hand car, a click on one of the pictures of available cars is enough to display the technical features and the financial details. Interestingly, on-line buyers get a discount!

Services

The sites visited offered a heterogeneous range of services. We found a very wide range of services ranging from the very simple to the very sophisticated. We also found some surprises in terms of the type of organisations which feel that they have to be on the net. Amongst the greatest surprises was the fact that the Vatican has a very convincing on-line service where visitors have access to daily reports and to texts of the Pope's decisions. According to the Pope, John Paul II, the Vatican has to be on the internet because "the Church must adapt to the evolution of life".

Some companies have only established a very basic internet presence. Visiting their sites, one gets the feeling that they use the internet merely to have an on-line presence; such sites show advertisements and, sometimes, give information about the company. However, these basic sites were not as numerous as we had found in our previous studies in previous years.

Box 9.3: Taipei World Trade Centre

This site presents very detailed information regarding the different events taking place in Taipei. Detailed information about each particular trade fair is available, including general information, exhibitors, programmes, information regarding the products on display, etc.

In order to facilitate travellers who want to stay in Taipei, the site provides the addresses and the approximate rates of many international hotels. The site allows virtual visits of two of these hotels. Once inside the virtual hotels, general information is available as well as a map of the area. Then a guided tour of the hotels begins, with pictures and explanations. Bookings and registration can be made either by phone or by e-mail.

Because it is a very complete site, there is even a service which shows the weather in Taipei. A link with the newspaper MSNBC provides access to additional weather forecasts.

In addition to this, there is a virtual shop in the site. Visitors can buy food or other gifts on-line.

Finally, this site establishes connections with companies in Taipei, including presentations of the firms, a map showing how to reach them and companies' pictures.

We also found companies which used the internet in a commercial way, for example where visitors are allowed to buy on-line. A majority of the WWW sites seem to be in this category, which represents a significant evolution of the Web.

Other sites, but very few, were more sophisticated and offered virtual spaces that can be 'visited' from any browser; this was the case for example for Singapore Airlines which provided a virtual museum.

In order to be more attractive, other sites propose quizzes and games to test their visitors' knowledge of the information given in their site. They sometimes have a questionnaire and visitors can win a prize if their replies are selected. These practices are reminiscent of what supermarkets used to propose in order to make their customers more loyal to a particular shop and are mere updates of these old merchants' practices for the purpose of the net. Nevertheless, such ideas represent a real attempt to initiate some interaction between the company and its visitors.

In order to access certain services proposed by a site, users needed a password. Saab allowed reporters to buy pictures of their new models via the internet but, they had to enter their press number. Passwords were also used for on-line buying: at Siemens before visitors were allowed to buy, they needed an access number and a password. Nevertheless, the use of passwords was not common.

More commonly, site owners would require visitors to register upon their first access to the site and allocate them a login name which they could use for future access (the *Financial Times'* site operates on this basis). This enabled site owners to monitor the number of new logins and the regular visitors to the site.

A great number of companies offered job opportunities and there were significant differences between these sites. Indeed, some of the job opportunities provided had to be replied to by normal mail so that applicants still had to write a letter and send it with their CVs besides filling up the on-line questionnaire. Thus, many sites provided job opportunities but the application could not be made through the internet.

Nevertheless, we found one site that allowed applicants to submit their CVs via e-mail. Regarding career opportunities, a number of companies proposed internships for students and, actually, this service was only available on the internet.

Box 9.4: Singapore Airlines

This site presents general information regarding the company; for instance, the firm's background or information about planes, such as brand, their engine or the number of planes that the company is holding.

On-line check-in is available for first and Raffles class passengers and members of the company's priority list providing that they leave from Singapore. They just need to fill an application form and submit it to the webmaster. Users even have access to a map, visualising the seats inside the aircraft, so that they can make a better selection.

The 'route map' service gives information concerning the town of arrival, including the cost of transportation, the duty free allowance and also the average temperature per month.

There is also a link with downtown Singapore where in addition to general information, visitors can obtain local recipes.

If the internet surfers are interested in museums, they can visit the on-line museum which presents previous, current and future exhibitions. Pictures and explanations are available.

Lists of hotels can be consulted which provide the rates, the location, the number of bedrooms and the services available in the hotel. However, on-line registration is not available.

In addition to the mainstream services, we also found a small number of sites offering much more specific services. For example, Volkswagen offered their visitors the 'best road' service which indicated the best way to reach the internet destination to which their visitors wanted to go. Internet travellers could sign the Singapore Economic Development Board guest book on-line. On the Telecom Éireann site, visitors could calculate the cost of a call from Ireland to other countries. In Space Image, a site which showed satellite view of various places in the world, users could retrieve pictures from a large databank and obtain more precise views by clicking on the mouse pointer.

Evolution

Nowadays, more and more companies are involved in the internet revolution; not only American firms but also those companies that are based in other countries, have a site. Table 9.1 represents a comparison between 1996 and 1997.

As evident in Table 9.1, the integration of the internet in companies' strategy has increased, even in *The Economist*, where the number of advertisements with a Web address has nearly doubled in one year. This now means that more than 50 per cent of all ads feature a WWW address in this magazine.

The other magazines also have followed the same trend, and the evolution is even more significant with an increase from zero to more than one ad in five in the French magazine *L'Express* and a more than tripled percentage in *Business and Finance*.

As far as the number of new addresses (addresses that

Table 9.1: Evolutionary Patterns of Magazine Advertisements (percentage)

	Ad with a Web address		New addresses		Addresses with e-mail	
	1996	1997	1996	1997	1996	1997
Time Europe	21.3	38	45	56	0	4.8
Business & Finance	6.9	22.6	50	80	0	40
L'Express	0	21	0	41.6	0	4.1
The Economist	25.4	53.3	41.7	49.2	5.5	6.1

appear for the first time in a particular magazine as opposed to repeats of previous ads) is concerned, the European magazines have the most significant growth as more of their regular advertisers redesign their ads to include information about their internet sites. This difference can be explained by the fact that in the US, the internet has been part of companies' communication strategy for a longer time than in Europe.

Another aspect of the evolution of the net between 1996 and 1997, is the fact that in 1996, advertisements which featured an e-mail address were extremely rare. However, in 1997, e-mail addresses can be found in all magazines, even though the practice of providing an e-mail address in the ad itself is not yet developed. The ads that were published in the magazine *Business and Finance* were an exception to this rule (40 per cent of them had e-mail), but they were mainly the addresses of universities and schools as opposed to commercial firms.

There remain marked differences between sites of different origins from the point of view of services provided, but those differences are due to the fact that some countries are more developed than others. For example, we saw that the internet sites of American or Asian companies offered more complete services than European companies. However, the number of European firms which have a Web address is increasing.

The Future of WWW Services

We also found that an increasing number of companies use the internet as an integral part of their commercial strategy. Many allowed visitors to buy directly from their computers. In addition, some sites were especially created to report on important events that were taking place. General elections seemed to be the best platform for companies to create a new service, indeed RTÉ, the Irish national television created a special elections service during the last Irish general election, as did *Le Monde* in France.

For those without the required equipment, access to the Web is now also available thanks to cybercafes. By cybercafes, we mean bars where customers are able to connect to and browse the internet using the computers which are available to them in the bar.

During the period of study, we had the occasion to observe the great dynamism of the internet phenomenon. Indeed, some companies who had already advertised in a magazine without giving a Web address started to mention their Web address while we were watching!

In addition to advertising in magazines, some companies also indicate their Web address in their television advertisements, *viz.* Microsoft. Kodak also has a Web address, which is given on television. Not all companies have introduced such a complete integration of their advertising strategy, but this must be the sign of things to come.

CONCLUSION

All in all, the signs are that, as technology evolves extremely rapidly, in a few years nearly all companies will possess a Web address; indeed, they might have to if they want to compete on an equal footing. Thus, the internet revolution can be compared to the discovery of the phone. As far as expansion is concerned, differences exist. Indeed, it took the phone nearly a century to develop, whereas the internet has already reached the same expansion in only a decade.

The evolution of the internet has indeed reached a frightening pace. When we studied Irish home pages last year, we found that many organisations used their WWW pages as glorified advertising posters and showed no creativity in terms of offering information or services to their virtual customers. In fact, most homepages did not go beyond presenting the name and postal address of their owner. In addition, we found that the most represented group on the net was the tourism industry – hotels and bed and breakfasts – hardly our idea of technology wizards and leading-edge organisations.

We concluded that companies, which underestimate the potential of the internet, may find themselves at a disadvantage when faced with international competition, which increasingly uses technology to obtain competitive advantage and gain faster access to remote markets at no extra cost. The abundance of weak sites was made even more obvious by the small number of very rich sites such as Apogee Software, the computer games' distributors, who have developed their advertising strategy around their website. Not only are all their products on sales on the site, but new releases can be downloaded free in reduced functionality versions and forthcoming games can be tested on-line. Such sites seemed to be indicating the way forward, but other companies were slow to follow in the leaders' footsteps.

The situation is changing fast. Only one year ago, nearly 25 per cent of the sites we visited did not work properly or were "under construction". Many did not even have an e-mail connection or when they did, it was faulty or provided a link with an internet service provider instead of the companies themselves. In 1997, most sites had e-mail linkages with the site owners and, more interestingly, more than 30 per cent proposed interactive services, such as job applications or customer enquiries. In terms of electronic commerce, there was much more evidence that it had become a reality as nearly 20 per cent of the sites were concerned with on-line shopping.

There is no doubt that the internet has now become a very complete source of information and an efficient means of communication for consumers, business people and academics. It is not certain, however, that it will provide such unmatched business opportunities as described in various magazines and newspapers. It is doubtful that the net will ever become a life or death issue for any organisation, as traditional means of doing business will be slow to die. To borrow Bill Gates's words: all companies which bet on the internet will not be winners, but those who don't bet on it may end up losing out.

There is now no denying that the internet has brought something radically new to our lives and will probably continue to develop as a source of information for more and more people. This is enough to give it a very high status in today's world; a status that probably exceeds that of the telephone or that of television.

10

Electronic Commerce: Extending the Enterprise

Patrick Finnegan and William Golden

INTRODUCTION

The defeat of the powerful Persian empire by a coalition of more than twenty Greek cities in 448 BC is an early example of a group of small entities co-operating against a larger enemy. This victory also illustrates the importance of the co-ordination aspect of co-operation as the Greeks directed the efforts of their 200 ships (rowing in unison) to create a series of projectiles to ram the attacking Persians. Outside of the military arena, such co-operation has traditionally been lacking in Western civilisations where individual initiatives are greatly valued and rewarded. However, in recent years, organisations have begun to recognise that creating greater links with customers, suppliers and other organisations is an important element of corporate strategy. In some cases strategic alliances, which result in virtual organisations are being used to produce goods and provide services, as well as to share information, ideas and expertise.

Telecommunications and information technology have contributed to the emergence of these modern forms of production and exchange of goods and services. Such developments include the growth of wide area and value added networks (WANs and VANs), electronic data interchange (EDI), e-mail and tele-conferencing, as well as the internet. These advancements in tele-communications provide the basic building blocks for a new form of commercial activity called electronic commerce.

ELECTRONIC COMMERCE

Dating from earliest times, the exchange of merchandise and services has been a basic element of every civilisation. Beyond the practice of barter, an important corollary to such commerce is the exchange of business documents, such as invoices. Indeed a key aspect of conducting business is managing and controlling the exchange of information, which acts as a co-ordination device, with customers, suppliers, shareholders and financial institutions.

The information that is exchanged as part of a commercial transaction is either in a structured or an unstructured form. Structured information includes business documents, such as purchase orders, invoices, statements, payments and company brochures. These have traditionally been paper based, and have been delivered between organisations through the postal system. Unstructured information includes person to person communication, telephone conversations and business letters. The exchange of both structured and unstructured information poses problems for businesses. The postal system slows down the business cycle due to the time that a document physically takes to be delivered to the addressee. Communicating by telephone is problematic because often the person you want to speak to is not there and the game of telephone tag ensues. Person to person meetings, while enabling enhanced business relationships, are often perceived as being expensive and time consuming.

Traditional delivery mechanisms prove problematic in the current business environment where time-based competition is often as important as cost competitiveness. Alternative electronic ways of completing traditional paper based inter-organisational business processes are shown in Table 10.1. Together, these provide examples of ways in which commerce is currently being conducted electronically. The creation of electronic links between different organisations is achieved technically with one or more of the following: value added networks, the existing telephone system, private data networks, integrated services digital network (ISDN) and the internet.

Such electronic delivery mechanisms, for building strategic relationships with trading partners, enable strong and durable alliances with suppliers and customers, as they provide permanent electronic links which facilitate easier communication. At the other end of the spectrum, electronic commerce can facilitate an ad hoc query from a prospective customer.

Table 10.1: Traditional Commerce versus Electronic Commerce

Communications	Traditional Delivery Mechanisms	Electronic Commerce
Business Documents e.g. Invoice	Postal Service	Electronic Data Interchange
Cash Payments	Cheque	Electronic Funds Transfer
Short Messages	Telephone Call	Electronic Mail
Group Discussions	Group Meeting	Electronic Bulletin boards Computer Conferencing Teleconferencing
Document Exchange	Fax, Courier Service	Electronic File Transfer
Promotional Material	Paper Company Brochure	World Wide Web Pages
Customer Product Queries	Paper Product Catalogue	Web-based on-line Database

Electronic commerce can take many different forms, which will be discussed in the next section. Information and telecommunications technology facilitates both structured and unstructured business communications and can be used to create permanent or ad hoc organisational linkages. Examples of specific applications of electronic commerce used in these different ways are shown in Figure 10.1.

Figure 10.1: Forms of Electronic Commerce

	Structured	Unstructured
Permanent	Electronic data Interchange (EDI); Inter-organisational Data retrieval systems; extranets	Electronic meeting rooms; Computer conferencing
Ad Hoc	Electronic catalogues; World Wide Web home pages	Electronic mail; Electronic file transfer

ELECTRONIC DATA INTERCHANGE (EDI)

Electronic data interchange (EDI) facilitates the computer to computer transfer of structured business documents between organisations using an agreed format. The contents of an EDI message are structured and conform to the main types of business documents, such as purchase orders, invoices and payment details. The creation of an EDI link between trading partners normally requires investment in software and thus, when it is set up, it is expected to form a permanent means of transmitting business documents. The benefits and problems of EDI are listed in Table 10.2.

Table 10.2: Positive and Negative Aspects of EDI

Benefits of EDI

- Brings cost savings due to a reduction in re-keying errors.
- Reduces clerical costs as business documents enter the computer directly.
- Reduces order lead times due to faster order cycle.
- Speeds up the transmission of information between organisations.
- Enhances the relationship with EDI partners.
- Improves customer service.

Problems with EDI

- Initially difficult to integrate the EDI system into existing information systems.
- Initially difficult to choose an EDI standard.
- Adoption of subsets of the EDI standards limits flexibility to extend the EDI system.
- Needs a high-level of commitment from prospective EDI trading partners.
- High volumes of data transfers are required before benefits are obtained.

For an application to be labelled EDI, documents must be able to move between the two computer systems without the need for human translation. This transfer of data occurs using agreed standards. The use of a standard enables an organisation to trade electronically with any organisation which has adopted the same standard.

These standards specify in great detail what each part of the message contains. Thus, for example, if a purchase order were sent via EDI each part of the message would have a specific code which would identify its content, e.g. required delivery date. This level of specification enables computer systems to interpret the documents received and thus enter them directly into the electronic purchase order files of the receiving organisation. International standards for EDI exist which provide organisations with standard dictionaries with which to compose and decompose electronic business documents.

In recent years *Edifact*, a United Nations regulated standard, has gained acceptance as the leading international standard. However, a number of EDI standards predating *Edifact* are still widely used in certain geographic areas and industrial sectors. For example, the preferred standard in the USA is *Ansi x.12* and the standard of the British retail trade is *Tradacoms*.

In addition to these standards, some organisations have set up their own proprietary standards. One of the main reasons for adopting a proprietary standard is to attempt to generate a strategic advantage *vis-à-vis* competitors. The adoption of a proprietary standard can result in competitive advantage because it creates a market in which a company's products can only be ordered using their unique product coding system. If the company is first to provide such a service, it can build up a large pool of committed, loyal customers, which is hard for competitors to break.

The implementation of EDI in the first instance involves identifying trading partners who are willing to conduct business electronically. The other main requirements are a computer system with appropriate software and a communications network.

The computer system can be PC-based with software to support a recognised international standard. Currently, within Ireland, there are several value added network service providers which offer organisations the ability to send EDI messages over their networks. The connectivity and the service are paid for on the basis of a monthly rental fee and volume charges on traffic sent across the network.

Figure 10.2: Model of Integration for EDI Software

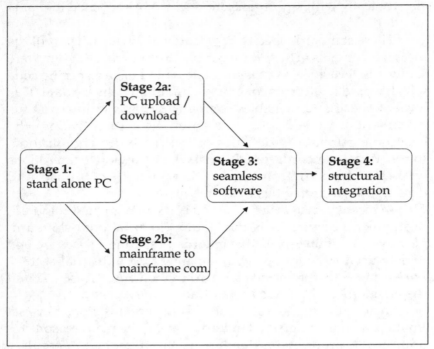

Source: Swatman & Swatman.

One model of EDI software integration within organisations[1] is shown in Figure 10.2. This consists of four stages with stage two being divided into two parts. Organisations can enter the model (i.e. start the EDI process) at stages 1, 2a or 2b.

The first stage consists of a stand alone PC with EDI software. A member of staff keys in the outgoing messages and prints those that are coming in. This stage has been likened to an expensive facsimile machine, as all it does is receive and transmit EDI messages. Some organisations who have been required to use EDI by powerful trading partners never progress beyond this stage. The main reason is that the integration of the EDI system into the existing information systems can be time-consuming and expensive. The problem however is that without integration with existing systems much of the expected benefits may not be obtained.

---

1. Swatman & Swatman, "EDI Systems Integration" *Information Society* (1992) 8(3) pp. 169-205.

Case 10.1

*In an Irish clothing manufacturer located in Dublin, which pro-
dces about 75,000 garments per week, the initial impetus for EDI
implementation was the result of formal requests from a large
customer to switch to EDI. While there is now integration of the
EDI system with the production system, this was not the case in
the beginning. The benefits of the integrated EDI system include
reduced stock levels, faster turnaround of orders, becoming a
preferred supplier of larger customers and easier auditing of
paperwork. The problems encountered include the set-up costs of
the initial EDI system and the fact that, due to the company's
relatively small size internationally, they are unable to persuade
other trading partners to adopt EDI.*

Stage two consists of two alternative paths. Firstly files created
on a mainframe or mini-computer are downloaded to the PC
containing the EDI software. This eliminates re-keying. Alternatively, the EDI software itself is on a mainframe or mini-
computer. This means that uploading and downloading is
avoided. In stage three, a seamless integration between the EDI
software and the application (mainly production) software is
implemented. Stage four is hypothesised as a state where EDI is
seen as an integral part of the organisation and influences the
functional structure of the organisation as well as other systems.

INTER-ORGANISATIONAL DATA
RETRIEVAL SYSTEMS

Inter-organisational data retrieval systems differ from EDI in that
they require human intervention to interpret the information being
received. They include on-line reference systems, electronic
distribution media, as well as inter-enterprise databases and
applications. In most cases, such systems operate in the same way
as they would internally. The difference is that a decision has been
made to allow external parties to retrieve data from the system.
The access to such data is normally curtailed and would typically
provide a person from outside the organisation with the ability
to read, but not to change, the data being viewed.

The application of such a system is normally confined to

specific individuals within certain trading partner organisations, with access being regulated by some security measure, such as passwords. In some cases the password enables an individual customer to retrieve information on his organisation's pending orders only.

> ### Case 10.2
>
> *A company, which manufactures sophisticated electronic equipment to customer specifications, has adopted an inter-organisational data retrieval system. The typical lead time on a specific order is thirteen weeks. During the period of construction of the equipment, the customers are continually in contact with the organisation to obtain information on the current status of the order. Answering these queries was time consuming as it involved accessing numerous databases. The company responded by putting a system in place which allows customers to access a database with information concerning the current status of orders that they have placed. By means of password protection and user identification, the customer is only provided with information on his/her orders. This eliminates unnecessary telephone calls regarding customer queries.*

The on-line reference, or database is normally stored on a computer owned and maintained by the host organisation. For security reasons, some organisations have made such systems available on stand-alone machines which are not permanently linked to the organisation's main computer systems. The data is updated via a write-only link from the main computer systems. Such systems often use internet browsers to access the data and have been called extranets.

ELECTRONIC MEETING ROOMS AND COMPUTER CONFERENCING

While EDI and inter-organisational data retrieval systems provide an avenue for regular communication of structured information between specified trading partners, a need exists to support more flexible, unstructured communications. Systems which support such unstructured communications on an ongoing basis are called electronic communications systems. These include multi-user editors, teleconferencing, electronic meeting rooms, electronic blackboards and computer conferencing. For a full discussion of groupware technology, refer to Chapter 14 of this book.

This technology, when used on an inter-organisational basis, creates a semi-structured environment to develop personal relationships and improve responsiveness to opportunities and problems. The benefits of such systems include reducing face to face meetings, enabling shorter meeting times, reducing the time waiting for responses, improving the speed of information transmission and retrieval, giving individuals greater control over interruptions, speeding up decision making and improving organisational learning. In general, such systems improve inter-organisational accountability and performance as staff activity is more visible.

Elaborate communications systems, such as teleconferencing systems, require specific formalised linkages between the co-operating enterprises. As such, they are generally implemented by organisations with a long-term commitment to co-operate with each other and provide a permanent basis for unstructured communication.

Case 10.3

A manufacturing subsidiary of a leading pharmaceutical company has implemented a groupware based IOS. The company is tightly controlled by a licensing authority in relation to new product development and production. Most of the research and development activities of the company are outsourced. The company uses computer conferencing and electronic meeting rooms to conduct meetings with the licensing authority and with the research and development institution. These systems allow participants to view documents, such as production plans and research results, during the meeting. This has resulted in reduced travel and has increased responsiveness to issues encountered in the area of new product development.

ELECTRONIC MAIL AND
ELECTRONIC FILE TRANSFER

For many organisations there is a need to have at their disposal an electronic communication medium which allows un-structured communication on a non-permanent basis. Electronic mail, commonly referred to as e-mail, provides such a system. It enables individuals to send typed messages and larger information files to anyone who possesses an e-mail address anywhere in the world.

The benefits of e-mail include its unobtrusive nature as a method of communication, the fact that it authorises asynchronous communication, its comparatively low cost, relative to other forms of communication, and the fact that it enables people to comm-unicate across time zones.

The problems with e-mail include security risks, delivery of unwanted junk e-mail, and the incompatibility of different e-mail systems which make it difficult to transmit large, complex e-mail messages, such as word processing files with complex layouts. Communication by e-mail with people outside your own organ-isation requires that you create a mail gateway from your internal system to an external network. The external connection requires an agreement with a service provider who will, for a monthly rental fee, provide you with an e-mail mailbox in which your e-mail will be stored.

You can then retrieve your messages at a time convenient to you and reply to them. Additional costs include the telephone charges for connecting to the service provider's computer. These charges are normally at local charge rates.

In addition to e-mail, communication systems often provide users with the facility to transfer computer files electronically. In the more advanced e-mail software packages, the file can be sent as part of the e-mail message.

However the system of the person receiving the e-mail must be compatible in order to reconstruct the file in the format it was sent. An alternative way to send files is via file transfer protocol (FTP). This standard is more robust and can operate in two ways: the sender actually sends the file to a number of addressees or alternatively he/she leaves it in a public area of the computer, such as a bulletin board, from which it can be retrieved elec-tronically by interested parties.

ELECTRONIC CATALOGUES AND WORLD WIDE WEB PAGES

The final possibility for electronic commerce is the provision of structured information for use on an ad hoc basis. One example of this would be the creation of an electronic company catalogue which is available to all users connected to the network. The most populated open network is the internet.

The internet is a collection of independent computer networks which are linked together for the purpose of exchanging information. While current estimates vary, it is believed that there are 70 million people worldwide who have access to the internet. The number of users connected to the internet has grown exponentially in recent years. This is due in large part to the arrival of user-friendly software in the form of graphics browsers. While the internet has been in existence for over 25 years these browsers have replaced the technical commands required to move around the internet with point and click technology.

Case 10.4

In October 1994, an Irish-based bookshop created its first World Wide Web pages on the internet. The pages included an on-line database of 40,000 second-hand books. The home pages were used initially to advertise only second-hand books. The trial proved so successful that they have further developed their (WWW) pages, which now includes a monthly newsletter, information on a book club and current publications of Irish interest. In the first year of operation, this system generated £50,000 worth of annual repeat business and this is expected to expand substantially as awareness of the product becomes more widespread on the internet.

This technology has enabled organisations to create graphically appealing, on-line company brochures in the form of World Wide Web pages. The creation of World Wide Web pages on the internet enables organisations to advertise and promote their company to a great number of potential customers. The main benefits of such homepages include extending the marketing reach of the organisation at relatively little extra cost.

One of the major disadvantages with the internet is the lack of security. This, however, can be overcome in a number of ways such as by placing your WWW pages on a service provider's computer, thus ensuring that they carry all the security risk.

IMPLEMENTING ELECTRONIC
COMMERCE SYSTEMS

The critical success factor for electronic commerce is the management of information rather than the implementation of the telecommunications infrastructure. The many available telecommunication options provide opportunities for choosing permanent or ad hoc linkages to send structured and unstructured information. The key issue for electronic commerce is an examination of the information required by trading partners and staff. By examining and simplifying the exchange of such information, an organisation is free to spend time on more important tasks. Beyond pure efficiency changes, an organisation can also pursue alternative business options with electronic commerce.

Electronic commerce can normally be implemented in three ways, which require increasing co-operation with external partners. The first phase is to replace manual and paper-based activities with electronic alternatives. This will normally improve the accuracy of the information and will reduce clerical costs. The next phase is to examine the information exchanged in order to determine possibilities for simplifying and eliminating this information. This normally requires working with trading partners to determine whether some of your exchange processes could be redesigned or eliminated. This requires a more long-term commitment to co-operation, but can increase the effectiveness of your interactions. Finally, an organisation can use electronic commerce to expand its current business interests or enter new activities.

The decision to initiate or participate in an interorganisational network can be based on two factors as shown in Figure 10.3, which is based on the research by Van Over and Kavan on EDI.[2] The first factor corresponds to the degree to which trading partners are likely to accept such a move, while the second factor corresponds to the likelihood that a competitor will establish electronic commerce connectivity.

• In cell 1 of the diagram in Figure 10.3, managers must realise that it is necessary to establish electronic commerce links in order to survive, as competitors are likely to seize the advantage.

---

2. Van Over & Kavan, "Adopting EDI: When and Why" *Information Strategy: The Executive's Journal* (1993) pp. 50-52.

Figure 10.3: Potential Electronic Commerce Opportunities[3]

		Market Receptivity	
		More	Less
Intermediate Competitor Adoption	Probable	Cell 1	Cell 3
	Improbable	Cell 2	Cell 4

- In cell 2, there are significant possibilities for competitive advantage by seizing electronic commerce opportunities ahead of others.

- In cell 3, firms have to decide whether or not to choose electronic commerce in the light of a probable introduction by a competitor in a market which is likely to resist much electronic commerce activity.

- Situations as in cell 4 offer firms an opportunity to pioneer advances in electronic commerce, but must face the possibility that such moves will be rejected by the market.

An important outcome of this examination is the decision whether or not to participate in electronic commerce as the leader organisation. This will determine the degree of risk exposure in the venture as well as the amount of systems development to plan for.

The implementation of permanent electronic commerce systems based on continuing co-operation is normally considered a strategic management issue, even if competitive advantage issues are not paramount. Therefore, it is necessary to have top management's commitment to continuing co-operation and to implementing such a system. It is necessary for managers to prepare a clear statement of objectives and to ensure that there is common understanding of these objectives, which should normally be

---

3. After Van Over & Kavan *op. cit.*

stated in the form of specific co-operation alliances rather than vague statements of intent.

The design of electronic commerce systems involves two processes. The first process is concerned with the design of a technical system to automate transactions by integrating technology into an inter-organisational procedure. The second design process includes considering the radical redesign of inter-organisational business processes and procedures as part of the structural integration of the co-operating entities. Such design has to be user-centred and requires good communication skills as well as a thorough understanding of communication technology possibilities and standards.

CONCLUSION

Electronic commerce presents real possibilities in terms of extended reach for many organisations. It is changing the way business is conducted by simplifying the manner in which goods and services are sold, ordered, delivered and paid for. The possibilities for electronic commerce are growing as the number of organisations that participate in this form of commercial activity increases.

A key issue for businesses is, therefore, to decide whether electronic commerce can be used to make their organisation internally more efficient and effective. In addition, as commercial activity moves more towards co-operation, rather than conflict, with important business partners, electronic commerce may be the key to nurturing a new type of business relationship.

However, while electronic commerce is based upon the establishment of a technical infrastructure, the exploitation of its possibilities is essentially a management issue. Discovering opportunities for electronic commerce is dependent on an examination of organisational activity and competition, that is largely independent of the technical issues. Electronic commerce, if it is to be successful, must be based on organisational strategy rather than technical ability, as it is the application of the technology to real business issues that will lead to success rather than the utilisation of the technology.

SOURCES

Swatman & Swatman, "EDI Systems Integration" *Information Society* (1992) 8(3).

D Van Over & C B Kavan, "Adopting EDI: When and Why" *Information Strategy: The Executive's Journal* (1993).

11

Using Internet Technologies for Training and Education

Colin McCormack

INTRODUCTION

Using the internet for education, more commonly known as Web-based education, is a practice which is attracting a great deal of interest in the academic and industrial areas. This chapter examines the reasons why an internet-based training system is necessary and looks at the possibilities offered by such a scheme.

WHY IS ELECTRONIC TRAINING NECESSARY?

The key asset of most companies will be knowledge, the only sustainable competitive advantage in the information society. Organisations will become learning enterprises, while lifelong learning facilitated by ICTs (information and communications technologies) will provide a new type of security for workers.[1]

Society is moving from an industrial to an informational base. This situation of having to keep pace with constant change in knowledge is known as 'lifelong learning', the idea that skills acquired to enter a profession will need to be constantly updated. Coupled with this idea is the notion of contract work, inherent in this notion is the idea that potential contract employees are responsible for retraining themselves.

What all this adds up to is a need for continuous training.

---

1. Department of Enterprise and Employment/Forfás, *Business and the Information Society, Report of Ireland's Information Society Steering Committee Information Society Ireland Strategy for Action* p. 38.

People can update their skill base to a certain extent but when it becomes necessary to change career, as is becoming increasingly common, some more comprehensive training effort is needed. One that will award recognition of a standard achieved so that individuals may obtain work in their new area of expertise.

We are constantly being reminded that we are in the information age, however, it comes a quite a shock to most people when it is pointed out that the means of imparting information in an educational capacity has changed little in hundreds of years. The 'chalk and talk' method is still the sole means of instruction in many universities and businesses. Computer-based training (CBT), also known as computer-based instruction (CBI), promised to free us all from dependency on the classroom by creating courses that could be followed on a computer. The method has been quite successful in a number of areas, however, it has not been adopted universally because of the expense of buying specialised CBT packages, the effort required to construct complete CBT courses and question marks over their overall effectiveness. CBT courses also usually have to be adjusted to fit specific requirements and most of them are not adaptable enough to do this. One major problem with CBTs, from a pedagogic point of view, is the fact that they involve no human contact, students need contact with fellow students to support them and an instructor to motivate and guide them. This is what has been the basis of our education system, the CBT may provide the training material efficiently but it cannot provide the training method.

What is needed is a new way of managing the educated and the education. One of the most successful means of educating is in small-group tutorials where courses can be tailored for each student and the particular objective of the courses. However, such tutorials are prohibitively expensive. The advent of the WWW allows us to implement a number of new and useful facilities for education which mimic in electronic form a small group tutorial and can offer many other facilities besides. Using the WWW as a distribution mechanism also allows us to change the structure of an education experience from purely teacher-centred to a system administered by an expert with local group leaders encouraging students, fielding basic questions and calling in the expert for advice when needed. This means the skills of the teacher/expert are utilised to the full.

The Use of the Web for Education offers a Number of Possibilities

A Web-based education system can be used in addition to traditional methods of education, such as distance or face to face education. This is the most popular educational use of the Web at the moment as it allows educators to solve some of the problems they encounter in the current education system without radically altering their method of teaching.

- It can be used as a primary teaching method – i.e. we can use the Web as a means of delivering lectures, completing assignments and holding tutorials and discussions. It also means that we can use the Web as a form of electronic campus where students and staff can interact much the same as on a normal campus. On-line resources, such as libraries and social organisations (clubs, user groups, etc.), can be set up to support the students.

- The Web can also be used as a means of 'knowledge networking'. Knowledge networking is a loose education system where people interested in various topics can share information and create their own mini education systems (e.g. a how-to guide on a particular topic). Knowledge networks usually have no single teacher but a group of people who help to teach each other.

In reality, many of the tools that provide the functionality of the Web-based classroom have very little to do with the Web at all. A Web-based classroom may use internet applications, such as e-mail, Usenet News, FTP and other computer applications, such as databases. However the development of the Web provides a system that can provide a single, universal interface to any computer application. By using the Web, interface educators enjoy the benefits of a single, easy to use program without being restricted in any way.

WHAT COURSES ARE WEB-BASED CLASSROOMS GOOD FOR?

One of the first questions we must always ask ourselves when planning to put a course on the Web is not whether it can be done but what is the best way to do it. Certain subjects are ideal for delivery using just a Web-based classroom, others are best accomplished using a variety of teaching methods. The most important thing to remember about a Web-based education system is that, similar conventional teaching aids, such as videos and slide projectors, it cannot teach the course on its own. It is not intended to replace completely the role of a teacher merely to act as a new form of educational tool.

Most types of classes can be put in whole or in part on the Web without any great impact on the way the class is taught. Most ideal for the Web are courses which emphasise in-depth coverage and discussion as these can be easily supported, or given entirely, on the Web. Any course which involves extensive writing on the part of the student would also be ideal as the students can share ideas and hand in their assignments rapidly using the Web.

One thing to note is that it has been found that a Web-based classroom is more suitable in a learner-centred role. This means that, if you make the information available for the students to go through at their own pace and provide facilities which allow communication between the members of the class or the lecturers, then you are encouraging the students to take more control of their own education. This differs from the traditional method of education where students sit in a large lecture theatre, dutifully write down a lecture and follow a course of learning suggested by their lecturer. It is worth remembering that students brought up on this force feeding education method may have difficulty in adapting to any new method of education. With careful design and appreciation of the students difficulties, it is possible to introduce the students to a more effective way of learning using a Web-based education system.

As regards the substance of a course, most topics can be taught using the Web as all forms of communication and inform-ation distribution are supported. Audio, video and graphical information can be distributed over the Web. This means, for example, that students can listen to music in a music course, view a demonstration of a chemistry experiment or look at slides from a biology lecture. Communication facilities can allow students to talk to each other using bulletin boards or using live audio links.

WHAT USES HAS A
WEB-BASED CLASSROOM?

What can be done with a Web-based classroom is limited only by the imagination of the educator and the abilities of the tools available. Since a Web-based classroom is an extension of the educator who built it and the situation in which it is used, the range of possibilities for a Web-based classroom is almost endless. To show what is possible in a Web-based classroom we have divided up the areas of possible use into four main categories: information distribution, communication, assessment and class management.

Information Distribution

Some different ways in which Web-based classrooms have used the Web to distribute information include the following.

- *Distributing Existing Computer Material*

   Many educators already make use of computers to support their teaching. Some educators use wordprocessors and presentation tools, such as PowerPoint, to produce learning material. Others use computer programs, such as simulations or computer-based teaching, to aid the learning process. Thus, the Web can easily be used as a medium to distribute existing computer-based materials.

- *Providing Resource Material*

   An equally simple use of the information distribution powers of the Web is to provide pointers to resource material available on the WWW related to the class.

- *Converting Information*

   We can convert paper-based information and make it available on-line or in disk file form (if we wish to distribute the course on disk). We can also convert existing material, such as Word documents, into HTML using available utilities.

- *Publishing Timely Information*

Information, such as lecture notes and examples, can be published at regular intervals. This has the advantage of encouraging students to access the system frequently to view new material.

- *Providing a Hypertext Course*

We can redesign the information which forms the main part of the course to make use of hypertext. This allows students to follow links to access related parts of the course. This means that a page of hypertext information explaining a topic could contain links to a glossary of terms, a link to an example, a link to the next topic or links to related topics.

- *Publishing Information Live*

It is possible to give a 'live' lecture over the Web. This means that student will access a specific Web page which will contain a transcript of the ongoing electronic lecture. The lecture can be given in different forms.

  - **Lecture can be text only**: the lecturer will type the lecture on a screen that the students can observe at certain time intervals, i.e. the students browser could download the information the lecturer has written every second or every minute.
  - **Whiteboard**: a piece of software called a whiteboard can be used. This allows a lecturer to draw, write text and paste pictures on a screen. With most whiteboard software the students see the changes being made live (or as near to live as the speed of their network connection will allow). The students can also put their own information on the board.
  - **Audio-based lecture**: if the network is of a reasonable speed a system such as the internet telephone can be used. This allows synchronous audio communication between the lecturer and the class.
  - **Video-based lecture**: some institutions are already transmitting live lectures over their local networks. This

enables students to view a lecture from their own computer.

- ## Limiting Students Access to Information

  We can make information available to students subject to certain restrictions. For example, we could prevent a student from accessing advanced material until they had read through basic material or passed a test (which can be delivered on-line). The idea of this is that it gives the students a sense of achievement to be allowed access to more advanced levels and it prevents weak students from skipping through the material.

  If the system is server based it also allows a record to be kept of the progress of the student because the server system will keep logs of which student has accessed what page.

- ## Giving the Students a Choice of Explanation

  We can allow our system to take account of the different types of student by using it to present a choice of explanations. For example, one student might like an explanation using a worked example, another might like an explanation using an analogy. Another reason to use choice is when your system is aimed at students with different goals. For example, students may like to know the relevance of a particular topic to them. So if we could provide explanations, showing how the topic being explained fits into the task that the student is used to performing, then it becomes clearer for the student why it is in their best interest to learn about it.

- ## Making Multimedia Presentations Available On-line

  We can create information in the form of multimedia (graphics, animation, video clips, sound) and make it available for distribution. Multimedia is a powerful way of explaining certain topics, unfortunately, it is usually limited by the logistics involved in presenting it to a class. With a Web-based multimedia system, however, we are sure that the students will be able to have a better view of the presentation.

Communication

An essential part of any learning experience is communication. In a classroom, a student may communicate with other students, with the teacher or with people from outside the classroom as part of the learning experience. Communication can take on many forms including one to one, small groups or the one to many format of a traditional lecture. The Web-based classroom provides tools to enable all communication methods including recent advances that enable live lectures. Some approaches that use communication in a Web-based classroom include the following.

*   *Individual Communication*

    Students can use the system to communicate with the lecturer either asynchronously or synchronously. Asynchronous communication, such as e-mail, means that students no longer have to wait for an appointment or visit an office as they can send their query and have it answered by lecturers whenever they are available.

*   *Group Announcements*

    We would like a system where we can send messages to students and they can send messages to us. This could take the form of a bulletin board or an e-mail system.

*   *Allow 'Live' Discussions or Classes*

    Tutorials or debates can be held where students are encouraged to make a contribution. The results of the debate can be stored in an archive.

*   *Allow Chat Groups/Bulletin Boards*

    Electronic bulletin boards can be set up where messages can be posted. Students can also have their own private bulletin boards. Groups of students can be assigned common bulletin boards when they start the course in order to encourage them to get to know other members of the class.

*   *Co-operative Work*

    This allows students to co-operate on project and exchange files, establish live discussions or have their own bulletin board.

- ### *Creation of Student Notes*

  Students often like to write their own notes on a page of lecture notes. If the lecture is in electronic form then this is usually impossible. However, we can set up a system which allows students to record their own notes on particular pages of the Web system and review and alter them when they want.

Assessment

Another task in the learning experience is assessment, finding out whether or not the students have understood the material. The Web-based classroom offers the tools and the integration that can make assessment more effective and efficient.

- ### *Self-assessment*

  Students can answer a set of questions after they have completed part of the course. Students can also take a quiz to satisfy themselves that they have the prerequisite knowledge necessary for the course. The quiz will be given by the computer and marked instantly by a computer program. The results will be returned to the student together with a list of recommendations based on the results (e.g. you got question 5 wrong, re-read section Y).

- ### *Checkpoint Assessment*

  On-line quizzes can be given at specific times to ensure all students are keeping up with the course. Students can automatically do the test and be marked by the computer with the computer sending notes to students (and staff) if they do not reach the required standard. Notices can also be sent to staff if the students do not do the test. On-line quizzes can also be given to allow the students access to further material.

- ### *Intelligent Tutoring*

  Intelligent tutoring systems which combine artificial intelligence to make certain assumptions about problems the student are having and direct material to the student accordingly can make use of assessments to provide a profile of the student.

- ### Exams via the Web

  Formal exams can be given via the Web. To do this we need some method of ensuring that the correct students are taking the exam and that the answers are secure.

Class Management

Management of the learning process includes tasks such as time tabling, tracking attendance, recording progress, calculating grades and identifying the learning needs of students. Many educators already use tools, such as spreadsheets, databases and specialised software, to perform these tasks. The Web offers an environment that can integrate these separate tools behind a consistent interface and make the whole process of class management more efficient.

The use of the Web in managing the learning process is still a new area. However, there are a few examples, including the following.

- ### Rapid Notification System

  A Web-based system can be a rapid means of making announcements or of sending messages to individual students.

- ### Monitoring of Students' Accesses

  If the system is based on a server, then we can examine the number of students accessing the system, what they are accessing and how often they are doing it.

- ### Submission

  Students can be permitted to submit their assignments via the Web and have them returned to them when corrected.

- ### Maintaining Class Records

  Students can use a Web system to register for a class and to select practical times. Class lists can be kept on the Web for access by administration and tutors. Changes in a students times or status can be made at any time during the course.

- ### Scheduling System

  Software which allow the co-ordination of meetings and resources.

USING THE WWW SYSTEM TO DELIVER EFFICIENT AND EFFECTIVE TRAINING

The two criteria we are interested in, when we talk about training, are its efficiency and its effectiveness. Efficiency is the cost, in effort and materials, of the training and effectiveness is the extent to which the training succeeds in its goals. Any training prog-ramme, be it university or commercially based, must examine itself from these perspectives. In this section we examine the advantages Web-based education has over conventional educ-ation systems.

Location and Time: Independent Delivery of Material

Students do not have to study at a particular time or in a particular place. They can study in the office, library, laboratory or at home. Practically anywhere they can bring a computer can be used. Courses need not be delivered on-site, you could co-develop a course with a university or head office which is located a thousand miles away and access the system through the internet.

Platform Independence

Unlike CBTs, the WWW is not dependent on any particular type of computer or operating system. This reduces the amount of effort and cost needed to use the system as individual machines do not have to have specialised software installed or a company's set-up does not have to be modified in order to install a CBT package. Web tools also require fewer resources than traditional CBT systems, thus minimising the strain on resources.

Dynamic Distribution of Information

Information stored at a central distribution site can be changed at any time. It can be corrected or new and pertinent information can be added immediately. It can be changed in response to students' requirements or comments, in response to changing management objectives or a change in the material being taught.

Support for Interactivity

The WWW allows students to talk with each other, individually or as a group, and to send questions or hold conversations, audio/video or text, with their educator.

Scaleable with No Additional Cost

The WWW system can be used to train five users or 5,000 users. As long as each user has access to a computer equipped with WWW tools capable of accessing a central site or local site at some time, the system can be used. The system can be stored at a central site and copies of it can be distributed around the organisation for fast local access. The copies would be update from the central site with new information at pre-set time intervals.

No Need for Proprietary Protocols or Expensive Software

The majority of the software needed to access the systems described in this chapter is available free and can be used on any computer, regardless of make or operating system.

Standardised

The procedure for presenting information on the WWW is standardised so tutors can concentrate on the content of the course they wish to present as opposed to the means of presentation. This also means the material will never become obsolete or assume a form that is difficult for users to read.

Simple, User-friendly Interface

Importantly for users, unfamiliar with computers, the WWW has a simple point and click user interface, which enables people to concentrate on the content of the educational system as opposed to wrestle with the mechanics of a computer system. Hypertext also allows keywords to act as links to more information.

Learner Dictates Pace

In many courses, the pace of the course and order of topics covered is dictated by the instructor. With a WWW information system, students can learn at their own pace and choose the information that is most relevant to their needs. If a student feels comfortable with a particular section of a course (and they can answer questions on it satisfactorily) then they can skip that module of the instruction. Moreover, if the student is lagging behind, then the pace can be dictated by the tutor.

Simple Information Addition Procedures

Information used by the WWW can be produced from many different wordprocessors, meaning course notes and manuals can be translated for use on the WWW with little effort.

More Opportunity for Learning by Trial and Error

Students can learn at their own pace and also can attempt exercises devised by their tutor and marked automatically by computer. These exercises can be attempted many times at any time of the day without relaying on the tutor to mark the material. The tutor can also prepare the exercises with explanations as to why the answer is wrong and automatically elicit questions from the student on why they are having trouble with the question. A list of material relevant to the question and contained on the WWW education system can also be provided.

More Direct Feedback to Tutor and Interaction

Tutors have an opportunity to send messages to a group of students, or to individual students, at any time and with a guarantee that the students will receive them. Students can also send messages to their tutor anonymously, which overcomes any problem of shyness or embarrassment on the part of students. Students can hold discussion groups with each other even though they may be quite a physical distance apart. Students can also interact with bulletin boards that could contain common questions, problems or hints.

Monitoring

The system allows a tutor to keep track of what material students are reading, the time spent on the tutorial, the pattern of accesses, the results of the students and the number of times the individual students have used the system. This allows a look out to be kept for problem areas in the course or problem students who would otherwise be left behind.

Can Personalise or Customise a System to Cope with Different Types of Learner/Learning Objectives

Different students have different methods of learning, they may also require different methods of instruction and need to receive different explanations. All this can be accommodated in a system which can offer alternative courses for students.

Phased Training/Flexible Schedules

Because an electronic system is continuously available and easily altered, schedules need not be rigid, employees do not have to be trained on multiple new tasks all at once because the tutor won't be available. Students can be trained on a particular task and can rest from training in order to familiarise themselves more with that task and return to the training programme when their workload and experience permit.

Groups of individuals with similar educational abilities can be accommodated with this phased system, i.e. we could have a group of quick learners or a group of people who are especially interested in one particular aspect of the course they are taking because it is of more relevant in their area.

Building on a Working System

There is no need to experiment with systems and software, all the necessary software and protocols have already been developed and extensively tested (Web browsers and servers). This means that no effort has to be invested in software development or testing and debugging. Some tools have already been developed to act as support for Web-based education systems: for instance, WBT (http://homebrew1.cs.ubc.ca/webct/) and TopClass (http://www.wbtsystems.com).

Low/Declining Cost

In general most companies already have an internet or intranet system already in place, so no new resources are required.

CONCLUSION

All of the software needed to implement the above scheme is currently available, what is needed is a recognition that the way training has been carried out can change for the better by combining all the positive attributes of the internet with relevant content. While this may, initially, seem to be a radical change in the way education is carried out, it is obvious on closer inspection that the internet facilitates the most basic and successful education mechanism, that of a focused group tutorial and an active user-based learning system (in contrast to passive instruction techniques, such as seminars). There is no doubt that the system proposed in this chapter can achieve greater efficiency and effectiveness than any current education system and investment in converting existing education systems and retraining educators is urgently needed.

While initial investment and adoption of these systems will be time consuming and expensive there is no other realistic way to solve the training and mobility problems provided by today's modern workforce and ever changing operating environments. Web-based education systems are now being adopted by universities and content is being produced for them by publishers and providers of traditional computer-based tutorial systems. A number of organisations have started to co-operate with universities in order to develop their own, more specialised, system.

It is recommended that companies slowly start to build their systems, beginning with their existing technical support structure, linking people who seek technical support with an on-line system set up which would be managed by technical support personnel. This would enable studies of how people use these systems to address basic problems before investing in more complicated systems intended to train the workforce. This testing phase is crucial to a successful implementation as each organisation faces unique challenges in such areas as requirements, equipment and personnel. Another critical factor is obtaining user interaction and participation. This is essential as the system should become not just a once only training resource but a learning network of individuals with a content that is constantly evolving and extending to meet the new challenges and opportunities of the organisation.

SOURCES

Department of Enterprise and Employment/Forfás, *Business and the Information Society, Report of Ireland's Information Society Steering Committee Information Society Ireland Strategy for Action* (1996).

C McCormack & D Jones, *Building a Web-based Education System* (New York: Wiley) 1997.

12

The Intranet Revolution

Brian O'Flaherty and Arthur Stanley

INTRODUCTION

Much hype and media attention has been focused on the internet and the ubiquitous World Wide Web (referred to hereafter as WWW). This attention is hiding the quiet corporate revolution of the intranet concept.

The intranet is defined as an internal corporate information sharing network based on internet technology, i.e. using a client/server architecture. The extent of this revolution is evident in the sales of servers by the market leader Netscape, which estimates that 70 per cent of its server sales are used internally to build intranets. According to a survey, 22 per cent of the top 1,000 companies in America are using an intranet. Presently, intranet sales account for 43 per cent of the $1 billion Web server market and the predictions are that this will increase dramatically.

At this point, a lot of questions must arise in managers' minds, such as: "What is an intranet?", "What can it do for an organisation?", "What risks are associated with it?" and "How would an organisation go about building one?" This chapter sets out to answer these questions.

BACKGROUND

Intranet technology is very much based on internet technology but because the information system is totally enclosed within an organisation, additional issues prevail. We will start with an overview of internet technology.

The interest in the internet (and the WWW in particular) derives from a critical mass of enabling technologies to meet the demand for new ways to link people and share information. The key enablers of this growth are:

- a proliferation of PCs and networks;

- the use of open standards for easier communication between computer users;

- crossplatform support allowing data transfers between computers of different types;

- multimedia support and ease of use;

- increased support for secure transactions.

The three essential technologies, which define the WWW today, are those which define the communication between a Web client (the PC used to access information) and a Web server (the computer where information is stored) connected over a TCP/IP (transmission control protocol/internet protocol) network. These are as follows.

- **HTTP – Hyper Text Transport Protocol**, which governs communications between a Web client and a Web server.

- **HTML – Hypertext Mark-up Language**, which is a document format for Web documents. Unlike standard word-processors, this uses standard directives to specify the format, which leaves the actual formatting to the client computer accessing the data.

- **URL – Uniform Resource Locator**, which is a pointer to a resource on the internet (or intranet). It serves as the global addressing scheme for pages stored on Web servers, containing the name of the Web server, any extensions which define a specific page or any other information to be used by the Web server. For example, the address of the Executive Systems Research Centre (ESRC) at University College Cork is: 'http://www.ucc.ie/esrc'.

Other useful protocols include file transfer protocol (FTP) – used for the transfer of entire files over a network and News Groups (Usenet) – where a forum for debate, via e-mail, is provided for people interested in particular topics.

Increasingly there are powerful PCs sitting on every desk in an office or building, all of which are connected to each other by local area networks (LAN) or wide area networks (WAN). This constitutes the physical infrastructure used to connect all machines into one network – i.e. a system for inter-communication between computer terminals, PCs and related equipment operating within the same general area. Thus the primary requirements for intranet connectivity are already present in most offices. The additional requirements are as follows.

- A dedicated server – for the sole purpose of providing internet facilities.

- Server software.

- Client software to install on all connected PCs.

- A communications stack (usually TCP/IP), which provides each client PC with a unique internet code.

- An HTML editor.

The beauty of intranet implementation is that all of the software components are available as shareware (i.e. public domain software), modestly priced commercial software or free from companies, such as Microsoft.

As a general rule the server hardware needs to be sufficient to run Windows NT, Windows 95 and/or a UNIX system. In addition you will also need to configure the hardware with LAN cards for TCP/IP connection over the network to the clients. This is normally easy as network operating systems, such as *Novell*, allow you to run different protocols simultaneously.

In essence, the Web server software enables an organisation to manage its internal WWW service. The package should provide the functionality to set up and manage homepages, develop WWW content based on HTML, perform text searches and integrate with internal corporate databases or back-office applications as indicated in Figure 12.1.

The HTML files are prepared using an HTML editor. It is not necessary to recreate all of the internal documents of the organisation. Using utilities, such as *internet assistant* from Microsoft, you can convert all of the organisation's electronic documents to HTML format which can then be used on the server. Using an HTML editor such as HotDog (available at 'http://www.sausage.com') enables an organisation to imbed graphics, sounds and animation into otherwise unattractive documents.

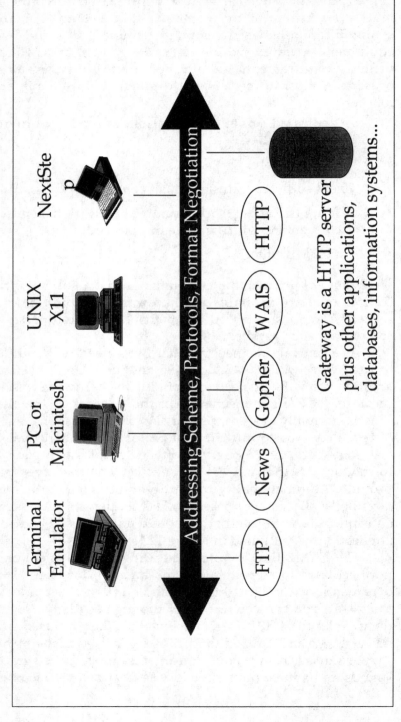

Figure 12.1: How Intranets Operate

BENEFITS OF INTRANETS

There are numerous possible benefits associated with intranet implementation, which are outlined in the list below. These categories of benefits identified for intranets are explained in the following section.

- Platform independence.
- Information transparency.
- Ease of use.
- Cost efficiency.
- Time efficiency.
- Universal client.
- Users have information control.
- Scaleable applications.
- Multiple distribution.
- Single dource of data.

Platform Independence

Information can be created, viewed and moved without modification across different hardware, operating systems and software. Web servers and viewers are available for all platforms, i.e. MS Windows, Windows 95, Windows NT, OS/2, Unix, MAC, etc. In addition, TCP/IP will run in conjunction with all types of network: ethernet, token ring, FDDI, etc., and network operating environments, i.e. Netware, Unix, IBM Token Ring, DECNET, etc. Therefore, in a multi-platform environment, the intranet can span all commercially available equipment and operating systems. The HTML documents are standard, irrespective of the nature of the Web server software or browser used.

Information Transparency

In the multi-platform environment, the user is unaware of where the data is stored and the type of machine, not to mention the physical location of parts of the documents. Information can, therefore, be accessed regardless of its location and without any knowledge of the means by which it is transferred.

Ease of Use and Universal Client

All Web browsers have an easy to use graphical user interface. Only one Web/client browser is required to allow each user to traverse the intranet. Producing Web pages is as easy as word-processing. Web pages also provide a common interface across multiple applications and data, including legacy applications.

Users Have Information Control

In an intranet environment, user control is distributed and given to individual users, who would normally generate the information in the first place. This may become a disadvantage from an information management perspective as people may pursue their own agendas or fail to maintain their documents reliably.

Scaleable Applications

Vertical scaling (adding new servers) and horizontal scaling (adding new users) is easily achieved, with bandwidth (the data transfer capacity of an internal network) being the only major limiting factor.

Multiple Distribution and Single Data Source

Documents can be distributed to, and accessed by, anyone in the organisation once they have been located in a single information repository, namely the server.

THE INTRANET VERSUS GROUPWARE DEBATE

In terms of groupware, *Lotus Notes* is now accepted as a reference amongst all commercially available products. Lotus have defined groupware as being "software that uniquely enables organisations to communicate, collaborate and co-ordinate key business processes".

Groupware is the convergence of a number of previously individual technologies, such as messaging, workflow, and conferencing, in an effort to help individuals work together in a better way. *Notes* aims to provide multiple users with simultaneous access to corporate information and to facilitate communication between users.

This process is built around an organisation's client/server architecture, where the users can communicate over the LAN (or WAN) with document databases which are located on a *Lotus*

Notes server (groupware and *Lotus Notes* are dealt with in Chapter 14). Other facilities which *Notes* offers are:

- a graphical user interface;
- e-mail facilities;
- server security;
- customisable templates for common business applications compatibility with a variety of server and client platforms;
- documents containing text, images, sounds and motion pictures.

Functionality

Though they are not directly comparable, some of the functionality of *Notes* can be offered in a non-proprietary and relatively inexpensive manner using internet technologies, which are based on open standards. Thus organisations, which wish to develop a more collaborative environment, now have an alternative approach.

Both *Notes* and intranets are associated with document storage and distribution. Some major differences exist between the two concepts in relation to the management of document flows within an organisation. Whereas one of *Notes'* main strengths is that it provides extensive support for the management of workflow and for collaboration-intensive activities, there is currently no single application available for the intranet providing this level of functionality, which requires that the users develop their own or use a number of different offerings. Netscape intends to introduce workflow automation functionality in the next version of their browser.

Cost Implications

Buying into a complete *Lotus Notes* implementation is obviously more expensive than setting up an in-house developed intranet. The average investment in a *Lotus Notes* site can amount to as much as $250,000 for a large organisation whereas a fully implemented intranet solution can cost as little as $10,000. However, there are differences in the quantity and quality of support and training available, with a tendency for most intranet solutions to have very little, if any, training included. Where training programmes are available for intranet solutions, they can vary dramatically in quality.

Document Focus

The main similarity between intranets and *Notes* is the document focus. The intranet documents adhere to the now standard HTML documents. These documents behave similar to a Windows help menu and can easily be created using a standard wordprocessor or an HTML editor.

The most important aspect of these documents is that the maintenance of the data on the site now reverts to the department that created it, thus making the content creators in marketing, sales or human resources responsible for maintaining their own data on the site. This frees valuable resources in the MIS department and also speeds up the circulation of valuable information as this now goes from origin to the point of publication in one step.

The best use of this type of technology is when each department sets up its own homepage. Any employee can then access the information as required. This, however, gives rise to important organisational issues that must be addressed. The organisation's ability to control the quantity and quality of information that is posted is reduced, as standards cannot easily be enforced and a situation may arise where some pages meet the standards of best practice and others fall far short.

At this point in time, both *Notes* and intranets support rich documentation and multimedia. *Notes*, however, allows many users to access and update documents whereas the intranet functions on the basis of a single user creating HTML code. For the moment, the intranet requires the use of specialised applications to enable it to interact with databases, though several suppliers, such as Oracle or Microsoft, are currently building WWW capabilities into their offerings or are developing software that enables a database to deal directly with queries of users via an HTML interface.

Open Standards

One of the fundamental differences between the two approaches is that of proprietary versus open systems. Lotus are working to make *Notes* more open, but underneath all of the new open features, it is still a proprietary system. On the other hand, any intranet solution is based completely on open technology derived from the WWW. There are an enormous number of tools available for Web client and Web server development. It is also simpler to incorporate new technologies, such as multimedia or Java (an object-oriented programming language for the internet), into an intranet thus cutting down on the development costs.

These tools have and are proving themselves easy to learn and use, to the point that it is now possible to have a small site up and running in only one day. But the enormous number of tools can be a disadvantage in that they can lead to a fragmented tool-set, whereas *Notes* is totally integrated.

Notes allows an organisation to leverage their current network investment to the maximum as it supports all major network protocols, whereas an internet set-up will only recognise TCP/IP. On the other hand, the intranet will run both clients and servers on all of the popular platforms currently available whereas *Notes* only recognises the major UNIX variants and will not run on a Macintosh server. Mac clients are available.

Future Evolution

Although fundamentally different approaches have been adopted by groupware and the intranet, the recent convergence in both technologies is leading to a situation where much of the functionality is now available on both platforms. Furthermore, recent releases of *Lotus Notes* now includes *InterNotes Web Navigator*, which allows *Notes'* users to browse the external Web. IBM also have intentions to provide native support for the key internet protocols HTTP, HTML and Java in *Notes*. This will lead to the ultimate aim of making a *Notes* server and a WWW server available to users on a single platform.

Initially, *Notes* was developed to provide internal access to information and the internet access to external information. The intranet products currently available allow access to internal information while still providing the option to market corporate services on the WWW. They also provide all the facilities which allow people to share information quickly, although without the full functionality of collaborative groupware applications. Following their purchase of Collabra, however, Netscape do intend to introduce workflow products into the most recent versions of *Netscape Navigator*.

In the control and security realm, *Notes* is far ahead of an intranet solution. *Notes* uses an RSA-based encryption to ensure secure transactions, but it also features a sophisticated user verification and security hierarchy. It is possible to establish global and private document databases, with features that allow users to share databases if they wish. All of these features are part of the *Notes* environment. On the other hand, an intranet is a full-disclosure type system, where all of the documents within the organisation are available to every user.

The solution an organisation chooses is dependant on its specific needs. If an organisation has a need for the type of work-groups for which *Notes* was developed, *Notes* is the obvious choice, however for the support of activities that require less group support, the intranet may provide a cheaper, more flexible and user-friendly option.

SECURITY

Thus, a prime issue associated with corporate use of internet technology and intranets is security. Put succinctly "if your staff can access the world, what is stopping the world from accessing you".

Security should be a prime concern of organisations where internet issues are concerned. However, many organisations are racing to establish a network presence without considering security issues.

The main way of controlling network access to your organisation is by using a firewall. A firewall is a system, or group of systems, that enforces an access control policy between two networks (the concept of a firewall is illustrated in Figure 12.2). The means by which this is achieved varies widely, but, in principle, it can be thought of as two mechanisms: one that permits traffic and one that blocks traffic. An important aspect of a firewall is that it facilitates the implementation of an access security policy. There are two well-established methods of implementing a firewall: through using a router (a device that enables the transfer of data between networks) or using a computer system.

The safest way to secure an intranet would obviously be to have no connection between the internal network and the external Web server at all, but this approach rules out the later development of potentially valuable externally oriented applications. There are two types of firewall presently available, namely a packet level filter or an application proxy.

Figure 12.2: Implementation of a Firewall

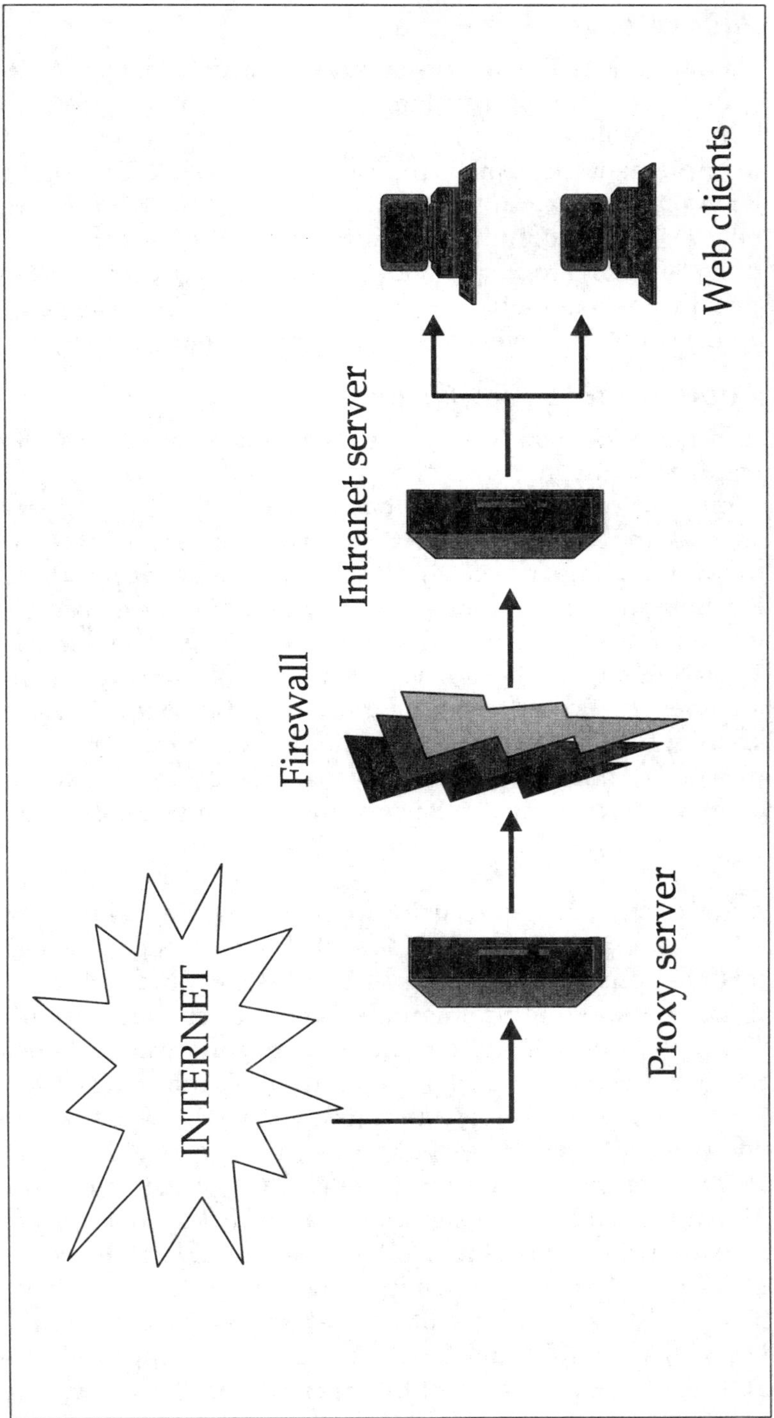

Packet Level Firewalls

An important thing to note about a firewall is that a router can be a firewall, a computer system can be a firewall or a firewall can be built from both a router and a system. Using a router on its own to implement a firewall is referred to as a packet filtering firewall. Each piece of data in a TCP/IP environment is transferred in a packet, which contains a source and destination address. A packet-filtering router provides firewall security by not delivering certain packets (called dropped packets). The packet filtering approach is, however, difficult to implement properly.

Application Level Firewalls

Another way to build a firewall is to put a computer system between the internet and the private network. This system is sometimes referred to as a bastion host or a proxy server and enables application level security. All packets must flow through the system, known as an application proxy. An application proxy is a miniature version of an already existing internet service that you want to allow through your firewall. The proxy server makes decisions on whether or not the user is allowed to use internet facilities, based on a wide variety of parameters. If the criteria are met then the proxy passes the packets on the internet. With proxies, application level firewalls provide much finer control over which packets can be transmitted across the firewall.

Security Policies

A more sophisticated security approach invariably implies a more intrusive approach. The BBN security framework clearly highlights this relationship, classifying security as a continuum that ranges from a paranoid to promiscuous policy, as shown in Figure 12.3. The promiscuous policy allows everyone unchecked access between the internet and the organisation's internal network. The permissive policy allows all traffic to flow between the internet and external network except that which is explicitly disallowed. Permissive policies are implemented via packet filter firewalls. The approach has two significant drawbacks. Firstly, it requires an exhaustive set of filters to block all possible addresses, which is difficult in an ever expanding internet environment. Secondly, it is almost impossible to block undesirable packets without also blocking desirable packets. A prudent policy approach prevents all traffic flowing between the internet and the internal system,

Figure 12.3: The BBN Security Policy

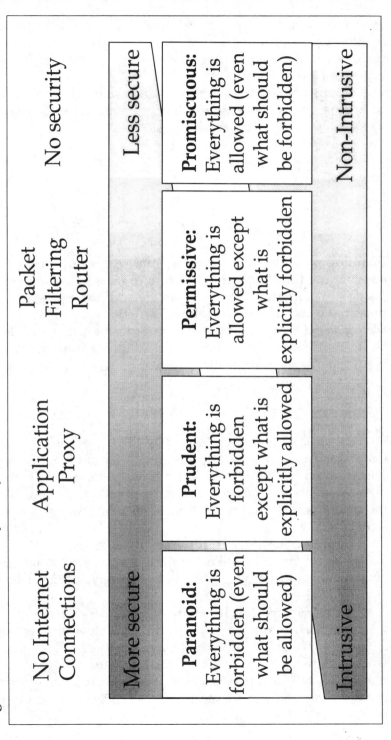

except that which is explicitly allowed. Prudent policies are implemented via a set of application proxies. Permissive and prudent policies act as network boundaries, they are referred to as perimeter security solutions.

It is impossible to make a network totally secure as the threat of 'inside' break-ins is difficult to prevent, but it is possible to significantly reduce the security risk.

PLANNING YOUR INTRANET

Planning plays an important role in a successful intranet implementation. Intranets can creep into organisations in an ad hoc fashion, making it difficult to manage and exploit their strategic potential. Amdahl have developed a methodology called *Intranet Methodology*,™ which "focuses on building the processes and skills that enable and encourage adaptive innovation". The methodology consists of three stages.

Step 1:   Goal clarification.

Step 2:   Implementation planning.

Step 3:   Infrastructure development.

Goal clarification generally involves a team-based workshop, which identifies Web goals that fit your organisation's business objectives. These goals are in turn used to "guide your team in the development and evaluation of specific strategies and projects".

Implementation planning involves assessing the organisational, technical and information status of your current environment, identifying shortfalls and developing a plan for change.

Infrastructure development involves three different aspects, i.e. technical, management and content development infrastructures. Technical infrastructure refers to developing the network architecture and in particular integrating all system components within the organisation. Management infrastructure refers to the training of key personnel. Content development refers to training in Web page design, creation and conversion.

This is an example of one possible planning method, it is not proposed as a definitive planning approach, but it does highlight issues that require consideration when developing an intranet.

CONCLUSION

Given the uncertainties that remain in relation to the future of the internet/intranet phenomenon, one potential method to make some sense of where this technology is going is to look at what the major players on the software market are planning. Indications are that they are all betting on a rapid development of internet/intranet applications.

It should, however, be borne in mind that Bill Gates has warned that "only some of the companies laying bets on the internet will be winners. But companies that bet against the internet will be losers". Box 12.1 shows how key players in the computer field have endorsed the whole internet concept.

Box 12.1: The Major Players Embrace the Intranet

Microsoft: Microsoft are taking the internet very seriously in an effort to become the main internet company in the future. Bill Gates referred to the internet as "the biggest development since the invention of the PC". Microsoft are adopting an aggressive approach to the internet software market, in that they have offered their Web browser free to all users. They are also offering server products and a site management product called Front Page. *They also provide HTML conversion add ons for* Word for Windows *and* Powerpoint, *which allow you to save* Word *and* Powerpoint *documents in HTML format by simply using the 'save as' option.*

Oracle: The major supplier of database technology and OLAP (on-line analytical processing) have developed Web server software, which allows connection between the internet and Oracle databases.

Lotus: Many commentators feel that the intranet is a major threat to Lotus's groupware market share. Lotus are embracing the intranet and have developed InterNotes, *a product which enables inform-ation exchange between* Notes' *databases and the internet.*

Novell: *Novell have developed* Netware Web Server *software, which allows you to store* HTML *documents on the internal corporate network. It is possible to use this server internally as an intranet server or externally as an internet connections, therefore establishing an internet presence.*

Section 4

Information Systems for More Effective Organisations

This section is made up of the four chapters listed below.

13. *Business Process Re-engineering.*
14. *Business Potential of Groupware.*
15. *Workflow Automation Systems.*
16. *Accounting Information Systems.*

Section 4 introduces various ways that information systems can be used to make organisations more effective and their internal processes more efficient either by analysis and creative re-engineering of current processes as described in the first chapter, or by implementing certain types of computer-based systems as explained in Chapters 14 and 15.

The area of business process re-engineering has been the object of much debate over the last ten years and managers are tempted by its potential, yet wary of its dangers. Chapter 13 attempts to present a balanced view of this debate based on the first-hand experience of the Executive Systems Research Centre (ESRC) with BPR. Chapter 14 presents a detailed introduction to another hotly debated topic of the 1990s: groupware. More than ten years after the development of the first groupware systems, the hype has died down somewhat, but the potential for drastic increases in group productivity remains and managers must be aware of it. Chapter 15 focuses more tightly on workflow automation systems, a particular type of systems that can be used to support organisational tasks that require collaboration between large numbers of staff. While such systems require large investments and often lead to drastic reorganisation of work practices, their potential in yielding significant improvements in efficiency, reliability and speed has been demonstrated in many industries and simply cannot be ignored.

The final chapter proposes a different perspective on the domain of information systems. Written by a non-IT specialist, it emphasises that accountants have a crucial role to play in the development of better, more relevant information systems. It suggests that collaboration between accountants and IT specialists may be the key to more efficient organisations.

13

Business Process Re-engineering

Brian Fitzgerald

INTRODUCTION

The business process re-engineering (BPR) concept, although not new, having first emerged in the literature about seven years ago, is currently very topical and is ubiquitous in recent organisational, management and information technology literature. The extent of the widespread popular interest in the BPR concept can be gauged from the fact that a recent book on BPR featured at the top of the US bestseller lists, competing with general-interest, romantic novels such as *The Bridges of Madison County*. This popularity is also reflected in the fact that many organisations claims to be undertaking BPR projects and many software vendors are offering products to support BPR. This scenario is not altogether unique as there have been many examples in the past of concepts that have achieved widespread popular appeal, some of which have been quick-fix, flavour-of-the-month fads. This chapter discusses the principles and concepts underpinning BPR and identifies the ways in which it differs from other approaches, such as continuous improvement programmes. Following this, a methodology specially devised by the Executive Systems Research Centre (ESRC) for use on BPR projects is discussed.

BASIC PRINCIPLES OF BPR

While BPR is usually portrayed as a new concept, a number of the principles and concepts underpinning BPR have their antecedents in other disciplines. An important contribution has come from industrial engineering, for example, where methods, such as process analysis, activity costing and value-added measurement, have been used for about 50 years. Other foundational disciplines include operations management and systems analysis. However, BPR is now coming to prominence in a very different business environment from that which prevailed heretofore. Certainly, the technological infrastructure is now very different, offering capabilities that were not feasible in the past.

Also, BPR attempts to reorient the axis of the organisation away from the traditional emphasis on control through vertical management channels; instead, it seeks to replace this with an emphasis on a customer value-added orientation, which in turn requires a horizontal organisational focus on processes. The latter orientation is one where real value may be added for the enterprise.

One of the basic principles of BPR is that of shortening and simplifying end to end processes. Business processes, which may have been clean and simple when originally designed, have often evolved to become more complex as additional control checks and work-arounds have been incorporated to cater for exceptions. The business processes in use in organisations today were designed in an era when a very different competitive environment prevailed. Based on the scientific management, they were deliberately designed to stifle creativity, simplify work practices and improve efficiency and control, much similar to the manner in which the 'qwerty' keyboard was specifically designed to slow human typists down to a speed at which the mechanics of the typewriter could cope. In the industrial climate following the Second World War, these principles were further reinforced and institutionalised in business practice. The legacy of this historical influence has been the excessive fragmentation of business processes, reflected in the hierarchical division of organisations into functionally specialised departments, which is now taken for granted in modern organisations.

Problems with Departmental Specialisation

There are many problems inherent in organisational compartmentalisation according to narrow functional specialisation. Firstly, it causes the organisation to be broken down into little cubby holes where individual or departmental goals displace overall organisational goals. Also, given the manner in which business performance is measured and managed, there is often no real incentive for departments to collaborate. In fact, with departments adopting entrenched positions, the relationship between them may be dysfunctional to say the least (see Box 13.1). The basic problem is that issues tend to fall between the cracks as processes transcend departmental boundaries and, even though most departments may feel they have optimised their own departmental operations, when the overall operations from each department are aggregated into a complete business process, the overall result may be far from optimal. This failure to achieve synergy is not altogether surprising given the conflicting departmental objectives in the first place.

Box 13.1: Some Examples of Dysfunctional Departmental Specialisation

The sales department in one large organisation was having difficulty keeping up with customer demand because the quality control department was insisting on strict adherence to quality standards. As a result the sales department began to refer to the quality control department as the "sales prevention department" and the resultant friction and hostility between the departments had a serious detrimental effect on the organisation.

A manager in the maintenance department of an airline company refused to allow a service technician to respond promptly to an aeroplane service request because it would have entailed an overnight hotel stay, By waiting until the following day to deal with the request, the technician was able to complete the job and return without incurring hotel accommodation expenses. This obviously helped keep the maintenance department expenditure down, but the 14-hour delay while the plane awaited service represented a huge loss for the company.

Bankruptcy of Existing Paradigms

In the past, the primary emphasis has been on process rationalisation, that is, the motivation has been to automate or expedite existing manual processes and the processes themselves have been largely left intact. The futility of this approach has been bluntly summarised by Drucker in his declaration:

There is nothing more useless than to do efficiently that which shouldn't be done at all.

Process rationalisation has resulted in incremental gains, but this is still a far short of the dramatic ten-fold improvement that has been identified as necessary. Also, the incremental benefits from continuous improvement programmes may be levelling out and are, perhaps, finite anyway.

The following analogy illustrates the central problem. If one's objective was to travel from Paris to Rome as quickly as possible, one could consider driving there by car. A new engine, new tyres and a device to detect speed traps could be installed. These might shorten the duration of the journey by several hours. However, regardless of the number of improvements made to the car, it would still be much quicker to fly!

This illustrates the fact that there is a limit to what can be achieved through rationalisation under an existing paradigm. History has repeatedly shown that dramatic improvements often require a revolution in thinking and practice as old paradigms give way to new. Yesterday's revolutionaries often become complacent and are recast as tomorrow's reactionaries. For example, IBM were aware of micro-computers for several year, but remained aloof, satisfied with the prevailing mainframe culture, until market forces made their involvement inevitable. Likewise, Microsoft, whose *Windows* product was not a major force at the start of the decade could find their market dominance threatened by new paradigms, such as the pen-based ones or personal digital assistants.

In the current business marketplace, which is characterised by shortened product life cycles, increased customer expectation, and continuous raising of the competitive threshold, the ground rules have changed. Indeed, the industrial era has been described as "bankrupt". There is a need to find new and imaginative ways to accomplish work, guided by processes which are more appropriate for the prevailing business environment. However, business analysts have been prisoners of institutionalised past practice and have failed to question the unarticulated ground rules which are obeyed unquestioningly because "that is the way things have always been done around here".

Consequently, the rationale behind each business process and its component steps should be fundamentally challenged. Any processes which are not critical, or which do not add value for the customer come in

> *The old emphasis on efficiency and control must give way as quality, service, flexibility and innovation become paramount concerns.*

for special scrutiny and are eliminated if possible.

SOME OF THE REPORTED BENEFITS OF BPR

The BPR philosophy recognises that not all companies should have to make the same mistakes. At the heart of this is the notion of predatory plagiarism, whereby organisations benchmark individual business operations against the best practice for that particular business operation, perhaps from a company specialising in such a business. The goal is to emulate this best practice. Paradoxically, however, many organisations are unwilling to share their experiences of BPR, or to make public any measured aspects of business performance other than the statutory financial ones. The following is a brief summary of the more noteworthy of the BPR successes reported.

Accounts Payable at Ford Motor Company

In the early 1980s, the Ford Motor Company in the US sought to streamline its accounts payable department, which employed more than 500 people. Management felt that rationalising existing processes could allow a head count reduction of about 20 per cent. Ford decided to look at how Mazda organised its accounts payable department and discovered that Mazda's department consisted of five people. When Ford investigated further, it found that, while Ford organised its accounts payable around matching purchase orders with invoices, Mazda organised its department around the more direct goal of matching deliveries with orders. This allowed Mazda to delegate responsibility to those who were working directly with delivered materials. Thus, while much of the work that Ford had been doing in the past involved resolving mismatches between invoices and purchase orders, Mazda's mode of operations helped prevent mismatches in the first place. By following the Mazda example, Ford was able to achieve a 75 per cent reduction in the company's head count.

Mutual Benefit Life Insurance (MBL)

The MBL insurance company discovered that new customer policy applications were being processed by nineteen people spanning five departments, with typical turnaround times for applications ranging between five and 25 days. By creating a new position of case manager, who was given overall responsibility for a new policy application, and establishing appropriate knowledge databases to support that individual, MBL was able to eliminate the inefficient and time-wasting activities that occurred as applications moved from department to department. MBL eliminated 100 positions and new policy applications can be completed in as little as four hours.

The Pre-sale Customer Quote Process at CIGNA Corporation

The time to deliver a quotation to customers at the CIGNA corporation was seventeen days. The process had fourteen hand-offs and seven authorisation steps. CIGNA re-engineered the process and removed physical partitions between departments, co-locating employees that needed to communicate. Following re-engineering, the process has a 3-day cycle time, three hand-offs (all electronic) and no authorisation steps.

A METHODOLOGY FOR BPR

Much of the literature on BPR has taken an evangelical stance on the issue, assuming that BPR is automatically good for an organisation. As a consequence, there has been little reporting of actual BPR failures. Estimates of failure rates vary from between 50 to 70 per cent. However, it is quite probably the case that many failures may go unreported since the organisation will understandably not want to publicise the fact or, indeed, may not even survive to tell the tale. Therefore, it is likely that the true failure rate may be even higher. Certainly, many companies only begin to consider BPR when they are faced with a survival-threatening crisis and radical surgery is required. For example, Rank Xerox was forced to re-engineer its business processes when its photocopier market share plummeted from 90 per cent to 9 per cent following the entry of Japanese competitors into its marketplace.

A key issue in business process re-engineering is the "how" question. Any significant undertaking, which BPR certainly is, requires that some method be followed. BPR projects cannot be planned meticulously and organised into precise steps, which can then be prescribed as universally applicable in all situations. Nevertheless, since BPR requires a fundamental reappraisal of business operations, a methodology, which can act as an anchoring framework to co-ordinate the complex web of BPR activities, is essential. Otherwise, there is a real danger that those involved in BPR projects will confuse motion with progress and charge about in random directions hoping that any recommended changes can be successfully implemented as a matter of course. Implementing BPR recommendations may require a fundamental change in organisational culture and mindset and this cannot be left to chance but must be carefully managed. Also, the adoption of some methodological support is appropriate.

The following methodology was devised by the Executive Systems Research Centre (ESRC) for use on BPR projects. The methodology is expressed as a series of phases (see Figure 13.1), each of which addresses a basic question, and is summarised below.

1. **Select process to be re-engineered.**
   This addresses the basic question, "Where are we going to start?"

2. **Establish process team.**
   Addresses the question, "Who is going to do it?"

3. **Understand the current process.**
   Addresses the question, "Where do our stakeholders see us now?"

4. **Develop a vision of the improved process.**
   Addresses the question, "Where do our stakeholders want us to be?"

5. **Identify the actions needed to move to the new process.**
   Addresses the question, "What do we need to achieve?"

6. **Negotiate/execute a plan to accomplish these actions.**
   Addresses the question, "How will we achieve it?"

It is worth noting that the methodology is expressed from a first-person point of view, reflecting the fact that culture and mind-set change are required in itself rather than from any direct actions which external consultants can take. However, the 3rd and 4th phases (understand the current process and develop a vision of the re-engineered process) adopt an external viewpoint as well, reflecting the fact that a detached stakeholder-oriented, outside-in viewpoint is necessary. The stakeholders include employees, management and customers, as the needs of all these constituents must be addressed when re-engineering processes.

Even though the above phases are presented as linear steps, a central tenet of the strategy is that it is based on an iterative approach. At any stage, it is permissible (and may indeed be desirable) to revert to a previous stage for further refinement. Also, the links between the 'understand current process' phase and the develop a vision of re-engineered process phase in Figure 13.1 are shown as dotted lines to indicate that this is not an automatic progression. Indeed, there has been considerable debate as to whether one should develop a vision of the re-engineered process before attempting to understand the current process. Those who advocate this sequence argue that discontinuous thinking and imagination are very important when it comes to developing a vision of the new processes, and it is important to escape the shackles of past practice. They suggest that an initial concentration on the current process will constrain later efforts to be imaginative and to re-engineer the process.

Figure 13.1: A Methodology for BPR

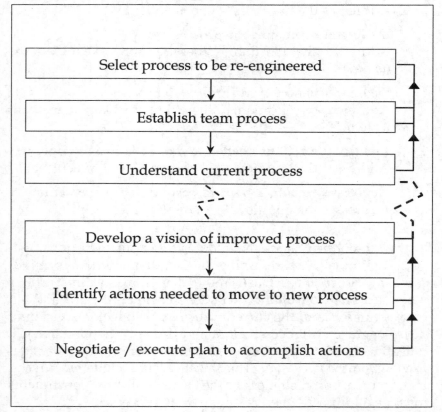

However, the counter argument runs to the effect that one has to understand the context of a process before one can consider redesigning it. To illustrate the importance of context, consider the following salutary, if somewhat apocryphal, story of a manager in an airline company who on analysing aircraft fuel consumption discovered that 2 per cent of the fuel was used during the first 30 seconds of the flight (the take-off run). Based on this isolated fact, the manager recommended that all aircraft should take off on half-throttle thus saving millions of dollars on fuel bills. However, the folly of such a proposal is immediately obvious when one considers the context. BPR requires a fresh and open mind, but the exercise must be grounded in a thorough understanding of the operation of the current process. As a consequence, the methodology outlined here, recommends that understanding of the current process precedes developing a vision of the re-engineered process.

Select the Process to be Re-engineered

BPR requires a global view and an integrated approach to business, rather than the traditional reliance on narrow departmental specialisations. There may be several candidate processes for BPR, however, it is necessary to focus in on a particular process to ensure that the project does not expand in many different directions. This phase ensures that such a focus takes place at the outset.

The scope of the process to be re-engineered must be defined clearly and unambiguously. Therefore, the specific deliverable from this stage is a 200-word (half page) preliminary description of the process to be re-engineered. This helps bound the area unambiguously and, even though it may be modified later, it helps in the next phase when team members must be selected and, in later phases, it facilitates other decision choices.

Establish the Process Team

BPR requires improved leverage of people and technology operating within the appropriate structure. The importance of people cannot be overemphasised and the selection of the process team is critical. Process change is about challenging even the most basic business assumptions, and may thus require significant cultural change. The process team must be empowered and empowerment can only be conferred by executive management. In this context, it is vital that an executive sponsor be appointed. This person will initiate the project publicly, ensure that doors are opened and necessary resources are available. Because of the intensive nature of the process re-engineering task, it is unlikely that the executive sponsor could be sufficiently involved and so a process leader should be appointed. This person would ensure that the project does not flounder and should, for the duration of the project at any rate, report directly to the executive sponsor.

The process leader then chooses additional members of the team. The team size should be kept as small as possible, as this reduces the potential for intercommunication problems and intra-team rivalry. Good candidates would probably be those who feel they are too busy to partake in such a team! Obviously, the people who currently perform the process should be involved, but it is necessary that the team be multi-disciplinary and cross-functional in composition, so that vital issues do not fall between cracks. There is a need to flatten management and functional hierarchies and to align processes away from bureaucratic structures to a more customer-focused one. Imagination and discontinuous thinking are vital for this team, so it is important that people are not chosen purely on the basis of existing management and functional structures. Another important member of the team is that of facilitator. This person should be independent, possibly a consultant, and co-ordinates research and prompts the team members who have the necessary domain knowledge and expertise.

Also, most organisations do not have a complete and uniform graphical representation of their complete business processes (the importance of such a model is discussed in the next section); rather, at best, individual departments may have their own idiosyncratic representations of the subset of the business process relevant to them. For this reason, the role of scribe is important. This person collates all relevant process information into a single repository using a standard graphical notation with each process component underpinned by a complete narrative description.

Understand the Current Process

This phase involves the team acquiring a clear definition and knowledge of the current process. The term 'process' in BPR indicates the need to focus on differentiating between the logical activity of what the process does, or should do, and the physical

---

Box 13.2: The Re-engineering Team

The selection of the re-engineering team is very important. However, a delicate balance is necessary. The team should be cross-functional and multi-disciplinary, but should be kept as small as possible. Imagination and discontinuous thinking are necessary skills, so individuals should not be chosen purely on the basis of existing management structures. The following roles should be considered when establishing the team.

Executive Sponsor: ensures the team is empowered and provides high-level public support for the project.
Process Leader: manages and co-ordinates the project on a daily basis on the executive sponsor's behalf.
Facilitator: independent consultant who researches current BPR projects and suggests ideas to stimulate re-engineering.
Scribe: responsible for documenting project findings in a single repository using standard notation for text and graphics.

---

implementation. This requires detailed analysis of the current process. It generally involves examination of relevant documentation, interviews with relevant personnel internally, and also externally as customers are important stakeholders whose concerns are vital in the current competitive business environment.

Benchmaking of the existing process takes place at this stage and other metric data on the existing process are gathered to assist later evaluation of the re-engineered process.

The explicit deliverable from this phase is a graphical model of the current business process. However, implicitly, the team amasses a large store of domain knowledge and have a clear view and thorough understanding of how the process functions. This is important for a number of reasons. Firstly, when processes transcend functional departments, quite often no individual can see the global picture or fully understand the overall process. By having a thorough description and unambiguous graphical depiction of the process, everyone can be made aware of precisely what the current process entails.

Develop a Vision of the Re-engineered Process

The explicit, deliverable from this phase is a graphical model of the new process which depicts, in logical terms, what the process should accomplish. The articulation of the current process in a graphical model helps to surface assumptions that may need to be challenged. To further stimulate desirable changes, the existing domain knowledge can be supplemented by examination of similar processes in relevant industries and from world leaders in the process.

The possibilities of more symbiotic relationships with customers should be investigated, as it may be possible to co-operate in ways mutually beneficial to all concerned – witness the virtual company concept between Apple, IBM and Motorola, for example. A central philosophy of this phase is the need to simplify end to end processes. Also, the individual component activities of the process must be evaluated and only those that add value should be retained.

As stated above, re-engineering requires the best leverage of people and technology is only a means to this end. However, at this stage, the team try to envision any role that technology might play. In successful process re-engineering projects, which have been reported to date, technology has usually been used to fill knowledge gaps created when a single generalist replaces the multiple specialist roles that existed before the process was re-engineered.

Identify the Actions needed to Move to the New Process

The actions needed to move to the new process must be detailed and prioritised. This phase involves the move from the logical model of what the re-engineered process must accomplish to the physical manifestation of how it will be accomplished. At this stage it is important to set audacious goals or 'stretch targets'. This is necessary to avoid a half-hearted approach being taken, whereby BPR lapses back into an incremental improvement programme without any radical substance. Visible metrics should be established wherever possible, so as to verify that the re-engineered process is meeting expectations. If the efficacy and value of the re-engineered process cannot be reliably assessed, then it is difficult to tell if BPR has been successful.

Negotiate/Execute a Plan to Accomplish these Actions

The plan must be negotiated, and, again, the executive sponsor plays a critical role here in ensuring that any cultural change will not be impeded. This is a vital but delicate stage and it is imperative that negative effects on employee morale be avoided. Relevant support mechanisms and management processes must be aligned. A formal presentation of the plan should be conducted to help win over those vital to ensuring its success. Not surprisingly, this phase proves to be very difficult. The organisation must present a 'business as usual' front, while at the same time accomplishing a smooth transition to new processes which must then be institutionalised.

Frequent monitoring is essential to ensure that the project does not fail at this stage, as this is where many BPR projects go on the rocks as radical change may not be fully undertaken.

Lessons Learned

BPR, while perhaps inevitable, is not an easy or automatic activity. A number of lessons have been learned by the ESRC from BPR projects which have been undertaken.

True re-engineering is extremely difficult to effect and requires total commitment on the part of all concerned – it is certainly not about half-measures taken by the half-hearted.

- The team must be established and empowered and, to this end, an executive champion/sponsor must be found. The team size must be kept to a minimum. In a BPR project with which the ESRC was involved, members were chosen from all the specialist areas relevant to the process, but the large team of experts resulted in meetings dragging on interminably as minor points of dispute were raised. Also, it was readily apparent that no single individual had a complete understanding of the overall business process. Compounding this, each team member represented their portion of the process with different graphical notations and narrative standards, thus making amalgamation difficult. These difficulties were resolved by reducing the size of the team to just a small number of core people who were able to elicit any necessary information from other personnel in the organisation.

- Achieving a thorough understanding of the current process, and representing this clearly and unambiguously in a graphical format, can be tedious, but it does confer significant benefits. Individuals in different departments tend to understand only the section of the process relevant to them and no one has the global view. A graphical representation of the overall process tends to highlight inefficiencies and anomalies.

- The early phases of the methodology: select the process to be re-engineered, establish the process team, understand which current process has been found to work well. The selection of the appropriate process – one capable of adding value and which can be clearly and concisely defined – has been found to be a key issue, as mistakes not detected at this stage prove costly to rectify later in the exercise.

- The latter phases of the methodology, from the development of a vision of the re-engineered process phase to the negotiation/execution plan phase are fraught with difficulties. While a radical change may be identified by the team as necessary, it is difficult for management to commit themselves to a high risk project, especially one which fundamentally alters the status quo. In the case of multinational companies, radical changes in business operations often cannot be mandated locally, but require head office approval.

- BPR projects, as reported, have almost always involved 'downsizing'. However, a reduction in the head count may not be palatable in many European organisations or cultures. For example, in the European context, lateral transfer is more widely used than dismissal as a means of dealing with personnel problems, but such a policy is anathema to BPR.

The question arises as to whether, given these constraints, it is worth initiating BPR projects in the first place. However, the answer must be in the affirmative. Firstly, from a thorough understanding of the current process, certain serendipitous or unanticipated, positive benefits may be achieved which do not require radical change. Also, it may be possible to identify stages in the process where a richer approach could add value for the customer without too much extra effort. Therefore, even if the radical changes required by BPR are not feasible, certain business process enrichment may be possible, whereby existing processes are enriched to add value whenever possible. For example, management may be satisfied with their current head count and overall budget and may not see a drastic reduction in these areas as beneficial. However, they may want to leverage these resources to better effect so as to optimise performance within these parameters.

Even when following a methodological approach, BPR projects are difficult to undertake and many fail or are abandoned without achieving the desired objective. Ptolemy long ago declared that there was no royal road to geometry and the same could equally be said of business process re-engineering. However, the journey may be just as important as the destination, as there are potentially significant benefits to be gained from undertaking the exercise. Furthermore, the rewards of a successful BPR project are great, from the very survival to the future prospering of the organisation.

14

The Business Potential of Groupware

Clive Holtham

INTRODUCTION TO GROUPWARE

Today's business environment has been characterised by a number of radical changes which threaten to undermine the most basic assumptions of organisational structure. Developments, such as the increasing globalisation of markets, the unstable economic situation, tensions on the job market, and the availability of new information technologies, require that managers reassess the way they look at their organisations and plan the work of their staff. Organisations must now be more efficient and more adaptable than ever. This has resulted in a focus on group processes in organisations and the benefits which can accrue from better utilisation of the possibilities of group work. Facilitating team work by re-structuring the operation of basic business processes to provide an environment which nurtures the development of these groups has become a common goal for many organisations. However, little is still known about what managers should do to benefit from better, smoother co-ordination. With this increased interest in the workgroup concept, has come attempts to support the work of teams through information systems. Groupware is the name given to this area of research.

Simply put, groupware, or *collaborative computing*, is a catch-phrase for a body of software and hardware that helps people work better together. A collaborative system creates an environment in which people can share information, knowledge and decisions without the constraints of time and space. Network groupware applications link workgroups across a room or across the globe. This type of software gives the group a common, on-line venue for meetings and it allows all members to labour on the same data in their own time. Collaborative applications include calendar management, video teleconferencing, integrated team support, and support for business meetings and group authoring, but messaging and e-mail systems represent the most basic type of groupware. At the top end of the scale, groupware products can put text, data and graphics together in an integrated groupware package, creating what is known as *comprehensive workgroup support.*

PRINCIPLES OF GROUPWARE

The advantages of structuring organisations to enable people to work as groups are that individuals, with very different psychology, expertise, and resulting approaches to problem solving, contribute their 'differences' to the group problem. It is well known that different people approach complex problems from very different angles. The potential for computer support is in the ability to allow people to make their own contribution and to integrate these individual results for the group as a whole. An e-mail system that simply sends messages back and forth does not nurture a strong sense of a shared environment among group members.

The complication in attempting to optimise the contribution of individuals to a group process is that the problem solving requirements of both individuals and groups must be catered for by the groupware system. The obligation for groupware to operate effectively at both individual and group levels often required its integration into the most basic communication channels of organisations.

The objective of a groupware system is to provide an opportunity for a group to exhibit 'collective intelligence'. This means that the result of the group communication process is better than the results that any single member of the group could have obtained alone. Collective intelligence is a very significant objective, because it is measurable in real situations and across the use of different communication alternatives.

A groupware system needs to support group communications 24 hours a day and offer the flexibility of being used synchronously or asynchronously. Individuals do not deal with problems only when they meet together as a group, nor do they operate, in most situations, as members of only one group. In real organisations, groups are very fluid in their nature and work problems involve overlapping and intersecting sub-groups. Consequently a number of different categories of collaborative interaction have been identified, each requiring very different technological assistance. The types of collaborative interaction that can take place are illustrated in Figure 14.1.

Figure 14.1: Different Cases of Groupware

	same place	**different place**
same time	Face to Face	Distributed Synchronous
different time	Asynchronous	Distributed Asynchronous

Time/space collaborative systems focus on the time and place of the interaction. Systems that support face to face, and synchronous communication enable interaction to occur at the same time and place, while systems that enable asynchronous communication allow interaction to occur in one place at different times. This means that people do not need to work simultaneously any more. Systems that support communication at the same time, but in different places, enable distributed synchronous interaction. Finally, systems that support communication at different places and times enable distributed asynchronous interaction. Many of the technical constraints that put software primarily into one or another of these categories a few years ago, no longer exist. It is now, therefore, possible to develop software solutions that are appropriate for all kinds of workgroup support.

THE FIVE CS OF INFORMATION PROCESSING
FOR GROUP WORK

Drawing on analysis of the business use of groupware, there appear to be five levels at which groupware systems can support and augment co-operation among staff members in organisations. These five levels are shown in Table 14.1 and are illustrated by the following examples.

The first and lowest level of group work – *connectivity* – involves making a physical connection between group members and the data they wish to share.

One of the largest users of groupware is Price Waterhouse. It implemented groupware systems, in the first instance, to achieve easy connectivity between its different offices, functions and management levels. It needed the ability not only to send e-mail, but also to share documents and proposals. Its groupware network operates both across the USA and internationally.

The second level is *control*, whereby managers access data relating to part of their group's functions to assess whether targets are being achieved, and to take remedial action.

Chemical Bank in New York use groupware to link 300 IS employees. According to project manager Gail McGee, in an application that tracks all development projects, employees in one group are able to "look at other projects and see synergies that may not be obvious to other people".

The third level is *collaboration*, i.e. individuals working together within a group, often outside the formal organisational structure, to jointly achieve a goal.

The Patricia Seybold Group in Boston, has made its reputation in the publication of high-quality newsletters. The organisation wanted to find a method of encouraging more interaction with its customer base and also of allowing customers to reorganise general newsletters for more specific and focused internal purposes. The answer to both problems was to create a database with a groupware package for both draft and historic articles. It was possible to get customers' feedback even before some articles were printed in paper form and customers could reorganise the historic databases to create their own customised internal publications.

The fourth level is *co-ordination*, which is required to ensure that

Table 14.1: The Five Levels of Potential Groupware Support and the Processes they Affect

Level of Group Work	Processes Affected
Change	Re-engineering; Speedier product development; Fast, flexible systems.
Co-ordination	Improved workflow. Customer service.
Collaboration	Added-value expertise; Document management; Integrate customers/suppliers.
Control	Status reporting.
Connectivity	Resource sharing. Messaging & Mail.

the activities of all individuals in organisations are perfectly synchronised so as to enable the achievement of corporate goals. In some cases, co-ordination can also involve the synchronisation of activities with external organisations.

Sun Alliance UK has developed the BASIL system – Broker Administration System Incorporating Laptops. It involved providing the account executives dealing with brokers with a notebook PC and modem, using dial-up groupware over a private network to the Oldham office. The first systems were developed for agency profile database, but executives are also now adding to this the softer data collected in the field.

Finally, the last and highest level is concerned with *change*. Leading and implementing change is one of the most important tasks of senior management, and requires immense skill in managing and motivating groups.

One of world's leading manufacturers of hearing aids, Oticon, has removed traditional job descriptions, office layouts and paperwork. It has adopted a very flexible team structure and moved to the use of electronic networks, and in particular electronic data processing, to enable information to be readily shared among all members of staff as and when they need it. At Oticon, all incoming mail is scanned into electronic format in the post room on receipt. It is one of the very few examples of the paperless office, although the finance department has still retained some paper records.

It is important to recognise that these five levels of group processes are largely interdependent. In particular, the benefits of collaboration and co-ordination cannot be achieved without physical connectivity and the lower-level processes, such as resource sharing and messaging/mail. In other words, in order to reap the benefits of groupware, companies must first stabilise their basic communication flows and ensure the efficient circulation of information among management and staff.

SUCCESSFUL APPLICATIONS OF GROUPWARE

A number of applications of groupware have already been successfully implemented in a large number of organisations.

Windows for Workgroups/Windows 95

This is the most basic and easily attainable form of groupware. *Windows for Workgoups* integrates groupware into the network environment. It provides users with e-mail, group scheduling, real-time conference facilities, network-monitoring utilities and file, printer and clipboard sharing. The Windows Graphical User Interface is an important part of *Windows for Workgroups*. Its clipboard sharing facility allows you to cut, paste and share pages of data, such as when you transfer pages of information directly onto someone else's clipboard. The Schedule + feature helps you plan meetings on-line by merging prospective attendee's schedules, finding a suitable time and mailing out invitations.

Collaborative Writing

Multi-user editors and group-authoring systems are able to bring a workgroup's collective input to bear during the creation and edition of a document. If the authoring systems is real-time, it allows several participants to edit a document at the same time by parcelling out logical segments of the document to members of the group. The system controls the read/write access to the various segments. Asynchronous editors, such as *Instant Update*, store both the original text and the reviewer's comments. This allows a document manager to evaluate all comments before making final changes. Conversational structuring permits the structure of a workgroup's conversations to be developed and used during what is normally an unstructured meeting. Messages that are most urgent can be seen at a glance.

Group Decision Making

Group decision support systems (GDSSs) are designed to facilitate face to face meetings. They provide tools for decision structuring, idea generation, voting and ranking. GDSS meetings are frequently conducted by a facilitator.

GDSSs have three levels of feature, but individual systems can have features at more than one level.

Level 1: Emphasises the improvement of communication, idea formation, discussion and messaging. Tools for level 1 include messaging, screen viewing, ranking/rating scales, agendas and voting.

Level 2: Systems incorporate the strengths of decision-support modelling and group decision techniques to enhance the system. Examples of these techniques include project planning and control/operations research tools, such as CPM (critical path method) and PERT.

Level 3: Systems, which are in the developmental stage, automate group communications patterns. They allow you to select and arrange meetings rules and include such tools as an automated counsellor.

Lotus Notes

Lotus Notes is the first commercially available product the functions of which permit all five of the process levels to be achieved (see Table 14.1), based on a single product. Its capabilities can be enhanced in combination with other products, and indeed *Lotus Notes* is often used in conjunction with a variety of complementary and even competing products in the PC environment, and usually collaboratively with mainframe and mini-computer systems. Even more significant than the functionality relating to individual segments of the grid, is the capability relating to the five Cs of connectivity, control, collaboration, co-ordination and change. In each of these five areas, there are examples of the *Lotus Notes* product being able to support remarkably different types of business process. In one environment *Lotus Notes* can meet relatively formal needs for tight management control. In another, it can provide an environment for the rich exchange of informal and unstructured opinions and ideas.

IMPLEMENTATION ISSUES WITH GROUPWARE SYSTEMS

Management, in general, is rooted in overcoming the barriers to implementing change, and to be successful in implementing groupware involves applying such management skills. There now exists a sufficient body of experience to be able to reach some conclusions on the areas needing specific attention when implementing groupware systems. The most important areas are the fundamental managerial roles, technical considerations and the approaches used in implementing groupware.

Fundamental Managerial Roles in Groupware Implementation

Four distinct roles were identified as having an important impact on the successful implementation of a groupware system.

- The first role is that of the *sponsor*, generally the Chief Executive or a very successful senior executive capable of championing the project.

- The second is the *technical leader*, someone who has a sufficiently broad understanding of all aspects of the hardware, software and networking issues in the organisation so that they can address and resolve the problems that arise.

- The third role is that of the *champion*. This could be a high profile business or IT executive or, more exceptionally, it can be a member of staff who has worked in a number of different parts of the organisation and who has, as a result, quickly identified the overlaps and gaps in the information that existed across the organisation. On hearing of the concept of groupware, people in such a situation can create a personal mission to encourage the organisation to use groupware for information sharing.

- The fourth key role is the *groupware administrator*. This is a technically competent person, working in either a business unit or IT department, who carries responsibility for the integrity of the groupware databases and is likely to be involved in fault finding, training, upgrades and the general smooth running on the technical side.

One area which needs to be specifically addressed is the role of external expertise in implementation, particularly consultants and vendors. It is noticeable that even in organisations with a wide range of technical expertise, it has often been cost effective to employ third parties with previous knowledge of groupware to support at least the initial implementation. This is because of the range of problems, both managerial and technical, that are raised by demands of more effective team work.

Technical Considerations

By and large, many of the most serious technical problems involved in implementing modern groupware products have now been solved and, increasingly, these are available at per user prices consistent with PC packages. The main outstanding technical problems relate to the question of standards, particularly in relation to hardware platforms, networking and data formats. In the absence of international, or even *de facto*, standards in some of these areas, it is essential for individual organisations that want to improve team work to set their own standards to ensure that basic data, networking and hardware compatibility exists.

Implementation Approaches

Many organisations, even those who have espoused the terminology of post-industrial organisation structuring and claim to have shifted the focus of their work from a task to a group-oriented approach, still display relatively strong tendencies to rely on multiple layers of managerial control. Therefore, it is essential for organisations to create information systems that can support the needs of both types of organisations. In addition, if a change is deemed to be necessary, information systems must also be able to facilitate the potential movement of an organisation, or units of an organisation, towards either style of structuring work.

The main reasons for this need for adaptability in the development of information systems are:

- **different needs of different functions**: a research and development department has much higher needs for rich interactivity than an accounts payable department.

- **uncertainty**: changes in the external environment or in ownership can create demands for new or changed processes. Greater decentralisation may be needed or new relationships with customers and suppliers. But equally, there may be a need for greater centralisation or a more control-oriented approach.

- **flexibility**: one of the major demands now being made on managers is to create systems and processes that are flexible, in particular to enable enhanced responsiveness to the customer.

BARRIERS TO THE SUCCESSFUL IMPLEMENTATION OF GROUPWARE

The implementation of groupware systems can act as a driver of great change in organisations. Consequently groupware systems will almost inevitably involve surmounting resistance to change in a number of forms.

Using the concept of the five Cs (introduced earlier in this chapter), a number of potential barriers to successful implementation of groupware have been observed in relation to each of the five areas. These barriers are illustrated in Table 14.2.

Group applications require a lot of pre-planning before implementation, extensive training and a willingness on the part of the individual group members to stick with it during the pilot period and up the often steep learning curve. The most successful groupware applications, such as *Lotus Notes* and various e-mail products, offer immediate satisfaction to the user.

But collaborative systems can meet stubborn resistance when they are introduced in a company, because they challenge the existing organisational culture with a new means of communication. Groupware can be capable of moving a company from a very hierarchical structure to one where each individual's input is accepted regardless of sex, race or office status. This can result in the creation of a new, on-line culture in an organisation. The challenge for managers is to define that culture in such a way as to increase the effectiveness of the organisation as opposed to destroying its current performance level. The higher one climbs in a company's organisation, the more one can encounter resistance to collaborative computing. These must be clear monetary incentives to sharing ideas and data, because personal

Table 14.2: The Barriers to the Successful Implementation of Groupware at Each of the Five Levels of Co-operation Among Management and Staff

Co-operation Levels	Barriers to Successful Implementation
Change	Lack of strategic vision
	Lack of accountability
Co-ordination	Currently separated units and islands of competence have to give up some perceived independence to share information.
	People deeply rooted in a PC culture can be resentful of attempts to network them.
Collaboration	People whose status derives from unique expertise are suspicious of having to share it.
	There are technical problems in collaboration across hardware platforms.
Control	More effective control is not always welcomed.
Connectivity	There has to be some "unlearning" of traditional technologies such as voice mail, fax and basic electronic mail.
	Technical problems between networks can be a significant issue.
	Achieving critical mass amongst users can also take time.

information is an individual's power base. Consequently, if the incentives for competition that exist in an organisation are not acknowledged, any effort at creating a collaborative system may be sabotaged.

A major problem with the successful implementation of groupware is that, as long as there are incentives for competition and control, people will use collaborative systems only to further their individual goals.

Companies, which have successfully integrated collaborative systems into their environments, have tended to be ones which have adopted flat organisational structures, where workgroups are the norm. In more hierarchically structured businesses, collaborative systems succeed best when they spread above and below from a focus at middle management level. The successful execution of groupware systems in this way often necessitates a shift in the organisation's culture. The technology on its own will not drive cultural changes, however, and management above all must be sufficiently dedicated to the concept of groupware to enable the obstacles, which will inevitably arise, to be sur-mounted.

Overall, for collaborative systems to be truly successful, you must change the way your organisation operates. Collaborative systems can provide that incentive to change, but dedication to the groupware concept at all levels of the organisation is necessary to ensure success.

GROUPWARE SCENARIOS
FOR STRATEGIC CHANGE

Three common scenarios are faced by management in relation to using computers in group work. They illustrate that the potential benefits from the implementation of new technology are constrained by both organisational and technical factors. These scenarios are summarised in Box 14.1.

Box 14.1: Scenarios for Groupware Implementation

1. Downsizing, but lack of resource to replace IT infrastructure.

2. Change possible in some areas, but not all.

3. Radical change led from top: resources allow comprehensive approach to IT review.

Scenario 1

This scenario involves organisations who are downsizing their workforce, reducing layers of management and putting emphasis on flexible teams. However, they lack the resources (not necessarily just financial) to replace their existing IT infrastructure. Organisations in this scenario are likely to be able to add groupware products at relatively low cost to existing networked PCs. However, the potential for strategic change could be assessed as 'medium'.

Scenario 2

In this case, radical changes are possible or essential, but only in some parts of the organisation. There is likely to be a comprehensive approach to groupware in only parts of the organisation, and in these parts the potential for strategic change could be rated as 'high'.

Scenario 3

With this scenario, radical changes in management culture and style are strongly led from the top. Resources permit comprehensive and integrated replacement of existing IT infrastructure to support the changes. An integrated client/server architecture with wide use of groupware is possible. The potential for strategic change can be 'very high'.

For each organisation, there are specific products that are highly specialised in meeting specific needs and support efforts to carry out strategic change of this nature. The fundamental issue here is balancing the needs of a single element with the needs of the organisation as a whole. Is it desirable for the marketing department to create a database that totally meets their needs, but cannot be related to the needs of the finance or service departments? Some of the exponents of the networked organisation approach argue the case for complete freedom of choice in software products, but this runs counter to the need of an organisation to have basic levels of connectivity. Complete freedom may be the correct business decision, but is essentially a strategic one which must be taken in a strategic forum. For managers in such a forum, four key questions must be asked of proposed software solutions.

- Can they support both traditional and more modern, networked organisational styles, and support the needs of different functions and the flexibility increasingly demanded by uncertainty?

- Can they support all of the five Cs of connectivity, control, collaboration, co-ordination and change?

- Are they scaleable across PCs and Apple computers, local area and corporate networks, workstations and mini-computers?

- Do they insure direct links with both mainstream large-scale office automation strategies and a wide range of small-scale PC and LAN-based products?

15

Workflow Automation Systems

Patrick Bowe

UNDERSTANDING WORKFLOW MANAGEMENT SYSTEMS

Since the Industrial Revolution, automation has revolutionised industry and initiated profound economic changes, which have occurred at an increasingly rapid rate since the 1950s. The extent of these changes in manufacturing is now such that further enhancements to manufacturing processes are becoming less significant. In the past two decades, however, while manufacturing productivity has seen substantial improvements, office productivity has remained practically unaffected. This has led researchers to focus on improving the efficiency of the service sectors. Workflow management systems, a new class of systems which seek to automate the flows of work in organisations, have been developed. These systems promise to tackle some of the inefficiencies inherent in office environments.

Background

The last two decades have seen manufacturing productivity improve by 75 to 90 per cent, while office productivity has virtually stood still at 5 per cent improvement over the same period. The significance of these figures can only be appreciated when the importance and magnitude of office activities in modern organisations are considered.

- American businesses alone have been estimated to generate 1 billion pieces of paper daily. Overall US companies spend $100 billion annually to purchase, distribute, store and process custom, pre-printed forms.

- Almost $2 billion is lost every year in destroying forms that have become obsolete or require changes.

- Large, American life assurance companies typically process 45 million claims each year at a cost of $2.50 each, thus totalling an annual $112.5 million outlay solely on claims processing.

Furthermore, gross inefficiencies inflate the level of costs associated with paper-based office work far beyond acceptable limits. In illustrating the inefficiencies of some workflow processes, Michael Hammer has described the case of an insurance company which estimated that while an application spent 22 days in processing as it travelled through the firm, it was actually worked on for a mere seventeen minutes. Inefficiencies tend to exist in the operation of these tasks for two main reasons.

- **Too much paper**: the retrieval of documents becomes difficult and subject to error.

- **Too many people involved in the process**: documents tend to be lost or are mislaid.

Despite these inefficiencies 92 per cent of information used in organisations remains on paper. Consequently the scope for productivity improvement is huge, making the cost of workflow management systems much easier to justify than many other types of technology using traditional cost accounting techniques. To deliver on their potential, however, workflow management systems have to answer the major challenge of bringing to the office the same benefits of efficiency, reliability and manageability that early automation brought to manufacturing industries.

What are Workflow Management Systems?

Workflow management systems are founded on the idea that business processes consist of sets of tasks carried out in a prescribed order which incorporate information from various sources. Workflow management can, therefore, be described as a methodology for managing the work of people who process documents. The activities of an organisation inevitably lead to the generation of a multitude of documents. The processing of a single document can require the input of several people, each of whom is concerned with different aspects of the document.

The office workers involved in the processing of a document vary, based on the details of the document. Thus, for example, if, on an application form for a health assurance policy, an individual indicates that he has had health problems in the past, the document is routed to the person who checks the severity of these health problems. Similarly the document will only need to be routed to other people when the premium is above a certain amount, others will only be involved when there is a need to check previous policies, and so on. Workflow management systems attempt to manage this flow of work around a business so that it takes place in a quick and efficient manner through the use of reliable and inexpensive computer-controlled procedures.

How Do Workflow Management Systems Operate?

In simple terms, workflow management systems are primarily concerned with applying computer-controlled intelligence to the task of organisational document management. This is achieved through manipulating the interrelationships between the five components of business process as displayed in Table 15.1.

Table 15.1: The Five Components of Business Processes

Component of the Business Process	Explanation
PEOPLE	The performers of various tasks at each stage in the business process
PROCEDURES	Rules that set the constraints of processing tasks
INFORMATION	The means by which a process is made visible to the people who use the system. Information makes the process visible, allows tracking of key factors and enables the creation of a historical record of accumulated work.
TASKS	The steps or activities that must be performed at each point within a business process. The tasks must be consistent with the workgroup's overall procedures.
MANAGEMENT	Capacity to monitor the flow of work and to take appropriate action if necessary.

Workflow management systems define the relationships between these five components, dictating the range of possible actions, events and occurrences which affect them, co-ordinating the flow of work as it passes though each stage of processing. Not all business processes are suited to workflow automation, however.

In fact, to date workflow management systems have been particularly concerned with one or more of the following functions.

- **Information routing**: which is the simplest form of workflow management. It involves the routing of documents based on a predefined set of processing steps for each document type.

- **Task processing**: which involves the computerised initiation of different stages of the workflow system based on the status of documents that are being processed. The workflow management system handles the monitoring to ensure performance of the necessary tasks without human intervention. It is, consequently, more complex than information routing. To carry out task processing effectively, a system of signals and responses must be in place.

- **Work-in-progress reporting**: which involves tracking the location of outstanding documents, which steps have been completed and whether or not processing is on schedule. This feature allows extensive monitoring of work-in-progress, and thus is particularly useful as a management tool. It also enables the identification of bottlenecks and problems in the processing of documents.

User demands are increasingly forcing the integration of all three of these functions into workflow management systems. As workflow management systems become more common, however, they are being used for functions beyond these three basic areas, with tasks previously requiring distinct applications, such as process re-engineering, electronic data interchange (EDI) and groupware, increasingly incorporating workflow components.

Furthermore, due to a relatively low cost and constantly improving functionality, workflow management systems are among the most rapidly growing applications in the IT field, fuelling continued movement of workflow technology into new business areas.

Why Implement Workflow Management Systems?

The appeal of workflow management systems lies in the often immediate and extensive cost savings they offer. This makes it quite easy to justify the cost of workflow management systems in comparison to many other types of information systems.

The benefits that can accrue to organisations can be both

immediate and long-term, both providing immediate 'hard' cost savings, and 'soft' benefits, in such areas as the quality of services provided and the quality of decisions made. Some of the potential benefits of workflow management systems are listed in Box 15.1.

The advantages of workflow management systems go beyond straightforward productivity benefits, however. The ability to track and record the location and status of documents as they are processed is increasingly becoming a standard feature of workflow management systems.

Box 15.1: Benefits of Workflow Management Systems

- Dramatic reduction and often elimination of the number of steps in most business processes, simplifying the structure of the entire document management system.

- Accelerated transaction processing time due to the support of parallel, instead of sequential, processing and the inclusion of parallel tasking facilities.

- Reduced potential for errors in the operation of the process due to computer-imposed checkpoints.

- Enhanced customer service due to higher throughput capability, the reduced possibility of error and decreased turnaround times required to perform the same functions.

- Increased internal productivity of typically 30 to 50 per cent.

- Facilitation of the streamlining of quality systems in organisations.

- Simplification of the training required for personnel on new systems.

- Increased flexibility in changing systems that are currently in place.

- Significant storage and photocopying cost savings.

Indeed most workflow systems now offer the capability to monitor actively the flow of documents throughout a system, thus making it much easier for central administrators to track the throughput of both individual agents and of the process as a whole.

The information contained in these tracking systems enables

management to identify who is or is not performing the necessary work not just on completed documents but also documents which are still being processed. Problems with the operation of the document management system in the organisation become much more evident as a result, and the need for management intervention can be recognised much earlier.

Furthermore, it is also a great deal easier to track causes of error and to pinpoint exactly who, and what, was responsible for problems in processing the work in question. Because many of the largest workflow management systems users are financial institutions, this ability to track and identify discrepancies in the operation of document flows is an excellent method of auditing transactions which have taken place.

This facility of workflow management systems, however, can lead to disillusionment with, or outright rejection of, a workflow management system by office workers.

User acceptance of the workflow management system at ICL was deemed the critical element of its success. Similarly, a small survey of Irish firms carried out by the author in 1996, verified the importance of ensuring users' satisfaction with the methods of operation of their workflow system. Managers at a number of large financial institutions expressed the opinion that consideration of users' wishes was a vital constraint on the scope of their workflow management system. Managers often used their intuition to determine how much latitude they have in monitoring subordinates. Either way, the issue of providing managers with the power to oversee the activities of every user of the system is a controversial one which must be tackled before the development of any workflow management system.

IMPLEMENTING WORKFLOW MANAGEMENT SYSTEMS

How are Workflow Management Systems Developed?

The earliest workflow management systems focused on managing flows of documents as they were processed, shared, manipulated and compiled in organisations.

Initially, workflow management systems sought to improve the efficiency of an organisation in terms of its paper flows, by automating the processing, routing and storage of documents. When this traditional approach is used, the actual changes implemented in the workflow process are minimal. The goal of this approach is not to maximise the benefits which can be gained from the technology, but rather to maximise the efficiency of the existing workflow procedures through the use of workflow management systems. The focus, therefore, is on maximising the efficiency of the existing document flows with little, if any, alterations to the structure of the underlying business processes.

For organisations unfamiliar with requirements of workflow technology, it is advisable to take this route initially. Organisations, which are more familiar with the nature of operation of workflow systems, can afford to apply their workflow systems to the co-ordination of other tasks beyond the traditional roles of workflow management systems. This has been particularly evident in the areas of business process re-engineering and groupware, development, which will be explored in greater depth later in this chapter. (See also Chapters 13 and 14.)

Consensus on a number of issues relating to the development of workflow management systems remains, however. The scope of a workflow management system should cover the entire range of the individual business processes it seeks to automate, spanning the whole set of linked activities involved in taking an input and transforming it into an output. Five elements must be clearly defined and incorporated into the development of the system to ensure effective workflow management. These five elements are as follows (see also Figure 15.1).

- The business process can be automated either as it currently exists or including improvements proposed after analysis. A thorough understanding is needed as a foundation for the workflow system.

- The processes involved are defined as procedures involving sets of tasks which are performed under a variety of conditions. Each execution of a process is called an individual case. Some of these tasks take place in parallel so that rendez-vous points may be necessary to collect output from several tasks. A system of deadlines and alarms is usually provided to support the completion of time-critical operations.

Figure 15.1: The Relationship Between the Core Elements of a Workflow Managment System

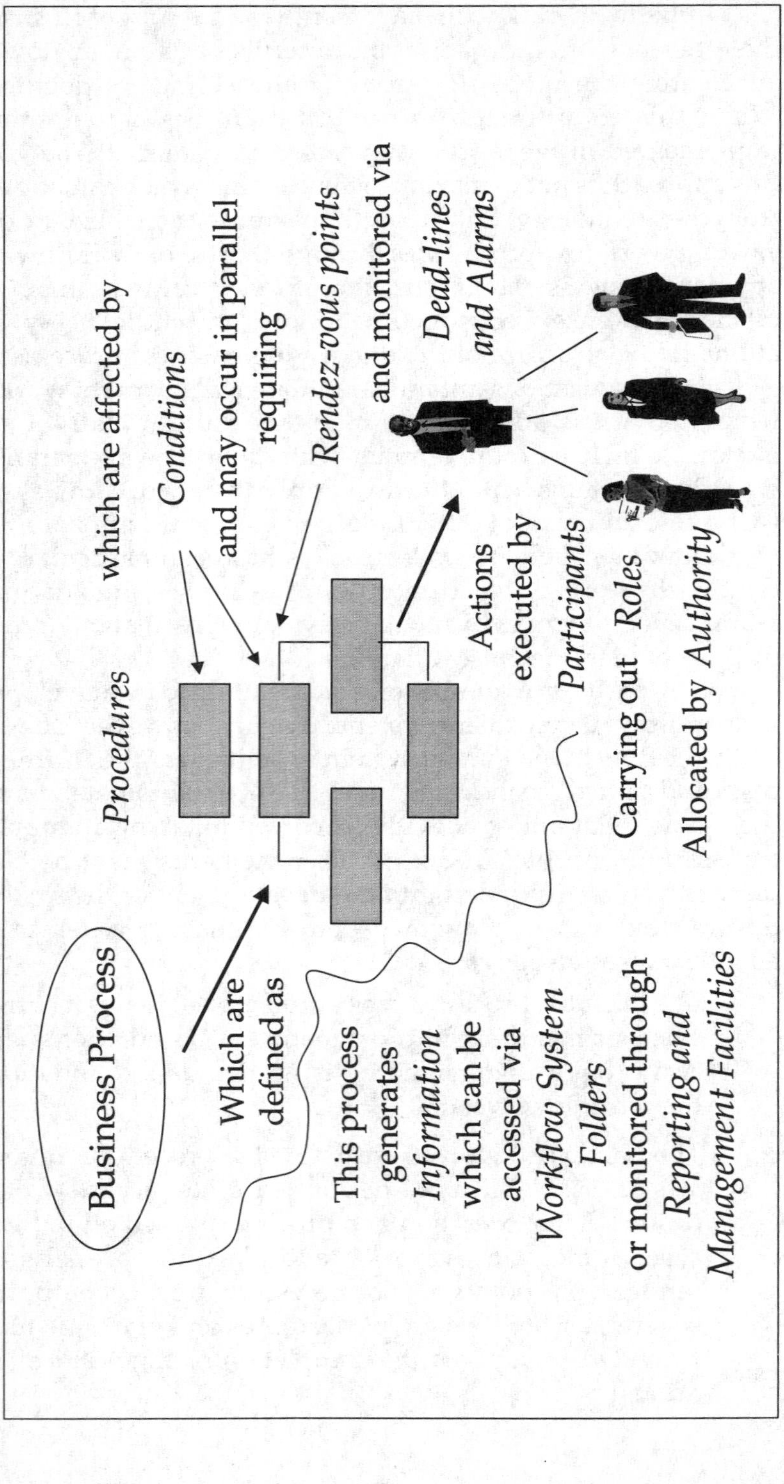

Business Process

Which are defined as

Procedures   which are affected by

Conditions

and may occur in parallel requiring

Rendez-vous points

and monitored via

Dead-lines and Alarms

Actions executed by

Participants

Carrying out *Roles*

Allocated by *Authority*

This process generates *Information* which can be accessed via *Workflow System Folders* or monitored through *Reporting and Management Facilities*

- Participants in procedures perform roles and can be allocated various degrees of authority to co-ordinate the approval policies of the organisations. There is a means of addressing participants in the system including titles, roles and references to in-built organisation structures.

- Workflow systems should allow flexible access to a wide range of data via a forms processing sub-system, which displays documents within folders.

- Reporting and management facilities allow management to assess the performance of subordinates through such measures as status reports, performance monitoring tools and audit trails.

Ensuring that these elements are unambiguously defined, before beginning implementation of the workflow system, will make coding easier and will lessen the burden of maintenance once the system is in operation. With these features in place, the introduction of workflow management systems should be relatively smooth.

The objectives of the workflow management system have an important role in the evaluation and development of workflow systems.

The primary objective behind most workflow automation initiatives remains improvement in the efficiency of organisational document flows. These gains are achieved optimally by implementing workflow management systems which initially focus on relatively simple and well-defined tasks. In this way, resistance to the introduction of workflow systems from office staff can be substantially reduced because improvements in the efficiency of existing office procedures occur without significantly altering the underlying structure of office work.

Implementation, in this manner, also enables management to assess the capabilities of workflow management systems to be used as an agent for more drastic change in the nature of operation of their organisational document flows. Ideally the development of workflow management systems should, however, sit comfortably within the business objectives of individual organisations.

However, changing rules of competition in the modern marketplace are forcing an increasing number of organisations to apply the technology in more ambitious and innovative ways.

Looking Beyond Straightforward Automation of Workflows

As with most modern technological innovations, the crucial factor in the introduction of workflow management systems is not the technology, but the need to know when, what and how to install it. Accordingly, it is vital that a significant amount of planning be carried out before the implementation of a workflow management system.

Plans drawn up for the introduction of a workflow management system should, at least, include a description of the operation of workflow processes as they are currently executed, the evaluation of alternative methods of operation and a detailed plan outlining the scope and roles of the proposed alternatives. It is recommended that a firm methodology be followed to maximise the benefits to be gained from the implementation of workflow technology.

The Executive Systems Research Centre (ESRC) has developed a 6-step methodology for use on research projects.

1. **Capture the existing flow of office activities**. Graphical tools are particularly useful in providing a clear and meaningful overview of organisational document flows.

2. **Identify the existing bottlenecks that impede the flow of office activities**.

3. **Suggest ways to streamline that flow in order to enhance organisational efficiency and effectiveness**. This includes using technological support systems and reconfiguring existing work processes to combine two or more activities into one; eliminating redundant activities and shortening the time duration of these activities.

4. **Assess the adequacy of the existing office support systems** (including communication tools).

5. **Assess the ability of the organisation to adapt**. Factors to be considered here include the maturity of workflow technology use in the organisation and the support which can be given to the workflow systems once they are implemented. Organisations which are mature users of workflow technology can afford to be more ambitious in developing workflow systems. The level of support that can be provided for the workflow management system,

incorporating initial installation, training of the users of the system, and continued support and maintenance are also vital. This is particularly significant because employees will tend to return to older, proven methods of operation if they believe that the workflow management system will be troublesome to use.

6. **Implement automation of the operation of workflow processes**. This requires establishment of technological support for processes previously handled manually.

This methodology is not intended to be implemented in a rigidly sequential fashion. Indeed, while implementing the methodology it may be desirable to revert to a previous stage for re-evaluation as improved understanding of organisational workflows is gained (Figure 15.2 illustrates this methodology). Using this framework, the most significant factors involved in the introduction of a workflow management system will be considered and a suff- iciently detailed plan can be drafted for the implementation of the system. The organisation's ability to use workflow technology to initiate changes of a drastic nature can also be discussed in an objective and balanced way, based on the information generated. As a result, the technology can be introduced in a way which maximises the obtainable benefits.

THE FUTURE OF WORKFLOW MANAGEMENT SYSTEMS

The capacity of workflow management systems to act as a catalyst for profound change in the operation of organisational document flows is one of the major factors in the continued popularity of workflow management systems, as organisations begin to look beyond the mere productivity improvements that they offer.

Workflow management software is changing in line with the dramatic shifts taking place in the modern business environment. At the level of the technology itself, workflow software is in- creasingly being forced to incorporate such marketplace trends as the move to client/server architectures, the popularity of graphical user interfaces, such as *Windows*, and the continuing growth of PC LAN-based networks.

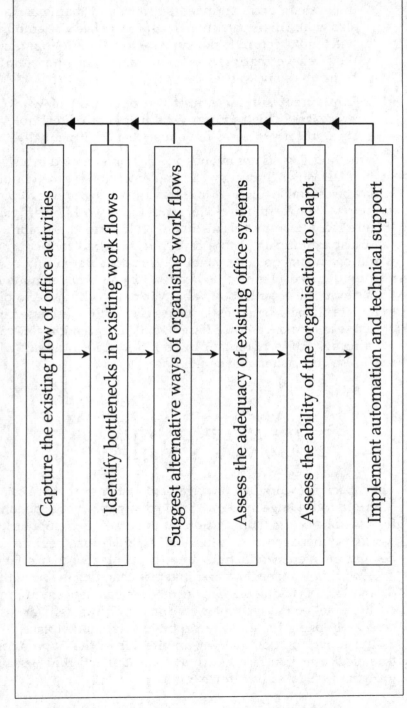

Figure 15.2: A Methodology of Implementing Work Management Systems

Capture the existing flow of office activities

Identify bottlenecks in existing work flows

Suggest alternative ways of organising work flows

Assess the adequacy of existing office systems

Assess the ability of the organisation to adapt

Implement automation and technical support

Consequently there is a growing need for open, flexible workflow management systems which can operate in varied environments under varied conditions and fulfilling diverse functions. This must occur in line with the evolution of the role which these systems play in organisations. Workflow management systems are capable of bringing about great change in the way business processes operate but in an orderly, structured fashion. This has led to an increasing tendency to integrate workflow software with a variety of other packages. The capacity to act as an efficient agent of change has also led to workflow management systems being linked with two other exciting areas of the computer field: business process re-engineering and groupware (see Boxes 15.2 and 15.3).

Box 15.2: Workflow Management Systems and Business Process Re-engineering

Business process re-engineering (BPR) involves the restructuring of organisations at a fundamental level. BPR demands that a company rethinks every aspect of its business, tackling the fundamental business processes around which the organisation has developed. It requires looking beyond the surface elements of issues and examining alternatives to the business processes which lie at the heart of the organisation's activities. BPR initiatives, therefore, generally involve drastic change when they are implemented in an organisation. Because most re-engineering efforts concentrate on rethinking of the nature of organisational work and the means of its execution, however, it makes sense to examine an organisation's workflow.

At a fundamental level, workflow assumes that business processes are composed of sets of tasks executed in a prescribed order which incorporates information from various sources. As a result examining the workflow of an organisation enables easier identification of the processes which need to be re-engineered or even discarded. (BPR is tackled in greater depth in Chapter 13.)

Control over workflow management software is currently in the process of migrating out of the computer-related departments of organisations and into workgroups, with development tools that empower end users to initiate workflows in response to market demands. This need, for end user development support, is manifesting itself through the development of tools which enable users of the popular software packages to integrate seamlessly feature of workflow software into their applications.

Box 15.3: Workflow Management Systems and Groupware

In simple terms, groupware refers to enabling technology that facilitates teamwork. It allows groups of individuals working together to solve common problems sharing system resources, irrespective of their location. These workgroups depend on the groupware technology to ensure that members can jointly access, work on and share the same information and documents. These activities tend to be relatively unconstrained by organisational policies to encourage communication between team members.

Occasionally, however, it is necessary that certain tasks be undertaken in a pre-specified way by members of the group, particularly in relation to conformance with standards. Furthermore, managers are often reluctant to commit to groupware initiatives without the ability to reliably assess workgroup productivity. Workflow management software is ideally suited to fit this gap in the groupware area, providing rigid document paths, document tracking facilities and easy access to measures of individual and group productivity. As a result, workflow components are becoming increasingly common elements of groupware systems. (Groupware is covered in greater depth in Chapter 14.)

This facility already exists for Visual Basic™ users in the form of *FileNet's Work-Flow Custom Controls*, which can be added to the Visual Basic™ development tools, and power builder users through *WorkShop's Callable Work-Flow*. This trend is set to continue as workflow components become increasingly ubiquitous in computer applications, thus continuing the evolution of workflow management systems far beyond their basic role of document management.

16

Accounting Information Systems: An Alternative View

Accountants and IT:
Information Management with Strategic Intent!

Margaret Healy

> *Information is data endowed with relevance and purpose.*
>
> Drucker

INTRODUCTION

Information in the Context of Modern, Hi-tech Manufacturing

The past decades have seen many changes in the state of knowledge and know-how existing within the industrial base of first world economies, with companies striving for ever-increasing levels of flexibility. Flexibility, however, refers to more than just the ability to facilitate changes in current volumes and manufacturing systems easily. It is no longer sufficient to produce at lowest cost or simply to seek to serve a highly specialised niche market in order to ensure survival. Today's high technology industry is characterised by shortening product life cycles, rapidly changing technological bases for industry, increasing marketplace uncertainty, multiple sources of new technology and expansion in the use of existing technology. Factors, such as ramp-up speed, time-to-market and time-to-money, now command a significant portion of management attention in the quest for profitability and continued industrial survival.

Changes in technology are accompanied by changes in methods and organisation as well. Angel, for example, in considering the semi-conductor industry, comments:

> *In an era of intensified global competition, it is the ability to develop and create new market opportunities, to develop new products ahead of competitors and to reconfigure manufacturing processes rapidly in response to changing production requirements that offers the best prospect for long-term profitability of firms and industries.*[1]

All of this, of course, requires information.

Given the context of modern hi-tech manufacturing outlined, management, and the task of managers, must be considered to include mainly the sourcing, processing and application of data and information, to various contexts, situations and opportunities, as presented and perceived by individuals, within the collective social entity commonly titled 'the firm'. From this perhaps overly simplistic, but still useful, starting point, the importance of the data and information through which such an action and reaction process is put into place is undoubtedly of major strategic, tactical and operational importance to the organisation, and is directly implicated in the maintenance of the organisation's competitive advantage in its industry and environment. Thus, the roles of accountant, IT professional and manager are inextricably linked and woven together by the common thread of organisational information; its gathering, processing, storage, presentation, use and evaluation towards sourcing and sustaining competitive advantage in organisations.

Strategy: Sustaining Competitive Advantage

Competitive advantage is that which sets an organisation apart from its competitors. Its source within the organisation, and the means to sustain that advantage once achieved, have been addressed by a number of authors and in a variety of research fields and traditions. This section briefly explores that literature, highlighting what I consider to be the three broad headings under which the various 'solutions' and suggestions offered by these authors can be classified. These are 'resources', 'activities' and 'capabilities'. The following sections, will attempt to support the case for sustaining competitive advantage through accounting

---

1. Angel, *Restructuring for Innovation* (1994) pp. 4-5.

based on the role of the accounting information system (AIS) in an organisation. Helping to sustain the competitive advantages of the firm thus needs to become a more explicit consideration in our conception of AIS and of the professionals detailed in their functioning.

THE ACCOUNTING INFORMATION SYSTEM: DETERMINING STRATEGIC RESOURCES?

Resource-based views of the firm point to differences in resource endowments across organisations operating in the same industry, and to the importance of those resources, in their being unique and difficult to replicate in other organisations, as the underlying reasons why some organisations consistently perform better than others. Such valuable organisational resources can be physical, for example the location of a manufacturing facility near a valuable source of raw materials, or the hardware configuration particular to that facility. Such resources may also be intangible, for example technological know-how or the existence of patents or copyright protecting valuable technologies or processes. Other less tangible sources for competitive advantage have also been offered: the ability of the workforce to learn and adapt to changing conditions, organisational flexibility and innovative product development.

In terms of the accounting information system, a resource-based view of the organisation considers the elements of that organisation from the numerate approach of the balance sheet – a document sometimes classified as a 'position' statement. A tangible, quantifiable identity is sought for that which is considered to be the assets and the liabilities of the firm. Through a combination of historical circumstance, prevailing budgetary ethos and the dominant influences exerted on the organisation in terms of its culture and its financial position, some of these assets come to bear the label 'strategic'. Each element is viewed as distinct, and capable of quantifiable expression; thus each represents a resource to be drawn on in the governance of the organisation, with the extent to which this occurs being reflected in the profit and loss account for that year.

THE ACCOUNTING INFORMATION SYSTEM: DETERMINING STRATEGIC ACTIVITIES?

To outperform its rivals, a company must produce goods or services perceived to be of greater value to the customer than those of its rivals, provide equivalent goods or services at a lower cost, or do both. Following the conventional approach of the management discipline, competitive strategy, as proposed by this strand of the literature, rests on deliberately choosing a set of activities different in some way from those of competitors, be it following a cost leadership strategy, a differentiation strategy, a focus-based strategy or some combination of them.

Emphasising the importance of thus positioning the organisation in relation to its strategy, Porter, for example, argues that the existing writings on strategy still have much to offer. Managers have become preoccupied in improving operational effectiveness and, in the quest to do so, have allowed issues of strategy to slip by in the drive towards implementing initiatives such as TQM, BPR, ABC[2] or other cost improvement programmes: "In many industries, however, what some call hyper-competition is a self-inflicted wound, not the inevitable outcome of a changing paradigm of competition."[3] This wound deepens and festers when the worlds of academia and consultancy collide, with marketing concerns rather than underlying substance and validity predominant.

Porter illustrates the basis of the 'activities' stream of thought in outlining competitive advantage at the Southwest Airlines Company as coming from the way in which its activities "fit and reinforce one another". Insufficient awareness of issues of organisational 'fit' will hinder firms attempting to adopt new techniques or methods of operation. Thus, simply automating areas of activity or installing the latest in computing technology may in fact be detrimental to the organisation if the 'fit' is not right. In similar fashion, simply adding areas of activity, based on quantitative identity may be of little, if any, use in the longer term.

---

2. Total quality management, business process re-engineering and activity-based costing, see Chapter 13, p. 203 above.
3. Porter, "What is Strategy?" *Harvard Business Review* (Nov-Dec 1993) p. 61.

THE ACCOUNTING INFORMATION SYSTEM:
DETERMINING STRATEGIC CAPABILITIES

Competitive advantage, as based in resources or in activities, has achieved recognition across a variety of discipline-specific literatures, supported in part by field research and statistics. However, to be sustainable, such advantage must transcend four key threats: imitation, substitution, hold-up and organisational slack. Consideration of organisation 'capabilities', rather than 'resources' or 'activities', seems to offer (to this author at least!) the means to maximise the benefits of both the latter, while minimising the possibility of threat, as expanded upon in the following paragraphs.

Imitation allows an organisation to gain the benefits of a given source of advantage, without incurring the initial development costs necessary to bring that advantage to the point of commercial usefulness. It may be minimised through characteristics, such as physical uniqueness, or the need for large capital investment, but can never be completely eliminated. Substitution, as a threat, is related to imitation and again refers to the 'uniqueness' associated with the given source of advantage. Organisational slack can occur through complacency, in particular upon having achieved a dominant position in the industry. Hold-up occurs when the ability of the owner of a valuable resource is limited, because of the power others can exert over that resource, in fully appropriating all of the benefits and value accruing from it.

While 'activities' and 'resources' are easily understood and reflected in the reality of an organisation's ongoing existence, both are open to varying degrees of vulnerability regarding the ability to sustain that advantage. I would advocate instead to you, the reader, a consideration of competitive advantage from within the 'capabilities' literature.

Identifying firm, specific capabilities, leading to sustainable competitive advantage, involves focusing on the strategy, structure and core capabilities of a firm. Strategy is defined as denoting the set of commitments the firm makes in defining and rationalising its objectives, and how it means to pursue them. Given this broad set of objectives, structure refers to the way in which the firm is organised and the ways in which decisions are actually made towards the achievement of those objectives. Core capabilities are seen as being those activities and skills required by the strategy-structure combination, which the firm is capable of completing 'confidently', and which are built from a hierarchy of practices or organisational routines. Nelson puts this more concisely in the following quotation.

At any time the practised routines that are built into an organisation define a set of things the organisation is capable of doing confidently. If the lower order routines are not there for doing various tasks, or if they are there but there is no practised higher order routine for invoking them in the particular combination needed to accomplish a particular job, then the capability to do that job lies outside the organisation's extant core capabilities.[4]

As will be demonstrated later, both the accountant and the IT professional have roles to play here and are indeed dependant upon each other.

General Motors provides another example of the importance of ideas of 'fit' and 'synergy' among the elements of an organisation's strategy, structure and managerial processes.[5] During the 1980s, $80 billion was spent on robotics and capital equipment, with little adjustments being made to process dev-elopment or manufacturing procedures. Thus, while General Motors had what should have been one of the most flexible assembly lines in the world at the time, the company was producing just one model and losing money. The need to consider issues of fit and complementarities is not solely a feature of modern day manufacturing either. With Model T production at the Henry Ford factory, for example, highly inflexible manufacturing and a narrow product line were well-suited to each other and to the prevailing technological and market conditions.[6]

In relation to the modern hi-tech organisation, the writings of Teece and Pisano further develop the notion of 'capabilities', and are worthy of further study. They offer a paradigm of the modern organisation based on the concept of what they term 'dynamic capabilities'. 'Dynamic' refers to the non-static nature of the environment a given firm operates in, where for a high technology company aspects, such as time-to-market and the

---

4. Nelson, "Why do Firms Differ and How Does it Matter?" *Strategic Management Journal* (1991) 12, p.68.
5. See Milgrom & Roberts, "Complementarities and Fit: Strategy, Structure and Organisational Change in Manufacturing" *Journal of Accounting and Economics* (1995) 19.
6. *Ibid.*

pace of innovation affecting the nature of future com-petition and markets are of vital concern. 'Capabilities' emphasises "...the key role of strategic management in appropriately adapting, integrating and re-configuring internal and external organisational skills, resources, and fundamental competences toward [that] changing environment".[7] Thus, competitive advantage lies in systems of assets, both tangible and intangible, and in the links and relationships between those assets. It is more than merely activities or resources. Accounting, in part at least, specifies many of those links and relationships, and they cannot simply be acquired through the purchase of a bundle of assets in the marketplace, and the simple replication of their existing organisational functionality. It is the links and complementarities between those assets – the difficult-to-replicate routines – within which competitive advantage is generated and sustained.

The source of competitive advantage stems from some combination of three factors, based on the strategic dimensions of the firm: processes, positions and paths. 'Process' refers to the ways in which 'things get done' in an organisation, and is similar to the 'routines' proposed by Nelson. Much of this can be determined as the work of the accountant and the means and measures which are used throughout the organisation. 'Position' relates to the current organisational situation in terms of its technological assets and capabilities, supplier relations, strategic alliances with competitors, the existence of any intellectual property rights and its customer base. IT-related assets are becoming an increasingly important element here; in particular when one broadens the definition of IT to include aspects of electronic commerce and internet-related activities. Finally, 'path' involves consideration of the strategic alternatives facing the organisation; how attractive are the various opportunities available to the firm and to what degree is the firm constrained in its ability to avail of those opportunities.

Focusing primarily on the IT system and its individual components of hardware and software, without considering its broader organisational existence and functioning within other relevant sub-systems of the organisational entity, tends towards a viewpoint based on elements of 'position' alone. This highlights the need for a broader outlook, and advocates that mangers

---

7. Teece & Pisano, "The Dynamic Capabilities of Firms: An Introduction" *Industrial and Corporate Change* (1994) Vol. 3, No. 3, p. 538.

should consider the accounting system in its broadest possible definition, as the means through which the 'practised routines' of Nelson are invoked for sustainable competitive advantage.

THE ACCOUNTING INFORMATION SYSTEM

Specifying the routines or mode of governance determining competitive advantage in any organisation involves consideration of four factors:

- firm boundaries;

- internal formal structures;

- internal informal structures;

- external linkages.

Accounting is implicated in the design, structure and maintenance of each of these elements. Accounting literature has concentrated, however, on aspects of the exercise of power and its consequences via accounting control processes, rather than on its role as ". . .a means of organisational survival".[8] Accounting is about constructing information to create an image of the world and as such can and is very powerful if used constructively. Just think, for example, of how many decisions are justified, even if retrospectively, by or through accounting numbers or calculations and of the number of decision making scenarios in which accounting formulations play an essential role.

Accounting does not, however, commence with the series of neat journal entries or transactions of the standard exam question type – rather accounting originates in the much more chaotic, diverse set of activities involved in the planning for and running of the modern organisation; the lower order routines of Nelson. Accounting also does not always take place over the convenient time period of the account horizon – decision making is not temporally bounded, but can have implications over the future of the organisation, beyond that viewed as 'current' or 'short-term'. The accounting system must also seek to deal with this and to reconcile the need for an information set to meet the

---

8. Otley *et al*, "Research in Management Control: An Overview of Development" *British Journal of Management* (1995) Vol. 6, pp. 531-544.

needs of company and revenue law requirements, accounting concepts and conventions, auditor regulations and the internal needs of management.

Definitions of accounting vary depending upon the orientation of the author and the teaching direction of the text. Financial accounting has been variously described as "financial plumbing for the terminally tedious" or as being "quantitative information, relates to an entity, is based on observation, and is prepared according to rules". Management accounting has been summed up as being that which involves the provision of information of significant interest to managers. It is common to categorise managerial activity under the following headings: strategic planning, management control and operational control. Strategic planning involves the setting of broadly based, corporate-wide objectives and strategies, whereas operational control relates to the day to day management of the functioning of individual areas comprising the organisational entity. Management control serves as the connecting link, in acting to co-ordinate long-term objec-tives with short-term activity. It has been argued that accounting information, and in particular management accounting information, was the tool used for achieving management control, primarily through the use of budgetary control systems. Since then this view of organisations, and of the role of management accountants/management accounting within organisations, has come to be synthesised into the ideal of it being that of meeting the needs of managers.

In essence, accounting is actually about information – information on a wide variety of things, people and activities, predominantly, but not exclusively, measured in the form of numbers. Information from the same data, set is used in a variety of formats, thus highlighting the most obvious role for the IT professional – how to manage all this data and information. The distinction between the two most easily recognised areas of accounting – financial accounting and management accounting – can perhaps be traced to the need to teach the techniques of each without completely overwhelming the student with a mass of numbers, and associated organisational theory, legal reasoning and legislation, economic fundamentals, and the theories of individual and market behaviour. Thus, while at the highest levels of abstraction, both exist to service the information needs of the organisation, the driving forces pushing the development of each as an area of expertise differ in their outlook and purpose, with a consequent difference in the perception and the realities of the organisational existence of each. It should be noted, however, that this difference seems to exist only in the eyes and minds of the accountants within an organisation. To all other functions, accountants are generically regarded as one; the rigid definitions of the accountancy education are perhaps mainly maintained by its graduates.

Accounting is often analysed as a series of activities that are linked and form a progression of steps, beginning with observing, then collecting, recording, analysing and, finally, communicating information to users. Thus we can say that accounting information has special meaning in that it is data organised for a particular purpose, and the task of the accountant is to transform raw data into information. Data exists in a form unable to influence decision making at any level of the organisation, and over any time-frame until it is transformed into information. From an unlimited set of data available, the accountant selects the set of raw data that will be transformed into information. The filtering process by which he selects this data is determined in part by the conventions of accounting and company law, but also by the use to which that information will be put, and the means and technologies available to the accountant regarding its storage, retrieval, processing and reporting.

While accounting may produce static reports of a mainly historical nature, the events it seeks to record encompass a wide scale of activity, most of which will in some way impact upon the role of the accountant. Behind books of prime entry and journal adjustments lie a series of activities, which must be tracked and in some way recorded in the history of the organisation. Many documents are involved that may never enter the formal accounting system, or the presentation of its results, but which are a very vital part of it – GRNs, delivery notes, order forms, etc. Issues of relevance here include the design of such documents, their sequence and flow throughout the organisation, decisions about what data must be collected and why, the types of 'checks and balances' that must be built into the data collection/ generation/collation phases. The computer has evolved into the most important information-processing tool available to the accountant, and thus the manager, today. Even the changing nature of traditional pieces of equipment illustrates this: the mundane cash register is now the entry point for a very sophisticated stock control and reorder system, and can provide much information of use to the marketing department regarding the purchasing patterns of customers. Thus, higher order routines can also be facilitated via simple pieces of technology.

The signalling effect of accountancy – in that it measures things and thus, by default, does not measure others – can become a tool for the manager in communicating the strategic intent of the organisation. The areas stressed by the accountant will be seen as those of importance and people will naturally focus on them – thus this is an important concern in the design of the accounting system – both for the accountant and the IT professional. Questions to ask include: What should be measured? How should it be measured? What are the behavioural implications of those measurements? Will different people and functional orientations use the same information differently?

While these initial questions may seem like obvious, and indeed oft-cited, requirements or prerequisites on any system designer's checklist, the important point to take from the discussion is that the answers determine much more that simply a list of metrics and a procedure for collecting them periodically in electronic or other form. The answers must come together towards a sustainable 'fit' with the overall organisation, and its current position/process/path combination. This calls on the accountant in particular to review that role which the function has come traditionally to be seen as serving.

Traditionally, management accounting served to monitor and control areas such as stock, work-in-progress, variances from standards, i.e. to produce the measures associated with worker groupings, and activities split along functional divides. When combined with the power and scope of modern information technology and communications infrastructure, the role of, demands made on, and possibilities offered for the accountant and accountancy change completely: "With their skills in data analysis and statistics, management accountants can help pioneer the development of real-time, customer-focused information systems that turn companies into genuine learning organisations".[9] In similar fashion, the IT professional must come to view such potential as an opportunity for the further development of both

9. Johnson, "It's Time to Stop Overselling Activity-based Concepts" *Management Accounting* (September 1992) p. 48.

disciplines, in terms of both its professionals and its competitive and sustainable organisational strength.

Management accounting can be used to influence as well as to inform. Measurements place emphasis on certain areas of activity. Thus rather than offer a "frozen view of reality",[10] accounting can be used to maintain or alter patterns in organisational behaviour, thus supporting the view that, as the information system of the organisation, accounting has and can play a key role in the maintaining of sustainable competitive advantage.

The past emphasis placed on financial measures, such as return on investment, has evolved into the mistaken belief that returns come from investments (i.e. physical assets) rather than from competitive market position. ABC and ABM have shifted the focus towards collating and analysing costs around activities and away from the traditionally taught and accepted allocation approaches. In one sense, however, this is simply just a reallocation of the total overhead pool using a different set of mathematical means. More than economic measures, expressed solely in numerical terms, will be required to meet the future information demands of management, in particular within the context of a rapidly changing manufacturing environment, as outlined in the opening sections of this chapter.

The traditional role and status of the accountant is changing. The increased emphasis on decision making is bringing together many skills once viewed as separate domains of knowledge, and as belonging in distinct, separate areas of the organisation – e.g. data processing, computing, etc. Too often information systems are thought of as being groups of computers linked together, housing databases of information. An effective corporate information system will encompass more than just hardware and formal, predetermined communication and data flow channels – there will also be informal, transient and invisible channels, through which data will be collected, stored, manipulated and presented as information. An efficient accounting information system will seek to recognise this and to structure itself accordingly.

10. Roberts, "Strategy and Accounting in a UK Conglomerate" *Accounting, Organisations & Society* (1990) Vol. 15, No. 1-2, p. 107

CONCLUSION

Recognition of the need to broaden the focus and traditional viewed role of the accountant is evidenced in the growing body of literature appearing in professional and academic publications of the discipline. Accountants need to view their role in the organisation as that of providers of information, rather than that of providing retrospective justifications in support of decision making and searching for measures in support of short-term control and performance evaluations.

Focusing beyond the technical dimensions of the IT area, and the possibilities IT offers in terms of increased efficiency, cost reduction, change management programmes, teleworking, internet advertising and other such areas of topical interest, and instead towards consideration of IT, within the dynamic capabilities framework outlined earlier, offers the scope of a more concise definition of the discipline, at least in terms of its functioning, as that of being the facilitator and conduit through which organisations manage. Simply translated, this means that both disciplines exist to help organisations and their managers to 'work smarter'.

Accounting, as illustrated by Llewellyn, is a resource to be drawn upon in the governance of economic life.

> *The attention-directing, performance-monitoring and information coding functions of management accounting contribute to time-space zoning by reducing, absorbing or denying the uncertainty which is endemic to organisational life.*[11]

Financial accounting sets the boundaries of the organisation through its quantification of assets and liabilities, expenses and revenues, thus establishing organisational 'thresholds'. For management accounting, such boundaries also can act as 'binding structures', within which some form of internal unity is achieved for the organisational entity and to so facilitate the creation of higher order routines invoking and invoked by lower order routines, building and sustaining the competitive advantage of organisations; leading the accountant and the IT professional towards reconsidering their role as that of jointly managing information – with strategic intent!

---

11. Llewellyn, "Managing the Boundary: How accounting is implicated in maintaining the organisation" *Accounting, Auditing and Accountability Journal* (1994) 7 (4) p. 14.

FURTHER READING

D Angel, *Restructuring for Innovation* (New York: Guildford Publications) 1994.

H T Johnson, "It's Time to Stop Overselling Activity-based Concepts" *Management Accounting* (September 1992) pp. 40-49.

S Llewellyn, "Managing the Boundary: How Accounting is Implicated in Maintaining the Organisation" *Accounting, Auditing and Accountability Journal* (1994) 7(4), pp. 4-23.

P Milgrom & J Roberts, "The Economics of Modern Manufacturing: Technology, Strategy and Organisation" *American Economic Review* (1990) 8(3), pp. 511-528.

P Milgrom & J Roberts, "Complementarities and Fit: Strategy, Structure and Organisational Change in Manufacturing" *Journal of Accounting and Economics* (1995) 19, pp. 179-208.

R R Nelson, "Why do Firms Differ and How Does it Matter?" *Strategic Management Journal* (1991) 12, pp. 61-74.

Otley *et al*, "Research in Management Control: An Overview of Development" *British Journal of Management* (1995) Vol. 6, pp. 531-544.

G Pisano & S Wheelwright, "High Tech R & D" *Harvard Business Review* (September-October 1995) pp. 93-105.

M Porter 1996, "What is Strategy?" *Harvard Business Review* (November-December 1996) pp. 61-78.

J Roberts, "Strategy and Accounting in a UK Conglomerate" *Accounting, Organisations & Society* (1990) Vol. 15, No. 1-2, pp. 107-126.

R Rumelt, D Schendal & D Teece, "Strategic Management and Economics" *Strategic Management Journal* (1991) Vol. 12, pp. 5-29.

R Simons, "The Role of Management Control Systems in Creating Competitive Advantage: New Perspectives" *Accounting, Organisations & Society* (1990) Vol. 15, No. 1-2, pp. 127-143.

D Teece & G Pisano, "The Dynamic Capabilities of Firms: An Introduction" *Industrial and Corporate Change* (1994) Vol. 3, No. 3, pp. 537-556.

D Teece, "Competition, Co-operation and Innovation, Organisational Arrangements for Regimes of Rapid Technological Progress" *Journal of Economic Behavior & Organization* (1992) Vol. 18, pp. 1-25.

D Teece, "Firm Organization, Industrial Structure, and Technological Innovation" *Journal of Economic Behavior & Organization* (1996) Vol. 31, pp. 193-224.

The Caring Economy:
Internet Business Principles

Gerry McGovern

The Caring Economy is based on a number of fundamental beliefs. These beliefs are that the forthcoming digital age demands new thinking and a new philosophy, requires a new set of business principles, governing everything from research and development to customer interaction, and is a time when technology will become transparent and people will become paramount.

If businesses want long-term success in the digital age, they need to care about people, and about the issues that are important to people. The Internet is a revolution in communications, and not in technology. This is not a book about computers or the Internet, nor is it about bandwidth, faster processors, information technology, e-commerce, digital television, video on demand, nerds and hackers. It is not about cost savings and downsizing and automating people out of the picture. *The Caring Economy* covers and explores all these technologies and issues, but it is not about them.

It is rather a book about people - both business people and consumers - and how we all interact with each other, in life and on the Internet. It explores the relationship between people and the tools they make and use. It seeks to establish some philosophical foundations and basic principles for living in the digital age.

The book is written from the standpoint that community and commerce are inherently intertwined - you cannot have one without the other. It explores the whole meaning of what a 'network' is, what 'networking' is about and how best to live and work ethically and effectively within a networked environment.

The Caring Economy is about attempting to give people a route map for a journey to a new age. It says to the business person "Do not be scared, do not over-react." Things are not going to be all that different. The digital age will be more than anything else about people communicating, interacting and trading with other people.

The Author:
GERRY MCGOVERN is the Managing Director of NUA, a Dublin-based Internet consultancy that has won many key US and international contracts.

320 pages:
1-901657-61-2 hbk: May 1999
1-901657-60-4 pbk: December 1999

Managing Information Systems:
A European Perspective

Pat Finnegan & Ciaran Murphy

Managing Information Systems: A European Perspective examines prominent issues facing European organisations in the management of information resources. The book provides an integrated examination of issues in information management at all levels within an organisation, using empirical examples from a range of European organisations.

Likely to be of vital benefit to final year undergraduate and postgraduate students of information systems management, the book includes chapters on the following.

- The role of information in organisations.
- The IS function in context.
- Operations, management and inter-organisational systems.
- Systems development and operation.
- Technology issues.
- The challenges facing organisations in this area.

The book includes a range of contributors from across Europe, and contains a combination of empirical case studies, research reports and critical commentaries provided by European academics. It will be the first book to take an integrated approach to the individual topics covered, and the only book to tackle IS issues from an internal and external perspective at all levels of an organisation. This gives the book a distinct advantage over competitive texts.

The Editors:
PAT FINNEGAN is a lecturer in Information Systems at University College Cork. Professor **CIARAN MURPHY** is Professor of Information Systems and head of the Department of Accounting, Finance and Information Systems at University College Cork.

160 pages
1-901657-63-9 £18.99 pbk: September 1999

The Concise Dictionary of Information Technology

Donal Lynch

The Concise Dictionary of Information Technology is an accessible, user-friendly guide written to help readers distinguish a RAM from a ROM, a bit from a byte, ASCII from EBCDIC, a bridge from a gate, and the Internet from an intranet. The book, previously published by Chartwell Brat, is unique in that it is based on in-depth research, and yet written in user-friendly, accessible language that will be understood by computer experts and laymen alike.

The book defines the most frequently used terms relating to IT hardware, IT software, networks, data communications, computer programming, computer language, operating systems, electronics, digital technology, computer codes, the Internet and much, much more.

It makes the special terminology and jargon, which can confuse people new to this subject, readily understandable, and includes detailed cross-referencing for ease of use. It is a presented in an easy to read format for ready use at home, in the office, or at school or college. It is completely up to date, and is likely to be of invaluable use to anyone who needs to familiarise themselves with the terminology used in this increasingly vital area.

The Author:
DONAL B LYNCH is a Senior Lecturer in Computing and Information Technology at Bourneville College of Further Education, Birmingham. He has taught for over twenty years on a wide variety of IT and computer-related courses.

192 pages
1-901657-45-0 £14.99 pbk: April 1999

The above books can be purchased at any good bookshop or direct from:
BLACKHALL PUBLISHING
26 Eustace Street
Dublin 2.
Telephone: +44 (0)1-677-3242; Fax: +44 (0)1-677-3243;
e-mail: blackhall@tinet.ie